THE PINK SCAR

TROUBLING
DEMOCRACY

Troubling Democracy focuses on the past, present, and future of democracy. Often heralded as an ideal mode of governance, democracy—as ideology and practice—has long been fraught, full of possibilities and failures, great promises and persistent exclusions. That these tensions exist alongside deep scholarly interest and ever-evolving public conversations about democracy attests to a need to trouble—interrupt, refuse, reimagine, and reclaim—it.

Intentionally broad, interdisciplinary, and global, Troubling Democracy features books that treat matters of discourse, language, and symbolic action as they are at work in the world to advance conversations around power and to break open democracy's possibilities.

The Pink Scar

How Nazi Persecution Shaped the
Struggle for LGBTQ+ Rights

Thomas R. Dunn

The Pennsylvania State University Press
University Park, Pennsylvania

This volume is published with the generous support of the Center for Democratic Deliberation at The Pennsylvania State University.

Library of Congress Cataloging-in-Publication Data

Names: Dunn, Thomas R., author.
Title: The pink scar : how Nazi persecution shaped the struggle for LGBTQ+ rights / Thomas R. Dunn.
Description: University Park, Pennsylvania : The Pennsylvania State University Press, [2025] | Series: Troubling democracy | Includes bibliographical references and index.
Summary: "Examines how American LGBTQ+ activists invoked Nazi persecution of homosexuals to advance rights before the HIV/AIDS era. Highlights how early narratives of suffering shaped advocacy and influenced a distinct American vision for LGBTQ+ rights prior to the pink triangle's emergence as a dominant symbol"—Provided by publisher.
Identifiers: LCCN 2025024204 | ISBN 9780271100159 (hardback) | ISBN 9780271100166 (paperback)
Subjects: LCSH: Gay liberation movement—United States—History. | Gay rights—United States—History. | LGBT activism—United States—History. | Gay people—Nazi persecution—Germany. | Collective memory—United States—History.
Classification: LCC HQ76.8.U6 D86 2025 | DDC 306.76/60973—dc23/eng/20250616
LC record available at https://lccn.loc.gov/2025024204

The Pennsylvania State University Press is a member of the Association of University Presses.
It is the policy of The Pennsylvania State University Press to use acid-free paper. Publications on uncoated stock satisfy the minimum requirements of American National Standard for Information Sciences—Permanence of Paper for Printed Library Material, ANSI Z39.48–1992.

To those who stayed true to themselves,
even in the face of fascism.

Contents

Acknowledgments

Every book project is challenging. In the case of *The Pink Scar*, those challenges were far more than I anticipated at the start. I began this book two weeks before my daughter's first birthday, the first time in many months when writing a single word even seemed possible. I spent several months researching and writing this book while suffering from the onset and aftermath of a severe case of shingles. My long-planned research travel to Poland, particularly a visit to the Museum and Memorial at Bełżec, was thrown into flux for a few days by the Russian invasion of Ukraine. And the entirety of the research and writing of this project took place amid the unfamiliar and discomfiting realities of the COVID-19 pandemic. In sum, there were simply so many reasons why and occasions when this book could have fallen to pieces. This makes it all the more important at the book's completion to recognize the incredible support and encouragement of so many wonderful people who got me to this point.

I would first like to thank Colorado State University for supporting this project through my appointment as a 2020–23 Monfort Professor. The recognition, encouragement, and transformative research funding that came with that title made the project possible. I am particularly indebted to my department colleagues who nominated me for this professorship, the members of the university selection committee who put their faith in this project, and the Offices of the Provost and the Vice President for Research that supported my work during this three-year period. I am especially appreciative of the flexibility I was afforded in using my research funds in the face of COVID-19, including a one-year extension that allowed me to complete extensive research travel that was simply impossible during pandemic restrictions.

Much of this research travel in support of the book took me to libraries and archives throughout the United States, and I am deeply appreciative of the archivists, librarians, and staff at these institutions who supported my work. Among them, many thanks to the professionals at the Brooke Russell Astor Reading Room for Rare Books and Manuscripts at the New York Public

Library and the archives and research center at the New York Public Library for the Performing Arts at Lincoln Center. It was also a particular joy to get to write a handful of chapter drafts in the magnificent Rose Reading Room in the New York Public Library's Stephen A. Schwartzman Building. My sincere thanks also go to the staff at the McCormick Library of Special Collections and University Archives at Northwestern University, who facilitated numerous visits to the reading room during some of the worst days of the pandemic. A special thanks to Mel Leverich at the Leather Archives and Museum in Chicago for their flexibility in helping me access the archive's rich pulp collection during two different visits. Much appreciation as well to the various professionals at the United States Holocaust Memorial Museum, particularly at the David and Fela Shapell Family Collections, Conservation and Research Center. I would also like to extend my thanks to the staff at archives I could only visit digitally due to COVID-19 restrictions, particularly the good people at the ONE Archives at the University of Southern California Libraries.

This book also required two intensive international research trips to various sites of Nazi persecution. I could not imagine writing this book without spending time at these locations, and each visit eminently increased the quality of this book's claims. One of these trips was to Poland, a rich, beautiful, and large country I could not possibly have navigated on my own with the time and resources I had. I am therefore very appreciative of the staff of the Cultural Experience tour company, who impressively guided me and a dozen other travelers across the nation to often remote and far-flung locations in just a few days. I am particularly indebted to Dr. Isabel Wollaston for sharing on this tour her extensive knowledge of Poland and the Nazi concentration and death camps inside its borders during World War II. While I was fortunate to be able to navigate a research trip to Germany on my own, a special thanks to Insider Tour Berlin and Radius Tours for their insights at two German concentration camps. Most of all, I am deeply appreciative of the tour guides, staff, and professionals at the Sachsenhausen Memorial and Museum, the Ravensbrück Memorial Museum, the Dachau Concentration Camp Memorial Site, the Treblinka Museum, the State Museum at Majdanek, the Museum and Memorial at Bełżec, and the Auschwitz-Birkenau Memorial and Museum. Preserving these spaces of memory is essential for the horrible lessons they teach, and the careful and professional maintenance they receive as sites of memory is commendable.

I learned a great deal about the book project from a few insightful audiences who listened to in-progress drafts over several years. In this vein, I want to thank the students, faculty, and staff at the University of Richmond, Northwestern University, Colorado State University, and the University of Kansas for invitations to share my ideas in classes visits, colloquia, and lectures. Special thanks to Drs. Mari Lee Mifsud, Angela G. Ray, and Dave Tell for extending those gracious invitations. Thank you also to the staff at the Denver Public Library and the Mercer County Library System of New Jersey, who afforded my book a wider audience outside the academy. The opportunity to think through these ideas with each of these audiences contributed immensely to this final document.

This book would also not have been possible without a wonderful set of professionals in the Department of Communication Studies and the College of Liberal Arts at Colorado State University, who helped facilitate the many everyday tasks necessary for doing good research. Among them, many thanks go to the outstanding team of Azumi Solbrig and Zel Gabriel, who supported my travel and processed reimbursements for tens of thousands of dollars, often one tiny receipt at a time. Thanks also to Catherine Kane in the College of Liberal Arts, who did Herculean work on short notice to help me prepare a realistic budget for the project at the proposal stage. And a special thanks to my dear friend and colleague Eliza Chew, who endured my nagging questions, indulged my anxieties, tracked down answers to my strange questions, cut through bureaucratic red tape, and pushed me to get the most out of this unique research experience.

In writing *The Pink Scar*, I was lucky to have the support of two outstanding graduate research assistants, who did critical work for me at either end of this project. As such, an effusive set of thanks go to James O'Mara, who helped gather initial research for the introduction in summer and fall 2020, and Jamison Warren, who offered a smart reading of the final manuscript and helped draft this book's index in summer 2024. This book would have been a much heavier lift without their efforts.

I consider myself quite fortunate that Penn State University Press has agreed to be the home for this book. I am very grateful to my two readers, who pushed my thinking on the first version of the manuscript while remaining wildly supportive. Their questions and suggestions made this book significantly stronger. Thank you also to Josie DiKerby, Alex Ramos, and Nicholas Taylor for their proactive and helpful support in moving the book into publication. And to my editor, Archna Patel, thank you for your enthusiasm for this project from the start, stellar advice, care and attentiveness, and thoughtful shepherding of the manuscript (and its author) through this process.

Having near and dear colleagues who have supported me during the execution of this project has been an absolute joy. They have been fonts of knowledge, sharers of experience, compassionate listeners, exceptional mentors, voices of encouragement, co–problem solvers, and dear friends. Thank you to Drs. Eric Aoki, Kari Anderson, Greg Dickinson, Julia Khrebtan-Hörhager, Joe Sery, and Elizabeth Williams for all that you do.

Amid all the travel, I am also thankful for the many strangers and acquaintances I met along the way who buoyed my spirits, kept good company, provided many laughs, and even joined me on some adventures. Some of those people are old and beloved friends, like Kristin Witters, who shares my interest in the Holocaust and is a delight to see on any occasion. Others are brand-new friends, including rowdy tour mates, fellow travelers, the Aussie family that referred to me only as "our American friend," and the joyful patrons and staff I met at small and embattled gay bars in a few Polish cities. In particular, a special thanks to Andrea and David, who made visits to several sites of human suffering an unexpected occasion for friendship and restoration.

Closer to home, there are more than a few people to whom I need to say thank you. To the Commune, thank you for welcoming us into your community, becoming fast friends, and helping care for my family during my many weeks of travel and writing. To the G&T Club, thanks for always offering a respite, a few thousand laughs, and the best tagline for the project that I could have imagined. To Holly and Maisy, I can't imagine having completed this project without your love and support. I am so grateful for the family we have all built together. To Gary and Barbara, I get to walk this road thanks to your constant love, support, and encouragement. You guide me in everything I do. I love you both.

To my husband, Craig, thank you for sticking around for each of our crazy adventures and always saying yes to the next one. All our successes are shared, so this book is just as much yours as it is mine. Thank you for caring for our amazing little family and *always* being you. I love you.

And to Ada. You have been the greatest gift during this book's complex journey. You are my whole heart. Everything I do, I do for you.

Abbreviations

ALI	American Law Institute
AS	Elledge, *An Angel in Sodom*
CH	Coolen, *The Concentration of Hans*
GDA	Davidson, *Go Down, Aaron*
MFY	Kepner, "My First 64 Years of Gay Liberation"
MG	Zilinsky, *Middle Ground*
NN	Kearful, "The New Nazism"
PT	Lautmann, "Pink Triangle"
SNM	Itkin, *Silent No More*
QWB	Itkin, "A Question Written in Blood"
VH	Itkin, "Visitors from the Holocaust"

Introduction

When US lesbian and gay activists undertook the movement's very first White House picket on April 17, 1965, their animating concern was something not seen since the Nazi persecution of homosexuals during World War II: the return of concentration camps for homosexuals.[1] The activists' trepidation was not unfounded. Within weeks of the picket, US newspapers reported that Cuba's Fidel Castro regime had "launched a campaign against homosexualism." The earliest reports by the Associated Press were short on specifics but explained the crackdown via an ominous government statement that argued "homosexuals do not represent the revolution and the virile Cuban people" and that in a "Socialist society, there is no room for it."[2] Previous reporting by the *New York Times* crystallized the threat. The newspaper explained that the Castro government had grown "alarmed" by a perceived "increase in homosexuality" in its major cities. Quoting from a party newspaper, the *Times* shared that the Castro government did not propose to "persecute homosexuals," but did intend to "break their 'positions, procedures, and influence,' by applying 'revolutionary social hygiene.'" For readers unaccustomed to the regime's political doublespeak, the *Times* clarified that "revolutionary social hygiene" should be understood "as a warning that homosexuals would be rounded up and sent to labor camps."[3] As such, US news reports made clear to readers—both heterosexual and homosexual—that the alarming practices of mass arrests and internments of homosexuals undertaken by the Nazis three decades earlier were once again underway.

The day following the *Times* story, the Mattachine Society of Washington—a regional chapter of the earlier national gay rights organization—responded with atypical haste and resolve. In 1965, protests by lesbian and gay rights organizations were almost unheard of.[4] Yet at 4:20 p.m., ten men and women representing Mattachine Washington—including movement leaders Frank Kameny and Lilli Vincenz, a lesbian immigrant from Nazi Germany—situated themselves in "a choice spot directly in front of the White House" in Lafayette Square.[5] Dressed in their most respectable professional attire, the picketers raised their signs in the air and walked in formation for one hour before the gaze of the White House and the general public.

While even today this protest is remembered almost exclusively as a response to the Lavender Scare, the sweeping crackdown on alleged homosexuals employed by the US government, the message the protesters *actually* sent that day was far more complex.[6] Indeed, both the timing of the event and the signs picketers carried reveal that the group's concern for American homosexuals was deeply intertwined with memories of Nazi persecutions years earlier and the looming Cuban threat to do the same. For instance, a prominent picket sign framed the protest clearly: "Members of the Mattachine Society of Washington Protest Cuba's Crackdown on Homosexuals." Three other picket signs also noted the situation in Cuba while connecting those events to the US treatment of homosexuals: "Cuba's Government Persecutes Homosexuals. U.S. Government Beat Them to It"; "U.S., Cuba, Russia United in Persecuting Homosexuals"; "Employment for Homosexuals isí! Labor Camps NO!" Yet another sign drew a straight line between the events in Cuba, the United States, and Nazi Germany: "Jews to Concentration Camps Under Nazis; Homosexuals to Work Camps Under Castro. Is the U.S. Much Better?"[7] Three other signs appeared that day without reference to the specter of the internment of Cuban homosexuals or the Nazi regime, and the extent to which picketers conflated the experiences of Jews and homosexuals in the camps in their rhetorical appeal is hard to disentangle even today.[8] Yet Mattachine Washington asserted powerfully for the watching world in 1965 that US lesbian and gay activism was deeply attuned to how persecutions of the past—particularly the Nazi persecution of homosexuals between 1933 and 1945—would animate their work in the present and into the future.

As a persuasive undertaking, the White House picket produced mixed results. The urgent and evolving nature of events in Cuba demanded an immediate response but permitted little time to gather more picketers or alert the press. In fact, only one newspaper, the *Washington Afro-American*, covered the day's events, an early act of coalition-building between Black freedom activists and white homosexual leaders in the Washington, DC, area.[9] Nor did the picket demonstrably affect US policy toward Cuba or the fate of its large homosexual population. In fact, the Castro regime's promised crackdown against homosexuals and other undesirables was swift, including the expulsion of homosexuals from universities and the military, persecution in civil society and on the streets, and, as promised, the internment of homosexuals between 1965 and 1968 in the regime's Unidades Militares de Ayuda a la Producción (Military Units to Aid Production, or UMAP). The UMAP camps ultimately interned thousands of homosexuals, both male and female, without charge and subjected them to sixteen-hour days of forced labor, surrounded by barbed-wire fences and regular beatings of effeminate men by camp guards.[10] Nonetheless, the picket demonstrated that the specter of homosexuals jailed in concentration camps was a powerful and motivating appeal in the movement's politics. For an organization like Mattachine Washington, once notoriously cautious and insular, the protest was a bold step into a new era of forceful and public lesbian and gay advocacy in the United States. Despite the great suffering and many laments of American homosexuals in the decades before 1965, it is remarkable that it was the sudden and provocative internment of Cuban homosexuals that broke through the organization's trepidation about public protest and brought it, as later generations would demand, out of the closet and into the streets.[11]

Acknowledging that this germinal moment in lesbian and gay rights protest was, in fact, just as much about remembering the internment of homosexuals in concentration camps as it was about discrimination against US homosexual federal employees is a provocation—a provocation that prompts further questions. How, for instance, did lesbians and gays of this era come to know about the internment and persecution of homosexuals in Germany in the 1930s and '40s so they might reference these events in their persuasive appeals? Were the circumstances of the Cuban crackdown uniquely similar to the Nazi persecution, making it ripe for comparison? Or did the lesbian and gay rights movement remember the Nazi persecution in other ways and at other moments to advance its aims? What was the nature of these remembrances and to what purposes were they put? And what might rediscovering such a campaign of commemorating this persecution mean for how we should remember these events today and deeper into the twenty-first century?

This book answers these questions and more by analyzing how the early homophile, homosexual, and lesbian and gay rights movements in the United States understood and drew on memories of the Nazi persecution of homosexuals between 1933 and 1945 to advance their own social, political, and cultural aims between 1934 and 1981. More specifically, this book shows that the early lesbian and gay rights movement in the United States made remembering the persecution of homosexuals by the Nazis a central, animating, and indispensable part of their rhetoric and politics in the postwar era time and time again.

This claim counters much of our received wisdom about how early lesbian and gay communities in the United States understood—or did not understand—these events. For decades, historians and activists alike have suggested that most homosexuals could not have known about the persecution of their kin across the Atlantic until well after the war. When these events were known, we are told that these memories remained in small conversations among isolated groups—insufficient to be considered the stuff of a homosexual public's consideration or lacking in world-making potential. Rather, we are to believe that memories of the persecution of homosexuals by the Nazis were lost and forgotten for decades, only to be rediscovered years later when a meaningful post-Stonewall community was established. Only then would these memories reach their full potential, particularly as a rallying cry for the community as it faced the threats of homophobia, heteronormativity, and government inaction during the HIV/AIDS crisis—a moment exemplified in ACT UP's infamous 1987 poster slogan "Silence = Death."

But as the picket example and the remaining chapters of this book show, substantive homosocial, homosexual, and lesbian and gay publics of the pre- and postwar era were not unaware of the events that transpired against homosexuals under the Nazi regime. Rather, American activists remembered the Nazi persecution of homosexuals and wielded those memories in nuanced and diverse ways to advance a burgeoning lesbian and gay rights agenda. In fact, as this book demonstrates, the repression of homosexuals by the Nazis was an incendiary force within the community's discourse and imagination from some of the earliest moments of US homophile, homosexual, and lesbian and gay organizing. In short, it was simply impossible for the budding American homosexual movement between 1934 and 1981 to envision itself without reckoning with the harassment, arrests, blackmail, incarcerations, experiments, and murders of homosexuals at the hands of the Nazis.

Asserting that early American activists deployed these memories of the Nazi era over several decades should not, however, imply that these remembrances were simplistic, similar, or stable. To the contrary, rooted in different decades and facing disparate challenges in their efforts to advance a more just, fair, and equitable nation for lesbian and gay Americans—including issues of motivation, self-concept, and expertise—activists remembered the Nazi persecution of homosexuals in wildly disparate ways. Examining different moments in this struggle reveals that activists disagreed about which facets of the persecution were most meaningful and interpreted the same events for homosexual audiences with great variability. For instance, a homophile activist writer of the 1930s who remembered victims of an anti-homosexual massacre by Nazi leaders only a few months earlier drew on very different readings and features of this event than did well-organized California political leaders in the 1970s. In some cases, as we will see, the diversity in how the Nazis' homosexual victims were remembered—or even who could be considered a victim—can be explained by limitations in what was knowable about the persecution at different moments in time. But more often, these variations reflected rhetorical choices made by specific homosexual actors in particular situations to render their reminiscences of the past with certain emphases to achieve specific political and personal aims. These variegated deployments of memories and their desired effects are among the central considerations addressed in the pages to follow.

By necessity and choice, our concern here is not, with rare exceptions, what mainstream heterosexual discourses said or what heterosexual audiences knew about the homosexual persecution during this era. By contrast, the following chapters focus on how, in particular instances, a nascent lesbian and gay community—whose members described themselves alternately as inverts, androgynes, homophiles, homosexuals, and eventually lesbians and gay men—spoke about and imagined themselves in the looming shadow of the Nazi persecution months, years, and decades earlier. Simultaneously, this book offers important insights about the general features of remembering the Nazi persecution of homosexuals before HIV/AIDS. More specifically, I show that while homosexual victims were remembered through 1981 in ways that made sense in key political and cultural moments, those remembrances were also shaped by uniquely American understandings of Nazism and the Holocaust as well as very particular social, cultural, and political events unfolding on American shores. Ultimately, better understanding what these memories meant will inform how we remember, teach, and communicate about the homosexual experience under Nazism in the decades to come.

To that end, in this introduction's remaining pages, I devote significant time not only to recounting the core events of the Nazi persecution but also to demonstrating that the US media regularly reported on the Nazi persecution of homosexuals between 1933 and 1945 in assorted mediums that reached diverse American audiences—including homosexuals. As a result, we should absolve ourselves of the idea that the Nazi persecution was unknowable to US homosexuals before, during, or after the war. With that point established, the remaining chapters of this book build chronologically to advance three primary arguments:

1. Not only did American homosexuals know of these events, but they made remembering the Nazi persecution of homosexuals a central and animating rhetorical resource in their efforts to envision themselves as part of a more inclusive America in the years before HIV/AIDS.
2. In this work, homophile, homosexual, gay liberation, and lesbian and gay rights movements and activists each in turn used these memories of persecution in highly varied, dynamic, and sometimes contradictory ways to achieve their stated and unstated aims.
3. As opposed to "pink triangle" commemorations often aimed at heterosexual audiences after the mid-1970s, remembering the persecution as more than the experiences of homosexuals in the camps and addressing those memories almost exclusively to homosexual or lesbian and gay audiences were essential to their success.

By book's end, readers will walk away with a far richer appreciation for just how important and influential remembering the homosexual victims of the Nazi regime was in building the postwar homosexual world—and how the twenty-first century might again require that we remember these events in force to preserve that world for queer and trans generations to come.

Memory Matters, Matters of Choice

Writing a book like *The Pink Scar* requires making choices—choices that influence not only its scope and shape but also the questions it can ask and the answers it provides. In the wider realm of Holocaust scholarship and remembrance, the significance of choice is palpable, for what in other topic areas might appear to be a relatively minor selection of scope, emphasis, or representation has weighty implications here for who is counted as a victim and whose story is told at all. Scholarly conversations and memorial commissions have gotten bogged down on these very issues for years, even decades, for exactly these reasons. With this in mind, I have made several choices in this text that at the outset are essential to explain in order to place the book in its proper domain.

The first choice is to write this book at all, given the existing work in this area. Since 1975, academics and scholars writing in English have studied the history and implications of the Nazi persecution of homosexuals. Two well-appreciated works, both appearing in 1975, are notable: James Steakley's *The Homosexual Emancipation Movement in Germany* and John Lauritsen and David Thorstad's *The Early Homosexual Rights Movement (1864–1935)*. Both texts appeared in truncated forms and smaller circulations as early as 1973. These were followed by Richard Plant's now definitive *The Pink Triangle: The Nazi War Against Homosexuals* in 1986, which, despite theoretical and historical updates in recent years, remains most American readers' entry point into the subject. Essential contributions by other scholars like Rüdiger Lautmann, Günter Grau, Claudia Schoppmann, Geoffrey J. Giles, and Laurie Marhoefer have deepened and extended this work. Today, these events again appear freshly in print in a new wave of scholarly investigation, most notably W. Jake Newsome's *Pink Triangle Legacies* and Sébastien Tremblay's *A Badge of Injury*. For nonacademic audiences, stories of the Nazi persecution of homosexuals are available in films, graphic novels, young adult literature, and even children's books. Each text is a vital piece of an important infrastructure for sharing the stories of the Nazis' homosexual victims and defending us today from repeating the tragedies of this persecution.

Despite this still understudied but rich reservoir of scholarship, there remain unanswered questions and uninterrogated perspectives that justify writing this book. In particular, this book addresses an overlooked aspect of the literature by making two correlated choices to guide its scope and design. The first choice is to highlight the American experience of remembering the homosexuals persecuted by the Nazis. To date, scholars have completed significant work reconstructing the Nazi persecution of homosexuals and its role in the development of LGBTQ+ identities and politics in Germany. This work is exceptional and needs no retreading here. Less work has been done on how American LGBTQ+ communities have remembered these persecutions—but almost all this scholarship focuses on the period after 1975. As such, second and relatedly, this book intentionally avoids considering these memories in the post-HIV/AIDS memory landscape, an era that has been well studied, has received a veritable explosion of commemorative attention, and is fundamentally different from the memory work of the pre-HIV/AIDS moment. Understanding and reconstructing the role of the Nazi persecution of homosexuals as a rhetorical touchstone in the decades between 1934 and 1981 is therefore the exclusive focus of this book and fills a needed gap in our understanding.

This book also emphasizes how the Nazi regime's persecution of homosexuals is remembered by later generations, as opposed to investigating these historical events themselves. In doing so, it invokes the most agreed-on academic accounting of events where needed and devotes the bulk of its focus to memory. The study of memory has been a powerful tool for examining how collective articulations of the past are used to advance contemporary aims. Indeed, scholars debate but largely agree that our contemporary interest in memory—as both an academic interest and a dimension of cultural life—can be traced at least in part to a global need to reckon with the aftermath of the Holocaust, beginning in the middle of the twentieth century.[12] In some articulations of this work, the line dividing memory from history has been sharply drawn, with history seen as an objective telling of the past and memory presented as its more malleable and contingent other.[13] However, from a rhetorical perspective, all discourses—by their very nature as symbolic expressions—seek to persuade, advance a perspective, or change the worldview of others.[14] As such, both history and memory are mediated representations that pull the past forward in a meaningful way.

Nonetheless, by choosing to emphasize memory in this book, several key aspects of its relationship to the past are highlighted. For one, a memory focus foregrounds the *meaning* of the Nazi persecution of homosexuals through time. As such, how these events mattered to US homosexual activists and leaders at given moments in the postwar period and how they chose to understand them for rhetorical effect take precedence in the analysis to come. For another, a memory focus values the multifaceted, variegated, and contradictory ways these memories appear over the decades in US discourse as key sites of inquiry. Last, our memory focus places on equal footing a diverse set of texts, discourses, and artifacts for consideration. In this investigation, both grand documents at key turning points and cloistered, little-studied, and everyday artifacts from small archives are taken seriously for the articulations of the past they provide. In fact, as we will see, it is only by weaving together texts of stratified and diversified types that we can bring to light a picture of how the persecution was remembered, revealing aspects not previously visible.

This choice to emphasize memory also has significant implications for the project's approach. In some instances, methodological choices for this project were straightforward, such as relying on textual documents between the years 1934 and 1981 to examine and analyze remembrances of the persecution. This decision was self-evident, given the era I emphasize and my training as a rhetorical scholar specializing in highlighting shifts in memory in documentable remnants of discourse. However, other choices in this book are more innovative, intentionally diverting from those in other memory projects to identify a single, stable key term and trace its influence through time and across a narrowly defined set of memory texts.

Instead, my method deviates from this course in three novel ways. First, rather than fixate on a single term, this project identifies numerous closely related but not synonymous terms and phrases signifying homosexuality under the Third Reich to inform its analysis. This choice was essential, for relying on a common and more modern umbrella term that tries (and fails) to capture all the complexities of the persecution (like *pink triangle*) would have inevitably privileged certain decades and experiences, leading to an incomplete picture of the memories between 1934 and 1981 we do not wish to reproduce. I say more about this below. Meanwhile, to avoid this outcome, I opted to combine a diverse lexicon of unstable signifiers of historical LGBTQ+ people—drawn from a panoply of legal, political, scientific, medical, moralistic, derogatory, and slang discourses—with a handful of contextual terms about the Third Reich to conduct my search free from these earlier constraints.[15] These searches led, second, to a wide array of different kinds of texts that might be stitched together to tell the story of how the Nazi persecution mattered in US homosexual communities. More specifically, with substantive grant funding, access to historical databases, and travel to LGBTQ+ archival collections in New York, Chicago, and Washington, DC, I built an "archive" of mostly little-examined texts in early lesbian and gay history that serve as this book's primary source material. I also enhanced this archive with visits to key memory sites, including the US Holocaust Memorial Museum, the Memorial to the Persecuted Homosexuals Under National Socialism in Berlin, and four killing centers (Bełżec, Treblinka, Majdanek, and Auschwitz-Birkenau) and three concentration camps (Dachau, Ravensbrück, and Sachsenhausen) in Poland and Germany, respectively. Not every text I discovered appears in this book. Many were excluded due to their brevity, limited circulation, extensive attention by other scholars, or post-1981 publication. But this archive's richness is evidenced by the texts highlighted in the chapters to come. Finally, rather than defaulting to a rigid reading of static identifiers in a single text type, my method blends otherwise disparate and diverse homosexual victims of the Nazi persecution, strewn across widely variegated texts into a single, rich, and heretofore untold story of persecution and remembrance. As we will see, collapsing what others may view as distinct forms of homosexual suffering into a single story is unconventional and produces some strange bedfellows. Yet previous analyses have missed important rhetorical shifts and assertions in the LGBTQ+ past exactly because of methodological presumptions that render these diverse stories disjointed from one another. Here, I take a different approach, adopting an ecumenical view of who counts both as a homosexual and as a victim to tell a story of the Nazi persecution's remembrance that has yet to be unearthed at this scale.

Following from this last point, these innovative choices in method are undergirded by another choice that distinguishes this book from others: the decision to avert analyses of remembering "the pink triangles"—individuals who faced incarceration, mistreatment, and death within particular Nazi concentration camps due to their homosexuality—in favor of remembering a wider category of individuals here named under the variable rubric of the homosexuals persecuted by the Nazi regime. This choice was made for various reasons, including contemporary historical scholarship trends that have nuanced earlier depictions of "the Nazi persecution of homosexuals" as synonymous with the experiences of the pink triangles, and hard-fought conventions in commemorative culture that, while still imperfect, well capture contemporary research on this community of victims.[16] But perhaps most importantly, this shift away from the pink triangles is required by the simultaneous shift in this book to study memories of the homosexual persecution during the stated time period. As at least half of the chapters of this book demonstrate, for much of the postwar period, when homosexual victims of the Nazis were remembered by American homosexuals, it was often the experiences of these men persecuted *under* Paragraph 175 (the Nazis' enhanced anti-homosexual law) but victimized *outside* the concentration camps that were discussed.

The choice to adopt a wider lens through which to view the Nazi persecution of homosexuals produces numerous outcomes in the pages to follow. One of the most notable appears in chapter 1, which examines how Captain Ernst Roehm is remembered by an early homophile activist in the United States as a "victim" of anti-homosexual persecution.[17] As a homosexual who was himself a Nazi, did not experience the camps, and did not survive long enough to witness the persecution of homosexuals himself, Roehm does not meet the definition of a pink triangle by any modern standard. What's more, as an architect of the Nazi Party and a confidant to Adolf Hitler, Roehm can rightly be blamed as a contributor to the persecution of homosexuals, rather than its victim. Nonetheless, there is a good case to be made that Roehm— to the extent that he was targeted for his homosexuality—was a victim of our broader category of Nazi persecution. As a result, Roehm's remembrance is investigated in this book in a way that it almost certainly would not be in other such texts. By the same token, this shift gives serious attention to the tens of thousands of homosexual men who were harassed, blackmailed, and arrested by the Nazi secret police during the persecution but never entered a concentration camp. This segment of the homosexual community persecuted by the Nazis has too often been diminished, minimized, or entirely erased in public memory in favor of remembering the pink triangles almost exclusively. As a result, this book aims to provide a comprehensive overview and highlight who has been remembered at different times. It also sets up a consideration in this book's conclusion about what is lost when we narrow our scope of which homosexual victims of the Nazi persecution matter the most in our memory discourse.

It must also be stated that this investigation highlights both the remembrances of gay, white, cisgender American male activists, speakers, and organizers and the experiences of white, cisgender, male homosexual victims. As such, white masculinity and its rhetorical connections to US remembrances of the Nazi persecution of homosexuals are an important facet of this study. This emphasis on white, male rhetors and victims was not by design. From my initial research into remembrances of the persecution, I was hopeful I might discover a diverse group of LGBTQ+ people and their predecessors engaged in this work. To that end, I conducted searches with womencentric terms and keywords in LGBTQ+ inclusive archives and databases, intentionally devoted time to searches of available Black, Jewish, and Latino newspapers, and reviewed an incomplete run of the first national lesbian publication, *The Ladder*.[18] These searches were not for naught, revealing lesbian pulps and speeches, gender-spanning acts of protest, and intersectional Jewish gay and lesbian discourses that each in some way evoked memories of the Nazi persecution of homosexuals—all of which appear in the chapters ahead.[19] And it quickly became clear that the arrival of the HIV/AIDS pandemic radically expanded and diversified who in the American LGBTQ+ community recognized themselves in the memories of the Nazi crackdown.[20]

Nonetheless, the white cisgender male experience of the persecution is certainly the predominant frame through which this memory work was done in the United States between 1934 and 1981. There are several explanations for this focus. Chief among them is the fact that the law the Nazis most relied on to persecute homosexual crimes was exclusively concerned with policing same-sex desires and acts between men. This did not mean that women, transgender, and nonbinary people did not face persecution under the Nazis; current research reveals they did, often via a more generalizable crackdown mechanism against "asocials."[21] But because the Nazis explicitly identified homosexual acts between men as problematic in law, the persecution both hit them in significantly higher numbers and rendered this male-oriented persecution more easily legible to those commemorators who followed. Similarly, some of this same research demonstrates that cisgender "Aryan" men accused of homosexual "crimes" were more likely to be afforded a court hearing, a lawyer, and an appeal than non-Aryan or noncisgender individuals.[22] This was particularly damaging for homosexuals who were Jewish or Roma, as well as Afro-Germans, European Blacks, or Africans, all of whom were marked as non-Aryan through Nazi ideologies and faced increased chances of being sent to the camps or killing centers as a result.[23] Meanwhile, each of the affordances provided to Aryan homosexuals made it less likely they would face this same outcome and greatly enhanced the chances that these men's stories would be recorded and made available for memory. To these reasons, we can also add others, including gendered and raced archival practices and cisgender white men's greater access to speech, writing, and publication (even as homosexuals). But perhaps the most significant explanation for the prominence of white masculinity in US remembrances of the Nazi persecution of homosexuals between 1933 and 1945 is that the cisgender white men, who were overrepresented in positions of power in the American movement during this period, found it easy to see themselves reflected in memories of white, male, homosexual European victims. Meanwhile, both nonwhite homosexual men and white and nonwhite lesbian rhetors of the postwar era may have found these recorded memories that privileged the white, male homosexual experiences of victimization less rhetorically salient to their own personal and political goals. While such views would change later in the twentieth century, the ready-made identification between the Nazis' largest and easiest to recognize homosexual victims and the empowered white, male, homosexual activists in the United States after World War II likely proved a decisive factor in explaining the overwhelming amount of attention white masculinity receives in this volume.

In writing this book, I was also encouraged to reflect on the shifting nature of Holocaust memory in the early decades of the twenty-first century. Investigating the Nazi persecution of homosexuals in American memory today inevitably takes place against this backdrop. As this book makes clear, the Nazi persecution of homosexuals is not consubstantial with the Holocaust. Each event occurred on its own timeline and was prosecuted at different scales, using various methods, rationales, and horrors. Nonetheless, the moral imperative to remember the Holocaust often defines our modern commemorative culture, and the Nazi persecution of homosexuals has almost always taken place within that culture, sometimes within the very same commemorative zones and discourses. As such, remembering homosexual suffering in Nazi Germany between 1933 and 1945 is always anchored in a broader Holocaust memory infrastructure. But recent decades have seen profound shifts in the force of Holocaust remembrance. On one level, whereas Holocaust commemorations were once seen as the definitive examples of memory's power to hold successive generations accountable to the past, recent years have witnessed a declining resonance of these horrors with certain audiences. In particular, despite ongoing campaigns, today's youngest generations show a "shocking" lack of knowledge about the Holocaust, events that feel increasingly distant from their own experiences or responsibilities.[24] Simultaneously, far-right European political groups have found some degree of success in their efforts to forget, co-opt, or deny the Holocaust as part of their anti-Semitic and illiberal agendas. On another level, the atrocities committed by Hamas on October 7, 2023, and the inhumane prosecution of the war in Gaza by Benjamin Netanyahu's Israeli government in response have now scrambled the once nearly sacrosanct sense of morality implicated by remembering the Holocaust. In a world where even the most reliable supporters of the Jewish people must acknowledge an Israeli government seemingly hell-bent on carrying out its own acts of horror, long-standing connections between Jewish victimization and Holocaust memory may have been irredeemably upended. This book's investigation takes place within this larger context. While many of the particularities of the chapters are immune to these more modern shifts in Holocaust memory, the text overall cannot avoid the wider consequences of its context. As noted in several chapters, the fortunes and forms of remembering the Nazis' homosexual victims between 1934 and 1981 are often tied to implicit and explicit assumptions about the meaning of the Holocaust in American memory. In the book's final assessment, I return to the question of what remembering the Nazis' homosexual victims means today and what this flux in Holocaust memory portends for such remembering going forward.

To conclude this discussion of the choices that frame the text, I want to emphasize that I also write this book as a moral obligation in the face of the continued persecution of LGBTQ+ people. At the time of this writing, the American LGBTQ+ community—indeed, the LGBTQ+ community world-wide—is confronting just the most recent in a recurrent onslaught of assaults dating back to time immemorial. While this persecution takes many contemporary forms, it is imperative to note that these efforts extend to a campaign to further erase LGBTQ+ history and memory. Laws like Florida's nefarious 2022 "Don't Say Gay" law and Russia's 2013 antigay propaganda law have made sharing stories of the LGBTQ+ past in education, policy debates, and broader culture significantly harder than even a few years ago. Since the Nazis, we have rarely witnessed such concerted efforts by Western governments to destroy queer texts, silence queer voices, and police the acquisition of queer knowledge. At this moment, writing about the persecution of homosexuals by their own people and governments is a moral necessity that serves not only the victims who have long since passed but also present and future LGBTQ+ victims of intolerance, who might find in these past examples the tools of their own survivance and power. This choice to write into the headwinds of oppression is one I make without hesitation.

Much more remains to be said about this imperative as it relates to remembering the homosexuals persecuted by the Nazi regime. But recognizing the ongoing attempt today to disconnect LGBTQ+ people from their shared memories, history, and past, it seems prudent to remind ourselves—or perhaps to learn for the first time—about just what suffering homosexuals endured between 1933 and 1945.

Revisiting the Nazi Persecution of Homosexuals

The facts of the Nazis' homosexual persecution have been and remain incomplete and disputed. Many of the earliest US activists to reference these events had only partial insights into the true scale of the crackdown. Meanwhile, as generations further removed from the period took up these events, they also communicated them with incomplete—and sometimes wildly incorrect—information. Nor did a wider acknowledgment of the homosexual persecution necessarily bring more accurate depictions of these events. At times, more recent remembrances have been less accurate and informed than those from decades earlier. Even today, scholars continue to debate the details of this persecution. However, the last fifty years have seen a significant increase in serious academic work on these events that make a reliable set of facts possible. I do not recount the full picture painted by these scholars here. But to the extent that these findings function as the raw materials of the rhetorics discussed in the chapters to come, reconstructing the history of the Nazi persecution of homosexuals is essential for understanding this book's major arguments.

Many historians trace the particularities of the Nazi persecution of homosexuals to 1870, when the German Reichstag introduced Paragraph 175 in its newly created penal code.[25] Paragraph 175 set forth provisions against sodomy across the newly created empire, which previously held widely disparate attitudes toward sex in law and customs. The statute criminalized "unnatural sexual acts committed between persons of the male sex" and dictated punishment by "imprisonment" or the potential "loss of civil rights."[26] While the new statute was intended to chill homosexual proclivities, it did not eliminate homosexuality in the empire. To the contrary, Paragraph 175 was both interpreted and applied inconsistently by different governments during its first sixty years in law.[27] For example, Paragraph 175 was often reserved exclusively for sexual acts between men that "resemble[ed] 'coital acts'"—and anything short of provable copulation went unprosecuted.[28] But data also show that while there were periods of "passive enforcement," the decades preceding Nazi control also saw intermittent crackdowns, suggesting Paragraph 175 remained a threat to homosexuals.[29] As such, early German homophile activists like Karl Ulrichs organized to overturn or weaken Paragraph 175 both before and after passage.[30] But these efforts ultimately failed. Paragraph 175 remained in the German penal code into the Third Reich and beyond, establishing the infrastructure on which a more forceful anti-homosexual persecution would later be built.

Meanwhile, a rich homosexual subculture was growing in German cities between 1918 and 1933. Here, gender and sexual minorities found isolated pockets of tolerance that rivaled those found elsewhere in the modern world. Bars, nightclubs, and other establishments formed a rich "homosexual club culture," featuring both homosexual and gender-bending performers and patrons.[31] Twenty-five to thirty homophile or homosexual publications appeared in print between 1919 and 1933.[32] At least in Berlin, local leaders built productive relationships with police forces, even affording leniency to gender-nonconforming people for a time.[33] And academic and political leaders of the study of sexology, like Dr. Magnus Hirschfeld and his world-renowned Institute for Sexual Science in Berlin, established Germany as a base from which animosities against sexual and gender minorities were rebutted via scientific study and conversation.[34] Throughout this period, homosexuals became a common (though not always welcome) sight for both German and foreign heterosexuals, some of whom became enamored with the nation's sexual vitality, experimentation, and inconsistent regulation.[35]

But in 1920, a collection of small political parties joined forces under a new banner to form what would become the National Socialist German Workers Party, better and later known as the Nazis. At its founding were two leaders who would both become influential in how the party addressed homosexuality: Adolf Hitler and Ernst Roehm. Most historians agree that Hitler was largely ambivalent on the topic, even as other Nazi leaders and party organs condemned homosexuality outright.[36] But Roehm mattered in this calculus too. As a Nazi and known homosexual himself, Roehm was a weather vane for interpreting the fate of homosexuals as the Nazis took power. While rarely advocating for the homosexual cause, Roehm adhered to masculinist understandings of homosexuality popular among a faction of German homosexuals.[37] In addition to being a key ally of Hitler, he was a vital cog in the party machine and helped expand the Nazi Party with brute force as the eventual chief of staff of the SA (Sturmabteilung), an early Nazi paramilitary organization. But Roehm could also be a liability. He was attacked by the Nazis' political opponents for his sexual orientation, even while the Nazis themselves slung accusations of homosexuality at their opposition.[38] But as the Nazis steadily gained power, concerns about Roehm's sexuality ebbed for a time, confusing how Germans understood the Nazi Party's stance on the homosexual question. Did the Nazis oppose homosexuality? Or did Roehm's presence in Nazi leadership suggest that homosexuals would be afforded a degree of security in the Third Reich?

With Hitler's appointment as chancellor in January 1933, a string of anti-homosexual measures unfolded in quick succession. Three weeks after gaining power, the Nazis banned pornography as well as homosexual publications and organizations, which forced at least some homosexual establishments to close.[39] In the wake of the Reichstag fire on February 27, a Dutchman named Marinus van der Lubbe was labeled a homosexual, arrested, and executed for the attack on the nation—despite convincing evidence the Nazis set the fire themselves. Then, in May 1933, Hirschfeld's Institute for Sexual Science was sacked by a gang of young Nazi supporters, who subsequently set ablaze the world's largest archive of homosexual materials. And in fall 1933, a new category of inmates—"homosexuals and pimps"—was established at the Fuhlsbüttel concentration camp outside Hamburg.[40] For some scholars, these events constituted the start of the Nazi campaign against homosexuals (PT, 141). For others, these events did not yet rise to that level.[41] Regardless, meaningful machinations against homosexuals were well underway by the end of 1933. And yet many homosexuals remained inured, though perhaps more circumspect, to the growing threats around them.

Those feelings changed abruptly over a summer weekend in 1934. On June 30, Roehm and several dozen SA leaders were among the eighty-five people summarily executed in a spectacular "blood purge."[42] The operation was authorized by Hitler but masterminded by the likes of Heinrich Himmler, a fierce anti-homosexualist and Roehm political opponent. Unlike most of the day's victims, Roehm was not killed on the spot but taken into custody and executed in his jail cell days later. In a speech marking the Roehm purge, Hitler himself dubbed it the "Night of the Long Knives."[43] The purge signaled an acceleration of the Nazi persecution of homosexuals, even if many homosexuals did not yet realize it. For the Nazis used homosexuality as a public rationale for the mass murder of Hitlerite enemies, particularly the false pretense that Roehm and a homosexual cabal were plotting a coup. Thereafter, the message was sent to all Nazi functionaries: "Homosexuals are to be expelled from the ranks."[44] The Ministry of Justice also declared the purge—retroactively—"entirely within the law."[45] Thus, public discourse and private violence alike signaled to many homosexuals that any remaining hope for tolerance under the new regime was a mirage. But the purge also had a formidable functional effect: it eliminated the most powerful homosexual in the Nazi Party and replaced him with a leader keen on implementing a more systematic crackdown on homosexuals—Himmler, now head of the SS (Schutzstaffel), another Nazi paramilitary organization.[46] The Roehm purge thus helped secure Hitler's power—but quickly destabilized the place of homosexuals in the Reich.

Anecdotal evidence suggests that the purge immediately changed the demeanor of many German homosexuals. Newspaper reports indicate that some homosexuals attempted to flee Germany, an effort depicted in fictionalized accounts of this time as well.[47] And members of the SA soon reassessed their safety. Plant relates the story about a homosexual friend who had joined the SA under Roehm and felt empowered and respected. But in the purge's aftermath, he noted, "I'm afraid his SA uniform is no protection with Roehm gone."[48] For homosexuals who were less monied and well-connected, the purge forced them to fade into the background of German society. Some homosexual men did this by engaging (often lesbian) women in "lavender marriages."[49] Other homosexuals joined the German army, hoping their service would inoculate them from the prying eyes of the secret police.[50] Some homosexuals who feared arrest, refused to report on their friends and lovers, had already endured too many years of oppression, or refused to live a diminished life in a homophobic society opted for suicide.[51] Still others, unwilling or unable to dispose of their homosexual reputations, simply went about their lives and waited for the coming storm.

It came in October 1934. Unbeknownst to the German public, Hitler's secret police, the Geheime Staatspolizei (Gestapo), issued orders to police departments throughout Germany, requesting the names of all previously identified or suspected homosexuals. Within days, hundreds of men were swept up in the first wave of mass arrests of homosexuals in Germany.[52] US newspapers at the time reported that between three hundred and nine hundred were arrested nationwide, while Nazi statements placed the number at three hundred.[53] The fate of these men and those arrested in the following years varied widely, with the men's race (i.e., Aryan or non-Aryan) being a key factor in their stories.[54] Some were questioned and released or remanded for further investigation. Others faced trial and served time in local prisons. Homosexuals with existing records were sent to the earliest camps at this time, alongside Communists and other political prisoners. Nonetheless, historical reviews of data from 1934 suggest that homosexual convictions did not increase far outside historical norms, even with this crackdown.[55]

But on June 28, 1935, the Nazi persecution of homosexuals entered a grim new phase. As part of a larger revision to the German penal code, the Nazis aggressively modified the decades-old language of Paragraph 175. Among the changes, the statute was amended to broaden what qualified as same-sex acts beyond anal sex and to grant arresting authorities vague but significant latitude to consider mere gestures and looks between men as criminal.[56] Rüdiger Lautmann characterized these changes as a moment when "a kiss or an embrace became a felony" (PT, 141). In addition, subsections were added to the law that targeted what the Nazis deemed to be egregious acts between men, including male prostitution and sex with a male under the age of twenty-one.[57] The law's expansion resulted in a much wider array of potential criminal liabilities among German men—and a marked increase in their prosecution. Extant accounts suggest that 5,320 men were convicted for homosexual offenses under Paragraph 175 in 1936, representing a fivefold increase from 1934. This spike also correlated with new tools for persecuting homosexuals. In particular, Himmler created the Reich Central Office for the Combating of Homosexuality and Abortion, which took a lead role in documenting, tracking, surveilling, and arresting suspected homosexuals in the years to follow. By 1938, the combined impact of changed laws and enforcement were reflected in 8,500 homosexual convictions.[58] On the eve of the World War II, the Nazis had radically accelerated the persecution of homosexuals.

While most homosexuals experienced persecution by the Nazis in German courts and prisons, some homosexuals—particularly those considered non-Aryan—were sent to concentration camps, where a subset would later be marked by a pink triangle symbol.[59] Homosexuals were early arrivals in Nazi camps, which were smaller and piecemeal, and held prisoners in superior conditions compared to later facilities. In these years, homosexuals sometimes made up a larger percentage of those interned than they would later in the war (PT, 144–46). I have already noted that homosexuals arrived in Fuhlsbüttel as early as 1933. A limited number of homosexual inmates were also sent to Dachau around this time; they were reported to have worn the number 175 on their clothing to mark their crimes. An American journalist visiting Dachau in 1935 described thirty homosexuals in a camp of eighteen hundred prisoners, approximately 1.7 percent of its population.[60] As the number and types of camps grew, homosexuals' experiences within them changed profoundly. Unlike millions of Jews and some other categories of Nazi victims, homosexuals were less likely to be sent to killing centers in the East, unless they were also known to be Jewish. Rather, homosexuals were used in labor camps to bolster the Nazi economy and war effort. Reliable reports of homosexual internment occurred at Buchenwald, Dachau, Flossenbürg, Gross-Rosen, Mauthausen, Mittelbau, Natzweiler, Neuengamme, Ravensbrück, Sachsenhausen, and Struthoff (PT, 142). In a handful of cases, individual homosexual prisoners earned a degree of protection because of a special skill (like an expertise in medicine) or, far less often, service to the Nazis as *kapos*—complicit prisoners entrusted by the Nazis to supervise certain camp functions (PT, 158–59). More commonly, homosexuals as a group were subjected to intensive physical labor that few survived (PT, 150–53). These assignments included working in Dachau's gravel pits or Sachsenhausen's clay pits, collecting unexploded ordnances in Hamburg, and heavy construction work at Dora—all of which overrepresented homosexual prisoners in their work details (PT, 151–52). When commandants in select camps isolated homosexuals from other prisoners later in the war, homosexuals sometimes endured special punishments, like being forced to sleep without pants or with their hands visible at all times, lest they be tossed out into the freezing cold (PT, 148–49). Meanwhile, while many Aryan homosexuals avoided gas chambers, they did suffer starvation, whipping, exposure, unsanitary conditions, disease, and random violence. Lautmann's research team suggests that homosexuals received some of the cruelest beatings in the camps (PT, 153–54). In Bergen-Belsen, which had a large homosexual population at one time, homosexuals died in sizable numbers alongside other inmates during a typhus outbreak. In Buchenwald, homosexuals were subjected to unsuccessful hormone experiments that sought to "normalize" their same-sex desires and transform them into heterosexuals.[61] Scholars have shown that homosexuals had a very high mortality rate compared to their heterosexual peers (PT, 141, 156). Heterosexual survivors of the camps also noted that homosexuals were less likely to survive than other victim categories.[62] Figures vary widely, but many historians today quote Lautmann's team in estimating that between five thousand and fifteen thousand homosexuals were interned in concentration camps (PT, 146).

While male homosexuals made up the vast majority of victims persecuted in concentration camps, lesbians and transgender people also faced abuse and victimization by the Nazi apparatus. Long forgotten as part of the Nazi persecution, women were often targeted not for homosexuality (which was prosecuted under Paragraph 175 and concerned only males) but as asocials. In this way, women deemed troublesome, nontraditional, and defiant—including lesbians—were identified as threats to Nazi society. Many of these women were sent to German concentration camps that focused on female inmates like Ravensbrück.[63] Recent research has also shown that transgender people, too, found themselves persecuted by the Nazis and sometimes sent to concentration camps.[64] Neither the female nor transgender victims of the Nazi persecution are counted among Lautmann's numbers.

By 1940, civilian convictions for homosexuality under Paragraph 175 had dropped, but they remained elevated compared to 1934.[65] Data through the end of the war are incomplete but suggest that civilian arrests diminished until the Third Reich's collapse. However, as German men were drafted into the army, homosexual prosecutions that would have been facilitated under Paragraph 175 of the civilian code were instead addressed by the military penal code, which saw its own spike in homosexual prosecutions after 1940.[66] With the Allied advance and the liberation of some camps beginning in July 1944, some homosexuals could imagine the end of the war. Nonetheless, hundreds of homosexuals were still interned in camps as late as January 1945, including 194 homosexuals in Buchenwald (PT, 145–46).

Homosexuals fortunate enough to survive the war faced a cruel irony. Marked as homosexuals by their clothing and in camp records, many of these men were remanded into German custody to complete their sentences.[67] Indeed, while the Allies demanded the German penal code be stripped of Nazi laws, it allowed the Nazi enhancements to Paragraph 175 to remain—reflecting UK and most US state laws that criminalized same-sex acts. When freed, many homosexual men went into hiding, cognizant they remained at risk of prosecution in both East and West Germany. This fact was dramatized by the mass arrests of homosexual men in Frankfurt in 1951.[68] Until as late as 2017, German homosexuals seeking to expunge their convictions under the Nazis' Paragraph 175 or receive restitution from the German state were denied.[69] Varying kinds of homosexual acts between men would remain criminalized under Paragraph 175 in East Germany until 1968 and in West Germany until 1994.[70]

The history of persecution told here is not sacrosanct. Researchers continue to nuance our understanding of the persecution of homosexuals, even while the destruction of records and the passing of the last-known living homosexual survivors means some details will never be recovered.[71] The role of race as a factor in the homosexual persecution has increasingly become a focus of the most recent scholarship.[72] Yet the established facts of the persecution and the *meanings* of these facts to the LGBTQ+ community at different moments are not synonymous. Homophile, homosexual, and lesbian and gay activists have been undeterred from using a piecemeal history of this persecution in previous decades to advance particular and powerful memories that might secure the social and political needs of the community. It is to this shift from the facts of the persecution to its uptake in memory to advance the homosexual cause—particularly during the war years—that this book next turns.

Knowable Suffering, Ambivalent Audiences

For too long, scholars have operated under the assumption that, until recently, the Nazi persecution of homosexuals was largely unknown, and perhaps unknowable, to the average American—whether homosexual or heterosexual. For some scholars, like pioneering gay historian Allan Bérubé, this knowledge was reserved for the postwar period: "Few Americans knew until after the war that the Nazis had sent tens of thousands of homosexuals to the death camps, forcing them to wear pink triangles."[73] But even after the war, most scholars claimed that Americans in general and lesbian and gay Americans in particular were in no position to remember the Third Reich's actions against homosexuals. Historian Erik N. Jensen, for instance, argues that gays and lesbians "met silence in the postwar period regarding the Nazi persecution of homosexuals." Rather, Jensen asserts, "a shared memory of the Nazi persecution of homosexuals emerged in the 1970s" as a "newfound history" because, in his estimation, no large or meaningful gay or lesbian press or community existed to do this work until after Stonewall.[74] As such, Jensen begins his otherwise excellent account of US memories of this sort in 1973. Sociologist Arlene Stein, who likewise highlighted these memories of homosexual persecution, similarly focuses on more contemporary times, arguing that the lesbian and gay movement only deployed the "Holocaust frame" in "the early 1970s . . . the early to mid-1980s . . . and the 1990s."[75] Even contemporary scholars like Tremblay and Newsome, who rightly acknowledge in their respective texts the much longer (and wider) history of the uptake of these memories in the transatlantic LGBTQ+ community, devote almost no attention to such memories before the early 1970s, further perpetuating the late twentieth-century rediscovery narrative.

But while everyday Americans could perhaps never fully grasp the scale and brutality of the Nazi persecution of homosexuals between 1933 and 1945, it is simply untrue that this history was unknown at the time, let alone in the decades to follow. Rather, many Americans who could read and had access to a daily newspaper or major magazine, including homosexuals, had ample opportunities to encounter news about the persecution of homosexuals in Germany. The rich examples in this book suggest that many Americans, *particularly* homosexual Americans, did remember these events between 1945 and 1981—and that the fleeting accounts of the prewar and war periods served as their raw materials in this effort.

It should be noted at the outset that at least some homosexual Americans before and during the war had their own unique channels for learning about unfolding events in the Reich. For instance, recent German emigrants like Plant described letters written from friends and lovers who remained in Europe and narrated the persecution's opening months.[76] Bérubé also noted "rumors of German atrocities against homosexuals circulated through the gay underground in the United States" in the prewar and war period. He also shares the story of a US sailor who heard about the persecution from another sailor during a hushed postcoital conversation.[77] These accounts confirm the view that knowledge of the persecution circulated among pockets of US homosexuals before and during the war.

But an American did not need to be a homosexual to discover what befell the once-thriving German homosexual community under Hitler. While Bérubé suggested in 1990 from reports in the *New York Times* that only "some gay men read American newspapers reports about Nazi antigay attacks," ample evidence suggests this information reached much wider.[78] Today, digitized archives of local and regional American newspapers from the 1930s and '40s show that these events were actually hard to miss. In fact, news of homosexual persecution in Germany was accessible to everyday Americans of all classes in newspapers, magazines, and gossip rags in almost every state during the prewar and war years.

Wire services were a rich source of these stories. In fact, both the Associated and United Presses produced numerous news stories on the Nazi persecution of homosexuals that were picked up by small and regional US newspapers. An early instance—describing the Nazi police's first sweep of homosexuals beginning in October 1934—appeared in US newspapers that same December. Various headlines and texts described it as an "anti-homosexual drive" or a "campaign against homosexuals." A search of one newspaper database reveals that versions of this report appeared in at least forty-two local and regional newspapers in fourteen different states.[79] Each story focused on "an officially announced drive against homosexuals in German cities" or its aftermath, and most stories detailed that "about 300 persons were arrested."[80] A year later, wire services fed compelling evidence of the Nazi internment of homosexuals in concentration camps. Exemplary here was the Newspaper Enterprise Association wire correspondent Frazier Hunt, whose story about a visit to Dachau in December 1935 appeared in at least fifty-three regional newspapers in nineteen states over three months, in addition to larger newspapers.[81] In his reporting, Hunt described an inspection of the carpenter shop, where he encountered "a few [men who] bore a mystic '175' painted on their backs. They were the outcasts—the moral perverts."[82] The *175* Frazier described denoted inmates convicted under Paragraph 175 in some camps prior to the later use of the pink triangle. While most American readers would not have known about Paragraph 175, they certainly understood that "moral perverts" implied homosexuals. These two instances each had the potential to reach tens, maybe hundreds, of thousands of American readers, showing that the scope of what was knowable about the persecution of homosexuals was greater than anything considered to date.

Less political readers could also encounter in the sports pages similar evidence of the Nazis' crackdown. Allegations of homosexual activity by world-class athletes both demonstrated the fierce and growing Nazi antagonism toward same-sex desire and broke through to a different segment of the US reading public. For example, more than one hundred US newspapers covered the story of Dr. Otto Peltzer, a renowned German distance runner who was arrested, tried, and imprisoned for eighteen months due to homosexual acts (i.e., "offenses against morals") in 1935.[83] Papers also produced follow-up stories on Peltzer that included untrue reports that he had committed suicide or been "shot to death in his prison cell."[84] But no US papers I discovered reported Peltzer's second arrest in 1937 or his internment in Mauthausen in 1941.[85] Even more sports columns told the story of German tennis superstar Baron Gottfried von Cramm, the world's number two player, who was "seized by [the] Nazi secret police" in March 1938 upon his return to Germany. The *Chicago Tribune* stated on its front page that Cramm had been arrested on "suspicion of moral delinquencies," while the *Oakland Tribune* quoted Nazi police statements that Cramm was arrested "on suspicion of violation of paragraph 175 of the criminal code."[86] A series of stories followed. In one, newspapers reported that Cramm had pleaded guilty to an affair with a young Jewish actor. The paper detailed Cramm's sentencing, where the Nazi judge rebuked the star athlete for "not having remembered the lesson of Capt. Ernest Roehm . . . who was shot and killed in the blood purge . . . after being accused of homosexuality."[87] Cramm ultimately served less than a year in a German prison, but he was drafted and sent to the front lines in 1940.[88] Stories about the Cramm scandal appeared in more than 1,500 American newspapers in 1938 alone, representing every state in the nation.[89] Both the Cramm and Peltzer coverage made clear to US readers that Nazi Germany had become an incredibly dangerous place for alleged homosexuals.

Popular gossip columns and publications that targeted working-class and occasional readers also communicated the fate of homosexuals under Hitler. In fact, these seedier outlets were often the richest in describing the homosexual persecution underway in Nazi Germany, even as they tended toward exaggeration and scandal. A powerful instance occurred in September 1939, when the famed American satirist, humorist, and gossip Walter Winchell reported in his widely syndicated newspaper column that French authorities had arrested a "Nazi swish" in Paris. In Winchell's telling, the young German man had worked hard to avoid detection. At the time of his arrest, he was "dressed in femme finery" and well on his way to passing as another nondescript French ingénue until the gendarmes "spotted him by his huge feet." In his column, Winchell asked his readers to imagine the scene with him: a fairy of the Third Reich who, "since the beginning of the 'Heil-ing' with his right hand in the air[,] . . . never had a chance to rest it in on his hip." When the "swish" was asked by French police to explain his brazen and laughable crime, "the prisoner is said, unofficially, to have declared Germany had become simply unbearable under Hitler."[90] Despite Winchell's well-known disdain for the führer, his column revealed no sympathy for the arrested homosexual, who likely endured a harrowing experience while attempting to escape Germany.

US magazines with national audiences and wide distribution also told stories of homosexual persecution by the Nazis in the prewar and war years. Sometimes these stories appeared in magazines like *The Nation*, which drove political opinion or intellectual culture and discussed homosexuality in the Nazi ranks as early as 1932.[91] But a mention of the persecution likely to have affected many readers appeared in a cover story on Heinrich Himmler in *Time* on April 24, 1939: "The three big camps are now permanent prisons where Communist agitators, homosexuals, disgraced Nazis, Jewish university professors, [and] Protestant conscientious objectors are thrown together in common cells. They wear coarse, striped uniforms, their heads are cropped, they shave only once weekly. The Jews wear yellow badges and the homosexuals pink, and few steps are taken to prevent Jewish adolescents from being attacked or molested."[92] *Time*'s description of homosexuals could only generously be called ambivalent. No sooner are the homosexuals and their "pink" badges mentioned than the article raises the specter of sexual molestation. Thus, *Time*'s comment does little to depict homosexual internment as anything other than justifiable punishment. Nonetheless, given the magazine's hundreds of thousands of subscribers in 1939 and the article's national syndication, the mention almost certainly accounts for one of the largest contemporaneous acknowledgments of the homosexual situation in Germany.

These few case studies merely scratch the surface of what US audiences could know about the Nazi oppressions of homosexuals before and during World War II. While not a systematic analysis, they provide pointed evidence that the homosexual persecution was not a secret but a known fact that most literate Americans at the time would have encountered.

But if the average American had ample opportunity to encounter information about the Nazis' mistreatment of homosexuals between 1933 and 1945, why did this fact not raise moral outrage? At least two reasons help explain this collective shrug. First, through much of this period, Americans were taught to understand Nazism as akin to homosexuality. This equation drew from both the Eulenburg affair that rocked Germany's political leadership in the first decade of the 1900s and partisan mudslinging around homosexuality in German elections in the early 1930s. But the 1934 Roehm purge solidified the imprint of homosexuality on Hitlerism. As a result, we might surmise that few Americans believed homosexuals faced any actual threat from the Third Reich, given that they saw the Nazis as partial to homosexuals.

A second reason Americans seemed unmoved by the Nazis' evident persecution of homosexuals was that many Americans, to varying degrees, shared similar views with their German contemporaries regarding the treatment and punishment of homosexuals. While the United States did not have a national anti-homosexual strategy in the 1930s and '40s, a series of smaller, state-driven, sometimes coordinated campaigns of persecution against homosexuals and other "sex perverts" was in full effect during this era—many of which look eerily similar to Nazi strategies from the same time. Like the Germans, American states had laws on the books banning sodomy and other "crimes against nature." And while the Nazis' post-1935 Paragraph 175 greatly exceeded the severity of any US state law, both Nazi and American police forces regularly imprisoned alleged homosexuals with impunity. Both Nazis and American courts of the era took up the sterilization of homosexuals, and both nations' doctors and law enforcement officers approved of castration as a practical solution to what they considered sexual deviance. Indeed, the Nazis "frequently cited with approval a similar practice [of castrating homosexuals] in California."[93] Concomitantly, everyday Americans were just as likely to encounter newspaper stories of the Nazi incarceration of homosexuals as they were calls from their own law enforcement officials and state legislators to address the rising "homosexual problem" closer to home. Thus, they had little reason to pause at the Nazis' actions in real time.

In the years after the war, US animosities toward homosexuals continued, even as the worst atrocities committed against them by the Nazis had ended. In fact, as seen in chapter 2, there was a rapid escalation in the targeting of homosexuals in the United States during the immediate postwar period. As such, the years following World War II saw very few stories of homosexual suffering during the Nazi regime in the mainstream US press or political discourse. This public forgetting among mainstream US audiences would not change until the 1970s, when the Gay Liberation Movement began to incorporate messages about the Nazi persecution into their discourses aimed at *heterosexuals*. It is this transition that might best represent the rediscovery of the Nazi persecution of homosexuals in the 1970s that so many historians and scholars have pointed to in years past.

But this did not mean that the suffering of homosexuals under Hitler went unremembered between 1945 and 1975. Rather, in the absence of a general American public interested in the plight of homosexual persecution at the hands of the Nazis, these memories were directed inward to address the growing US homosexual community itself. In these decades and into the late 1970s, homosexuals recounted these stories of oppression among themselves, often in spaces where heterosexuals were uninvited or not looking. Through these tellings, US postwar homosexuals continued various memory practices related to the treatment of homosexuals in Germany, which ultimately shaped how the community and its members came to see and understand themselves in the decades that followed. It is in this arena that memories of the Nazi persecution of homosexuals became a powerful weapon and indispensable tool in the coming battles against homophobia, heteronormativity, medicalization, and anti–lesbian and gay politics.

Indispensable Memories: 1934–1981

In the decades during and after World War II, US homosexual activists did not just cultivate communities that remembered the fate of homosexuals under National Socialism. Rather, on multiple occasions, they also made those memories indispensable resources in their arguments with one another and the wider world for a better future for American homosexuals. The remaining chapters of this book tell the story of how these activists used these indispensable memories and the purposes they served at some of the most pivotal turning points in twentieth-century US lesbian and gay politics.

One of the earliest ways that memories of the Nazi persecution of homosexuals were marshaled by early American homosexual activists can be found in the years before World War II. In the wake of the shocking events of the Night of the Long Knives, how homosexual activists remembered the slain Nazi captain and homosexual Ernst Roehm in the months following his execution is an important inaugural case study. This instance is taken up in chapter 1,

"Virile and Valiant Anti-Fascists: Challenging the Myth of the Homosexual Nazi, 1934–1935." Here, we examine the case of Henry Gerber—a founding member of the nation's first homosexual rights organization, the Society for Human Rights. Gerber was an activist and writer who continued to speak out in support of homosexual causes, even after the Society was consumed by a Chicago police crackdown in 1924. So, when Roehm's murder was splayed across US newsstands in 1934, Gerber took note. Several months later, he published "Hitlerism and Homosexuality" in a small American periodical with a significant homosexual readership, *Chanticleer*. In this piece, Gerber attacks Nazism and holds up the figure of Roehm to public memory—as a victim of fascism and a role model for other homosexuals in a world of rising threats.

As a historical accounting of Roehm's life and politics, Gerber's commemoration of the Nazi captain in *Chanticleer* could only generously be called dubious. However, Gerber's celebration of Roehm as an anti-Nazi figure, while certainly incorrect, illustrates how figures like Gerber, particularly in the earliest years of homosexual advocacy in the United States, relied on murky and mysterious reports of Roehm's actions in US newspapers to build an actionable memory of the man. Nonetheless, while Gerber's factual accounting of Roehm was almost certainly wrong, the chapter illustrates a powerful rhetorical attempt by an early American homosexual activist to turn remembering the Nazis' initial targets of destruction into a "lamp," beckoning a nascent homosexual self-image.[94] Particularly, by making the case that Roehm—and by extension, homosexuals in general—was anti-fascist in orientation, anti-Hitler in actions, and "virile" and "valiant" in his performance of homosexuality, the chapter asserts that Gerber advances a powerful rhetorical memory for a homosexual audience, one that both attempts to cast homosexuals in a positive light and defend them from the growing presumption in the wider American public that Nazism was fundamentally a homosexual endeavor.

Chapter 2, "Vagrants and Outlaws: Remembering Nazi Laws to Fight the American Gestapo, 1949–1965," examines how a new generation of homosexual activists in the 1950s and early 1960s framed the domestic, postwar persecution of homosexuals in the United States by remembering secret police campaigns against homosexuals under the Nazi regime just a few years earlier. Key to this work was a newly formed US homosexual rights organization, the Mattachine Foundation, which would spawn two consequential offshoots: the Mattachine Society and ONE. Each of these groups and their contributors leaned heavily into conflating US and Nazi anti-homosexual policing to rally their cause. As we will see, far from being ignorant of the Nazi persecution of homosexuals in Germany before and during the war, the founders of the Mattachine Foundation explicitly framed their cause as necessary because of the suffering and persecution of homosexuals under Hitler. In fact, evidence of the indispensable reliance on memories of homosexual persecution can be found in both the group's earliest charter and certain founders' recorded anxieties about being discovered by an American equivalent of the secret police. Yet the bulk of the chapter's analysis comes not from Mattachine's founding documents, but from the writings, imagery, and conversations that emerge in the pages of two Mattachine-descended publications that ran between 1952 and 1967: ONE magazine and the *Mattachine Review*.

In comparison to Gerber's brief essay in *Chanticleer*, the repeated and diverse remembrances of the Nazi persecution of homosexuals in the pages of ONE and *Mattachine Review* demonstrated a profound evolution. For one, these American homosexual reminisces about the Nazi persecution entirely shifted their focus away from the befuddling Roehm to the thousands of European men who suffered blackmail, harassment, arrest, imprisonment, and violence at the hands of Hitler's secret police. In addition, at least some remembrances in ONE and *Mattachine Review* featured the first- or second-hand stories of actual homosexual victims of Nazi policies, rendering these commemorations more grounded in evidence and facts. And these memories of the 1950s and '60s also shifted the narrative toward a different victim profile: the homosexual subject of police mistreatment. This shift is important to note because it reflected the needs of US homosexuals at the moment and offers an instance where the typical victim of Nazi policies, as imagined by American audiences, aligns with the majority of homosexual victims in the actual persecution. Collectively, by advancing an image of domestic anti-homosexual policing as the acts of an "American Gestapo," both early gay male leaders and ordinary, mostly gay male citizens rallied support and energy for a new era of homosexual organizing that would increasingly combat this threat head-on.

After the early 1960s, American homosexual memory rhetoric shifted dramatically toward remembering homosexuals persecuted by the Nazis through the experiences of the pink triangles—those incarcerated in the concentration camps—as opposed to those who faced their own mistreatment in other institutions of German society. This important transition first appears in force in chapter 3, "Habitual Skeptics: Remembering Incarceration and Medical Experiments in Gay Nazi-Exploitation Pulps, 1966–1969." Drawn from an analysis of three diverse gay male pulp novels—*Go Down, Aaron* (1967), *The Concentration of Hans* (1967), and *Middle Ground* (1968)—this chapter considers how memories of the Nazi persecution of homosexuals are depicted and advanced in cheaply made erotic works aimed at gay male readers. Including these texts—two of which feature explicit and pornographic depictions of same-sex acts of all kinds—in this broader interrogation is untraditional in academic work around the Holocaust. It is likely that these texts have gone uninvestigated to this point exactly because they occupy the uncomfortable nexus of homosexual erotica and Nazi fetishization. However, following in the footsteps of more recent queer critics, this chapter takes these pulp novels seriously as both rhetoric and discursive evidence of what gay men of the late 1960s knew of the Nazi persecution—and how they incorporated that knowledge into their own gay dispositions in the United States at the time.[95]

The analysis of these texts in chapter 3 reveals three important shifts in how the Nazi persecution was remembered and used in the United States in this era. First, as we have already discussed, these pulps highlight a transition away from depicting persecution as the experience of police mistreatment and toward a more limited yet horrific form of persecution experienced in the camps. Second, chapter 3 notes that, while these gay male pulps are filled with exaggerations, inaccuracies, and misconceptions about the suffering of homosexuals in the camps under the Nazis, these texts also served as powerful vehicles for communicating important facts about the suffering of homosexuals to homosexual audiences who were less likely to have engaged these memories previously. Third, this chapter shows that gay male pulps also sought to cultivate skepticism toward science and the state within individual men's growing gay male habitus. More specifically, in an era when many new men were coming into their homosexuality and existing models of homosexuality emphasized citizenship, respectability, and deference to authority, these texts used depictions of the Nazis' callow treatment of homosexuals to nudge these new gay men toward a different disposition. By creating storylines in which homosexuals are mistreated by state actors and supposed scientists—and then adopting a skepticism toward these institutions—the pulps used memories of persecution to craft a new image of the American gay man for the coming 1970s. In doing so, they presaged the rowdy, in-your-face, anti-authority ethos of gay liberation politics that emerged in force soon after 1969.

Two very different ways of remembering the Nazi persecution of homosexuals take focus in the book's final analysis chapters, even as they are put toward a shared rhetorical goal: propelling lesbian and gay power. As opposed to earlier eras, when homosexual and lesbian and gay politics used these memories to reframe identity, reconsider a political issue, or reinvent one's self-image, by the 1970s, gay liberation politics was often fixated on getting homosexuals out of the closet and into the street. Motivating gay men (and some women and transgender people) to political causes in support of an emerging post-Stonewall lesbian and gay rights movement thus became a key reason to remember the Nazi persecution. Interestingly, as these chapters show, how these memories were leveraged to motivate action in the 1970s varied widely depending on who was doing the remembering and the political moment in US history in which they found themselves.

Chapter 4, "Spectral Siblings: Remembering Our Ghostly Brothers and Sisters as Martyrs for Gay Power, 1970–1977," considers how the fast-moving lesbian and gay politics of the early 1970s remembered the Nazis' homosexual victims as spiritual "brothers and sisters" to modern lesbian and gay audiences—fallen family members who remind us of the debt we owe them for our lives today. This transactional remembrance was fashioned largely by the Reverend Mikhail Itkin—a controversial homosexual and itinerant priest who mixed lesbian and gay spirituality with radical street protest to propel lesbian and gay men to action. In his role as a spiritual leader, Itkin was visited by two gay male survivors of the Nazi persecution, an event he found transformational. Over the years to come, Itkin would use that experience in writings, speeches, and poetry to urge lesbians and gay men not to take their newfound liberation for granted and to heed the call of the pink triangles, who, according to him, had fought bravely to resist their oppressors so that future generations of homosexuals might live.

In stark contrast to Itkin's remembrances, the late 1970s shows a marked counterpoint in commemorations of the Nazis' homosexual victims. At a moment when the Religious Right was ascendant and hard-fought lesbian and gay rights victories across the country were being rolled back by conservative forces, lesbian and gay political leaders reimagined the Nazi persecution at a different affective pitch: fear and shame. By the late 1970s—just a few years before the consequences of HIV/AIDS would become apparent and the "pink triangle" would find new meaning—the homosexual inmates of Nazi concentration camps were remembered in American essays, political speeches, and scholarship as ineffectual figures, weak lambs who walked helplessly to their slaughter. This shift in memory is analyzed in chapter 5, "Lambs to the Slaughter: Harvey Milk, Memories of Shame, and the Myth of Homosexual Passivity, 1977–1979." This discourse is seen most famously in

Harvey Milk's well-known Gay Freedom Day speech against the Briggs Initiative in 1978, but it was not uncommon in diverse discourses throughout the era. Taking Milk's speech and attendant interviews as exemplary texts, this chapter shows how a long postwar tradition of holding up homosexuals of the Nazi persecution as respectable victims is overturned—largely by combining homosexuality with ancient (and incorrect) repudiations of Jews as passive victims. In its place, post-Stonewall activists urged the movement to discard these contemptible German homosexual victims in favor of a new generation of US lesbian and gay heroes, who would meet their oppressors head-on and take control of their own destinies.

In the conclusion to this book, "Never Again, Never Forget, 1981–1987," I return to these case studies between 1934 and 1981 to consider from a broader perspective what it was for the lesbian and gay rights movement in its various forms to remember the Nazi persecution of homosexuals. In particular, I interrogate what a uniquely American tradition of remembering the Nazi persecution means and how it compares with this fuller view. Additionally, I show how this new accounting shifts our interpretation of these memories that have emerged since the HIV/AIDS crisis and what that shift portends for remembering these victims in the decades to come. In doing so, I show that following the old gay rights edict about the Nazi persecution—"Never Again, Never Forget"—is, in fact, far more complicated than it seems.

Chapter 1

Virile and Valiant Anti-Fascists

Challenging the Myth of the Homosexual Nazi,
1934–1935

On the one-year anniversary of his grisly execution, the *Times* of London published a brief but remarkable in memoriam for the notorious Nazi leader and
homosexual Captain Ernst Roehm: "In proud and most dear remembrance of
Ernst Roehm, Capt., June 30, 1934."[1] At first glance, this remembrance notice
appears unexceptional. The *Times* and other newspapers commonly published
this type of note in the decades after World War I, when columns burst with
"the names of those who were expected to be . . . leaders in the new century"
but "'who had been obliterated' by the war." And as a "public way for remembering the passing of a loved one," short commemorative notes to lost hus-
bands, sons, and fathers like Roehm's held "no hint of any glory of war."[2] In
these ways, Roehm's memorial notice was perfectly unremarkable.

Yet, upon closer consideration, Roehm's remembrance in the *Times*
is extraordinary in several ways. For one, that such a remembrance was
afforded to a known homosexual in a manner both "proud" and "most
dear" after his spectacular murder in the Nazis' 1934 blood purge is certainly
unusual. For another, it is surprising that this note appeared in the *Times*—
an English-language publication in a nation soon to be at war with the Nazis.
Roehm's commemoration also appeared in a special in memoriam section
intended for men lost in battle, suggesting that readers interpret his execution by his Nazi comrades as an act of war. Finally, this same note was placed
on Roehm's behalf not only on the first anniversary of his death but annu-
ally for years thereafter.[3] Clearly, whoever mourned Roehm in the *Times* did
not regard his life as a trifling fancy; they believed it was worthy of remembrance—and possibly celebration.

More broadly, as a public remembrance of the murdered Nazi captain, the *Times* note is also an outlier. Despite consternation over his 1934 execution in the global press, Roehm went relatively unremembered in the following years and received little scholarly or biographical scrutiny compared to other Nazi figures.[4] When Roehm was remembered, it was in one of two ways. In Nazi propaganda, Roehm was recalled as a homosexual traitor and a cautionary tale, reflecting how "the victors . . . shaped the writing of the history of June 30, 1934."[5] Meanwhile, Roehm's homosexuality was a useful, if intermittent, cudgel in US memory for berating the Nazis as morally perverse and psychotic. Interestingly, Roehm and the SA men who died at his side were almost never remembered as victims of the Nazi regime. But, as Roehm biographer Eleanor Hancock notes, these murders are "singula[r] in the history of Nazism" exactly because the "victims were themselves Nazis. Perhaps for this reason historians have not felt much of an obligation to them."[6]

But remembering Roehm and his men as victims *was* an important facet of early US homophile movement rhetoric in the months following the purge. In fact, a small cadre of US homophiles commemorated Roehm as a laudable martyr: an anti-Hitler and anti-fascist warrior struck down in a looming struggle against Nazi tyranny. Such a memory is peculiar, and perhaps even offensive from our modern perspective; his biographer asserts that Roehm was certainly not a martyr.[7] But in the summer of 1934, few American homosexuals knew much about Roehm, other than that he was a homosexual and the Nazis saw him as a sufficient threat to be eliminated. In other words, Roehm was a homosexual not to be trifled with. As a result, at least some US homosexuals of the 1930s found in Roehm a blank canvas on which they could project whatever intentions they wished. While a few homosexuals honored him by leaving flowers at his grave or praising him after his death, at least one American homosexual activist imbued Roehm with a proud and defiant homosexual character, circulating this memory among other homosexuals in the nascent, underground US homophile community.[8]

This activist was Henry Gerber, a founding member of Chicago's Society for Human Rights—the first documented US homosexual rights organization, created in 1924. A decade after the Society's dismemberment by the Chicago police and Gerber's arrest for lewd behavior, he moved to New York and embarked on a writing campaign in US and German periodicals to advance the homosexual cause. Among these writings was an essay he penned for the small US publication *Chanticleer* titled "Hitlerism and Homosexuality."[9] In the essay, Gerber sought to re-remember Roehm in the months after his death, in contrast to his memory in Nazi propaganda and US news commentary. Instead, Gerber wielded memories of Roehm and his fellow homosexual SA officers as virile and valiant anti-fascist crusaders who fell as the first victims in the struggle against the Nazi regime. Simultaneously, Gerber used Roehm's memory to recast homosexuals more generally in the imaginations of his largely homosexual audience as the vanguard, fighting an imminent worldwide threat.

In this way, Gerber's rhetoric represents some of the earliest American remembrances of homosexual persecution by the Nazi regime. As we will discover, these remembrances shaped how a small portion of the nascent homophile community was encouraged to see itself in the 1930s United States. At the same time, Gerber's rhetoric demonstrates how such memories functioned—and whom it imagined as a homosexual victim—during the brief period after the rise of the Third Reich but before the revisions to Paragraph 175 and the creation of the pink triangle.

Consequential Homosexuals: Roehm and Gerber

Appreciating US homosexuals' earliest efforts to leverage the Nazi persecution of sexual minorities requires understanding both the subject (Roehm) and the author (Gerber) of these memories. In some ways, Roehm and Gerber shared much in common: they were both German-born, veterans, similarly aged, half-hearted anti-Semites, and relatively open homosexuals.[10] Each man also suffered for his desires in ways that would forever mark his legacy. But Roehm and Gerber were also quite different. Gerber was an armchair intellectual and avid writer, whereas Roehm was a bruising military man; Gerber was an avowed Communist who never approached real power, while Roehm brutalized Communists for years and reached the highest echelons of Nazism. And though both men suffered for expressing their homosexuality, Gerber's actions led to his arrest and marginalization, whereas Roehm's desires became increasingly public and volatile. Nonetheless, Roehm's rise to power and Gerber's quest for a new vision of homosexuality placed them on a rhetorical crash course, ultimately realized in Gerber's 1934 essay in *Chanticleer*.

The facts of Roehm's life and death are particularly important for appreciating Gerber's remembrance of the Nazi captain. Born in Munich in 1887, Roehm built a prestigious military career before becoming disillusioned after Germany's defeat in World War I. Compelled by its rabid anti-Communism and masculinist order, Roehm joined what would become the Nazi Party in 1919.[11] Soon thereafter, Roehm met Hitler and quickly became an indispensable ally, particularly as a vital link to the Reichswehr—the German armed forces—from which the Nazis heavily recruited.[12] But his value to Hitler was perhaps best demonstrated during the Beer Hall Putsch in November 1923, when Roehm marched his paramilitary forces to the Munich War Ministry and occupied the building for sixteen hours. Within the day, the putsch had failed, but Roehm proved himself a key asset to Hitler.[13]

Unlike Hitler, Roehm escaped significant jail time for the putsch and resigned from politics. But when a paroled Hitler asked him to lead the SA as its chief of staff in 1931, Roehm again proved useful in leading the Nazis' antagonism toward their Communist enemies.[14] Roehm was an ideal SA leader: a trusted Hitlerite with military training and organizational skills, devoted to vanquishing Communist forces. While Roehm was also an anti-capitalist, he abhorred the Communists as a disorganized force that had to be eliminated, lest "Bolshevik chaos" rule Germany.[15] To that end, Roehm unleashed the disciplined SA as a brutal weapon against the Communists. By 1932, Communists and Nazis were engaged in open warfare on the streets. In June, at least eighty-two were killed and four hundred wounded in these battles in Prussia alone; in July, thirty-eight Nazis and thirty Communists were slain during larger riots.[16] Among such carnage, Roehm's SA also attacked strikebreakers, Jews, and Nazi political opponents, cultivating public displays of violence and intimidation that facilitated Hitler's rise to power.

However, as a Nazi-led Germany became more conceivable, Roehm's value to Hitler ebbed. Some contemporaneous journalists and historians attributed Roehm's change in fortune to his homosexuality—a view later promoted by Hitler himself.[17] But Roehm's sexuality appears to have mattered little. Hitler knew of it as early as 1925. And while some Nazi leaders loathed Roehm's sexual decadence, Hitler ignored it so long as it did not interfere with the party's rise.[18] When the German Socialist Party attempted and failed to make Roehm's sexual orientation an electoral liability, these homosexual concerns appeared moot.[19] Similarly, the long-held view that Roehm was vanquished for plotting a "second revolution" to overthrow Hitler is also inaccurate. Instead, historians today agree that "Hitler moved against the SA to retain army support . . . for the presidential succession."[20] Roehm was undone by his unpopular drive to incorporate the Reichswehr into the SA, an idea that Hitler rejected and that enraged the military leadership. Thus, the Reichswehr and other German elites supported Hitler's rise to chancellor on the condition Roehm's SA be diminished. As a result, Hitler's political aims best explain Roehm's fate.[21]

Roehm's fall took place in the early morning of June 30, 1934 (later known as the Night of the Long Knives), when Hitler and the SS converged on the Hanslbauer Hotel in Bad Wiessee and placed him under arrest. As Roehm was delivered to a Munich prison, Hitler and his new leadership carried out acts of retribution against perceived political opponents, including numerous other SA leaders seen as loyal to Roehm. Ultimately, at least ninety people were brutally killed, and more than one thousand individuals were placed in protective custody.[22] The following day, Hitler offered Roehm the opportunity to commit suicide. When Roehm refused, he was shot dead, ending the tumultuous, homosexual life of a onetime Hitler intimate. In publicizing the event, Hitler and his remaining lieutenants found both Roehm's homosexuality and the false coup narrative to be appealing angles for distracting the German public from the violent elimination of so many political opponents. In a speech before the Reichstag just two weeks after the purge, Hitler himself derided the executed for their supposed "treason" and "depraved morals":

> The life which the Chief of Staff and with him a certain circle began to lead was from any National Socialist point of view intolerable. It was not only terrible that he himself and the circle of those that were devoted to him should violate all laws of decency and modest behaviour, it was still worse that now this poison began to spread in ever wider circles . . . gradually out of a certain common disposition of character there began to be formed within the SA . . . the kernel of a conspiracy directed not only against the normal views of a healthy people but also against the security of the State.[23]

Hitler's Reichstag speech marked one of the most significant public accounts of this discourse, though similar propaganda around the purge continued for years. Such regular denunciations successfully desecrated Roehm's memory and contributed to his erasure in the decades to follow.

But where many saw a traitor, Henry Gerber saw an opportunity to reconsider the homosexual as a historical figure. Unlike Roehm, much of Gerber's life appeared unremarkable. He was born in Bavaria in 1892, immigrated to Chicago in 1913, and served in the US Army during World War I (*AS*, 8–10). Thereafter, he sufficed on a modest income, was unmarried, had no children, and lived alone, in relative obscurity, until his death in 1972 (AS, 167). But beneath this unassuming persona, Gerber hid the zeal of a homosexual advocate and the talents necessary to elevate Roehm's flawed legacy. These skills were threefold in nature. First and foremost, Gerber had accepted his homosexuality early in life, after a brief stint in a Chicago mental institution at the age of twenty-five (AS, 16). His incarceration only intensified his same-sex desires and practices—and his certainty that homosexuality was no crime. Second, Gerber was a proficient writer and publisher. He honed these expressive skills in the military, where he served as a printer and proofreader, and practiced them professionally and personally for most of his life (AS, 19, 55). Third, Gerber's military service afforded him a three-year posting in Koblenz after World War I (AS, 19). There, he gained firsthand experience with the percolating German homophile movement and became an avid consumer of both the homophile press and the work of Dr. Magnus Hirschfeld (AS, 24). When he returned stateside, Gerber maintained his subscriptions to German publications to the extent possible, giving him an unusual level of insight into successful homosexual organizing. Individually, many Americans had one or two of these experiences in the years after World War I, but Gerber was probably unique in bringing together all three to advance a new way of thinking as a homosexual in America.

The doomed Society for Human Rights and its short-lived periodical, *Friendship and Freedom*, were a manifestation of Gerber's unique alchemy; they would not be the last. Nearly ten years after his arrest and bankruptcy in Chicago, Gerber found himself in New York. He had grown cynical but continued to live a homosexual lifestyle amid New York's burgeoning homophile scene. There, Gerber also ran a successful pen pal service, *Contacts*, which brought in money during the Great Depression but also served as a cover for a network of homosexual letter writing, information sharing, friendship, and intimacy (AS, 58–65). In addition, Gerber once again found himself enmeshed in the publishing apparatus as a proofreader for the US Army's Recruiting Publicity Bureau. But he quickly grew tired of only reading the work of others. So, with some men he met through the Recruiting Publicity Bureau and *Contacts*, Gerber established the small monthly publication *Chanticleer* in January 1934 (AS, 69).

Unlike *Friendship and Freedom*, *Chanticleer* was not a declared homosexual periodical. It simply published on assorted topics of interest to its regular contributors (AS, 69). But *Chanticleer* was not hostile to homosexuality either. In fact, as a member of the publication's board and under his name, Gerber regularly published pieces that addressed homosexuality or made same-sex desire their central theme.[24] While the subjects of the pieces varied, many of Gerber's essays fixated on what he saw as a widening social campaign disparaging homosexuals and facilitating their persecution. Among these articles was Gerber's commemoration of Roehm, written about three months after the Nazi purge. The piece would become a vivid example of Gerber's limited efforts to change the public conversation on homosexuality in the United States—one in which Hitler and the Nazis played an increasingly prominent role.

Confronting US Depictions of Nazi Homosexuality

While the Nazis spent much of late 1934 remembering Roehm and his men as contemptible homosexual traitors whom the heterosexual and moral Hitler had expelled from their ranks, Gerber was tracking an equally brazen but very different remembrance of these events circulating in the US press: that the Roehm purge confirmed a long-standing American belief that Hitler and National Socialism were at least compatible with, and perhaps indistinguishable from, homosexuality writ large. Gerber recognized the specifically American version of the Roehm story as a greater threat to the nascent US homophile community than the Nazis' preferred interpretation. As such, Gerber's efforts to remember Roehm differently in the months after his death were an attempt to disrupt the growing perception among heterosexual and homosexual Americans alike that homosexuals were naturally disposed to fascistic and tyrannical movements like Nazism.

Such claims were not limited to the months after Roehm's demise. In the early 1930s, before Hitler came to power and well before most Americans saw the future führer as a threat, a surprisingly wide and diverse set of texts already circulated the idea that the Nazi Party was a homosexual cabal. This was certainly true in Germany, where both implicit and explicit allegations of homosexuality had become a common tool across the political spectrum since the 1907 Eulenburg affair.[25] Given the profusion of these allegations—including the well-publicized and mostly accurate homosexual charges against Roehm after 1931—it did not take long for foreign correspondents, visiting writers, and members of the US intelligentsia to recirculate stateside similar homosexual allegations against the Nazis.

However, there was not a rush to make such allegations the subject of public discourse. For instance, when Sydney Wallach published accusations of homosexuality among the Nazi leadership in his 1933 pamphlet *Hitler: Menace to Mankind*, a *Baltimore Sun* review syndicated in other US newspapers attacked Wallach for explicitly stating "the homo-sexual aspect of the Nazi movement which the press carefully avoids."[26] Similarly, the *Cincinnati Enquirer* lambasted Wallach's pamphlet as "an intemperate outburst against the Nazis, spreading their sins on the record for all to read."[27] As such, while stories about Roehm and other German homosexuals provided scandalous examples to portray all Nazis as homosexual, prudish gatekeepers within the US press corps strongly repudiated such allegations due to a general disposition against gossip and a specific reluctance to address the sordid subject of homosexuality.

But Americans readers did not rely exclusively on flagship newspapers to appraise the new movement sweeping Germany. Some Americans got their news from the era's popular scandal press, which freely reprinted homosexual accusations and similar sundry topics for a distinctly lower-brow audience. In fact, scandal, gossip, and exposé were the very stuff on which such papers' circulation and readership depended.[28] In 1934, New York (the new home of Henry Gerber) was perhaps the most notorious city for such vice publications, and few were as successful as *Broadway Brevities*. Throughout the 1920s and early 1930s, *Brevities* made a name for itself as the source of intimate gossip. Exposing homosexuality was a favorite subject, as evident in such dramatic headlines as "Fags Balls Exposed," "Third Sex Plague Spreads Anew!," and "Queers Seek Succor!"[29] And while *Brevities* almost always focused its ire on American debauchery, the paper's attention soon turned to the young führer in waiting, Adolf Hitler.

After ending a five-year publishing hiatus in 1930, *Brevities* and its competitors began to make direct connections between Germany and homosexuality. For instance, the front page of a 1932 *Brevities* issue, published three months prior to Hitler's appointment as chancellor, led with the headline "Fags Ram Heinies!" (*AS*, 77). In this campy usage, *heinies* was slang for both buttocks and Germans (*AS*, 246n2). The full story drew on earlier Weimar-era gossip to assert that "the Germans are turning queerer and the [German] Army is getting stronger" (*AS*, 77). In a 1933 story supposedly extolling "the oceanward trek of our little friend, the fagot," on US sea vessels, *Brevities* attributed such homosexual exploits to the sailors' "Teutonic extraction. Just a bit of the Hitler influence, it seems."[30] A few months later, the *Broadway Tattler* printed a political cartoon mocking Hitler as a "pans[y]" while simultaneously criticizing new Nazi sterilization laws for use on "sex perverts" (*AS*, 77–78). Suffice it to say, while highbrow newspapers refused to dabble in Nazi homosexual allegations, the lowbrow press and its readers quickly became adept recirculators of these allegations in US public discourse.

US-based political publications with anti-Hitler and anti-Nazi ideologies were another prominent site where homosexual allegations against the Nazis circulated in the early 1930s. Notable among them was the leftist and US Communist Party publication the *Daily Worker*. The writers and readers of the *Worker*, well versed in the clashes between the SA and Communist militants and the Nazis' subsequent internments of Communists in early concentration camps, were virulently anti-Nazi.[31] These American Communists had every reason to hate Hitler and were far quicker than other publishers to attack the Nazis in the starkest terms—including by characterizing their movement as homosexual. In doing so, the *Worker* had no reservations about merging gossip, innuendo, propaganda, opinion, and lies to make its point. Exemplary of these attacks was a 1932 *Worker* story reporting that a Hitlerite leader had allegedly resigned from the Nazi Party due to Roehm's homosexuality, which the newspaper reported as representing a wider "sexual corruption and demoralization existing in the Nazi headquarters."[32] Communist fury against the Nazis was also exemplified in a long exposé on Marinus van der Lubbe, the Nazis' patsy for the Reichstag fire, published in the *Worker* on September 28, 1933. The paper upbraided van der Lubbe repeatedly as a homosexual and faux Communist, one whose "intimate personal relations with high Hitlerite Officials . . . made him obedient and willing to play the firebug's part."[33] In the aftermath of the Roehm purge, the *Worker* again lambasted the Nazis as a "band of insane homosexual drug addicts" who "have to resort to sexual explanations for their bloody deeds."[34] When he recalled the Roehm purge months later, *Worker* writer Michael Gold called the Nazis hypocritical for their "great moral campaign . . . [to] purify Hitler's movement." Among a slew of other attacks, Gold asks readers, "Why should there be so many perverts among them?" He asserted that, because of their persecution, homosexuals "hate and despise society" and are "ready for the coward[']s road to revenge that the fascist movement offers."[35] Clearly, American readers sympathetic to Communism found plentiful support for the homosexual Nazi myth in their reading.

Meanwhile, some venerable left-leaning outlets like *The Nation* did publish accusations of homosexuality within the Nazi ranks at this time. Catering to an educated and intellectual reader, *The Nation* was a far more tepid promoter of this connection. For example, in a provocative piece in October 1932, a writer in *The Nation* claimed, "I hesitate to bring up a matter which has been conscientiously avoided for many years by the Berlin correspondents. It is a conclusively established fact that many of his close friends, notably Captain Roehm, leader of the shock troops, are homosexual. About Adolf himself, as about the whole Brown House menagerie, there is a discouraging atmosphere of effeminacy which can scarcely have endeared him to that part of Germany which adores the blunt masculinity of Hindenburg and Schleicher."[36] While tamer than the claims levied in the scandal press or the *Worker*, *The Nation's* accusations had a similar effect: construing Hitlerism and homosexuality as entirely linked in thought and deed in the US political imagination.

While *The Nation* may have been among the first to broach these accusations in respectable American journalism, it would not be the last. By the time the United States entered World War II in late 1941, characterizations of Nazis as homosexual had become not only acceptable in the press but also widespread across the American public. Even while American sentiments would not reach such heights for another decade, thousands of US readers were confronted with a rhetoric that maligned Nazi ideology as part and parcel with homosexuality by the mid-1930s—a practice most Americans viewed as sinful, criminal, perverse, or disturbed. Thus, the taint of homosexuality was quickly becoming a powerful tool for turning Americans against Nazi Germany.

At the same time, anti-Hitler homosexuals on the US home front worried the reverse was also true—that Hitlerism would soon intolerably taint homosexuals as pro-German, pro-Hitler, and, as such, anti-American. Disrupting this logic required a response—if not to turn it back, then to give US homosexuals an opportunity to imagine themselves otherwise. Into this breach stepped Gerber, armed with an unusual and potent new remembrance of Roehm and his compatriots as the Nazis' first homosexual victims.

Remembering Homosexuals as Valiant Anti-Fascists

"Hitlerism and Homosexuality" appeared in *Chanticleer* in September 1934.[37] In the essay, Gerber reconsiders Roehm's execution by the Nazis to critique the growing and problematic American viewpoint that homosexuality and Nazism were indistinguishable social phenomena. To that end, Gerber created a new public memory of Roehm and the other homosexual members of the SA murdered in the purge that countered the prevailing narratives about them in American memory up to that point. Specifically, Gerber imagined an idealized Roehm whose life and death repudiated homosexuals' problematic representation in the US press and offered homosexuals a different vision of themselves—one that might nurture a nascent American homophile community before it could again be snuffed out.

Gerber faced significant challenges in this task. For instance, the readership of *Chanticleer* was admittedly small. While no known circulation numbers survive, we can surmise that the subscribers likely numbered in the hundreds at best. As a result, any essay published in *Chanticleer* was unlikely to change American public opinion. Gerber's views on homosexuality also fell far outside mainstream US political beliefs of the 1930s, and there is little reason to think his essay could induce a wider readership to accept homosexuals. As a result, at least one Gerber biographer suggests that *Chanticleer* was more of a vanity project, an outlet for "self-promulgators" like Gerber who had strong opinions to share but few illusions about tapping the vein of American public discourse (*AS*, 69–70). But who then did Gerber imagine his intended audience to be if not the mainstream heterosexual public? And what did he hope that commemorating Roehm for this audience would achieve?

In my assessment, the audience for Gerber's memory work in *Chanticleer* is best understood as a narrow, committed, and not-unknown group of homosexual and homophile readers. Two pieces of evidence support this interpretation. First, Gerber had good reason to believe that some *Chanticleer* readers were homosexual. Gerber biographers suggest that, as the circulation manager for *Chanticleer*, Gerber used the subscriber list for *Contacts*—his correspondence club—to promote subscriptions to the magazine (*AS*, 69–70). Since Gerber very well knew that correspondence clubs like *Contacts* "were important to many gay men's lives in the first half of the twentieth century," he was confident his article's readers included homosexuals among them (*AS*, 2). In fact, Gerber himself cultivated long-standing homosexual letter exchanges via *Contacts* members by placing ads for the club that specifically targeted such an audience (*AS*, 64). And it worked: in his own letter writing, Gerber made homosexual connections with several homosexual pen pals due to his publications in *Chanticleer* (*AS*, 2). Second, while Gerber successfully published letters and essays in mainstream newspapers, we know that he also submitted and published his writing in international homophile periodicals that targeted homosexual audiences. For instance, historian James Steakley noted that Gerber's *Friendship and Freedom* was pictured among other homophile publications in a photograph in Hirschfeld's 1927 book chapter "Die Homosexualität."[38] Steakley and Jonathan Ned Katz have also shown that Gerber's writings appeared in German homophile publications in 1928, 1929, and 1930.[39] Gerber's biographer made similar claims (*AS*, 55–57). And later in life, Gerber would publish in the US homosexual magazine ONE.[40] Given Gerber's dual aims of cultivating a homosexual reading public with his magazine and targeting his ideas to homosexual audiences, it seems logical that he crafted "Hitlerism and Homosexuality" to address and persuade an American homosexual reading audience that he had captured in *Chanticleer*.

Nor should Gerber's essay be understood as addressing the prevailing homosexual-Nazi myth in the United States by happenstance. Rather, Gerber almost certainly recognized these discourses in real time and sought to address them explicitly. As we will see, Gerber's own references to *The Nation* in his essay supports this rationale. And Gerber's past as a Communist with roots in Chicago meant he likely also encountered these ideas in the Chicago-based *Daily Worker*. Similarly, as a 1930s New York resident, Gerber almost certainly came across *Broadway Brevities*. Collectively, this evidence suggests that Gerber wrote "Hitlerism and Homosexuality" as a direct rebuke to this pervading discourse.

Gerber sought to rehabilitate Roehm and his men for homophile public memory in *Chanticleer* with these points in mind. To this end, he deployed a two-part rhetorical strategy. First, Gerber disaggregated homosexuals from Hitlerism. Second, Gerber realigned homosexuality with anti-fascism and Communism while characterizing Roehm and the SA as virile and valiant warriors who deserved praise from their homophile contemporaries.

Discrediting Nazi Propaganda and US Press Memories

Gerber begins his powerful re-remembrance of Roehm in "Hitlerism and Homosexuality" by rejecting two earlier ways of remembering the deceased captain after his death. One of these memories was forwarded in Nazi propaganda, which depicted Roehm and the SA as homosexual traitors—figures to be despised and eliminated because of their moral failings and the threat they supposedly posed to the Nazi regime. The other memory was primarily shaped by the US press, depicting Roehm as evidence of a pervasive and deplorable homosexuality within both the Nazi leadership and the German nation. Of the two, the latter was particularly perilous for the nascent US homophile movement, which could ill afford to be maligned as somehow inherently fascist. But as shown in chapter 2, Hitler's construction of the "homosexual traitor" trope also threatened an emerging US homosexual community, prompting Gerber to repudiate both charges against Roehm as hypocritical, illogical, and profit-driven.

Gerber's two-pronged attack on earlier Roehm remembrances begins by assailing the Nazis' claims that the purge was justified by the captain's homosexuality. For Gerber, this claim was farcical, given that it was simply impossible that Hitler had not known of Roehm's homosexuality for years: "A few weeks ago Herr Adolf Hitler, in part justified the bloody murder of his intimate friends with the accusation that his Chief of Staff of Nazi storm troops and his clique had been guilty of . . . sexual aberrations. It seems strange that Hitler should have found that out so late. After having been intimately associated with Roehm . . . he must have been well acquainted with Roehm's inclinations. But such a little slip of memory does not bother the great corporal."[41] Here, Gerber uses heavy sarcasm to indict Hitler's supposed surprise at the discovery that Roehm and other SA leaders were homosexual. In doing so, Gerber critiques Hitler as deceptive and untrustworthy. This charge becomes clearest when Gerber characterizes Hitler's evasion as "a little slip of memory," a tongue-in-cheek retort to Hitler's attempt to minimize a lie, which had yielded significant consequences, as mere forgetfulness (MFY, 27).

But Gerber goes even further to denigrate Hitler's remembrance of Roehm after the purge by strongly intimating that the führer is a hypocrite. More specifically, Gerber playfully implies that Hitler's disavowal of Roehm's desire for men was rooted in a shared erotic experience. By using the words *intimate* and *intimately* in the paragraph to describe the Hitler-Roehm relationship, Gerber alludes to narratives from the US press that the entire Nazi leadership was homosexual (MFY, 27). As we have discussed, there is no evidence to support this accusation or any reason to suspect Gerber believed Hitler was homosexual. Gerber never makes this claim explicitly, which would only contradict his aim to sever the rhetoric linking Hitlerism and homosexuality. Rather, Gerber's jibe against Hitler is more jocular and further depicts the soon-to-be führer—and perhaps even the entire Nazi leadership—as disingenuous and hypocritical on the entire subject of same-sex desire.

After undermining Nazi memories of Roehm as a homosexual traitor, Gerber turns to concerns closer to home: the growing false belief among Americans that homosexuals were Nazis and vice versa. In this vein, Gerber paraphrases the charges in *The Nation*, stating that "the whole Hitler movement was based on homosexual Greek attachment of men for each other" (MFY, 27). Cognizant that this charge must be contested, Gerber swiftly turns his critical eye toward the claim's inconsistency and broader US press practices to disrupt this idea. Gerber points out that while *The Nation* suggests Americans remember Roehm as just another homosexual within Nazi ideology, the magazine simultaneously reveals the inconsistency of this claim. More specifically, Gerber amplifies *The Nation*'s broader argument that Hitler is rife with inconsistencies, what Gerber offhandedly calls "Hitler contradictions" (*MFY*, 27). By "Hitler contradictions," Gerber directs readers to what *The Nation* sees as Hitler's strange, illogical, and apparently incongruous choices during his rise to power. Exemplary of these contradictions, Gerber highlights how *The Nation* questions Hitler's decision to approve an attack on Dr. Hirschfeld's Institute for Sexual Science and its subsequent burning of thousands of homosexual books and documents. In said contradiction, Hitler—perhaps himself a homosexual—would be complicit in the destruction of the world's largest archive of his own people's literature. In pointing this out, *The Nation* overlooks this contradiction as a unique oddity of Hitler.

But Gerber challenges this interpretation, critiquing *The Nation* for trying to explain away a deeper flaw in its own logic by pinning it on the personal failings of a single man. He argues that *The Nation* simply has its facts wrong. In reality, its underlying claim is incapable of supporting the interpretation that Nazi ideology is undergirded by male-male attraction. Gerber argues it makes no sense that a (possibly homosexual) "leader" like Hitler would send a "heterosexual mob, led by homosexuals [i.e., Nazis]," to persecute a "Jewish doctor working for the interests of homosexuals" (MFY, 27). Instead, Gerber has a simpler answer: Hitlerism is not undergirded by homosexuality at all. In that case, the Nazi sacking of the Institute for Sexual Science is better characterized as a *heterosexual* leader (i.e., Hitler) encouraging a mob of *heterosexual* men (i.e., Hitler and the Nazi acolytes) to attack and destroy a homosexual organization housing homosexual literature. Gerber suggests that this alternate interpretation is more sensible than *The Nation*'s theory and more consistent with the long history of capitalist societies persecuting homosexuals. The only flaw Gerber identifies in his own interpretation is that it undercuts the idea that Nazism is a homosexual movement. But, of course, this is *exactly* what Gerber aims to do, despite *The Nation*'s attempts to contort itself in knots to prove otherwise.

Gerber doubles down on the absurd nature of these supposed "Hitler contradictions" discussed in the US press (MFY, 27). He asserts that such inconsistencies are not authentic homosexual experiences but creations of a profit-motivated press, incentivized to instigate homosexual scandals and condemn them immediately thereafter. Gerber berates "American journal-ists who profit from the publications of all the filthy details of heterosexual and homosexual perverts" (MFY, 27). He alludes first to the gossip press that fomented *The Nation*'s claims years earlier, scolding outlets that focus on the "'Pillars of Society' in Hollywood and New York" (MFY, 27). But Gerber also attacks "such a conservative and 'decent' paper as the *NY Times*," which revealed in its coverage of the purge salacious details about Roehm's "chief of police"—presumably Edmund Heines—who was "found in bed with a fair young man" (MFY, 27). Likewise, Gerber notes that "rumored" accounts of "homosexual orgies . . . around Roehm's headquarters" reported in the US press are easily understood as mere attempts to titillate readers and sell papers (MFY, 28). Most saliently, Gerber argues the coverage of the Roehm purge further illuminates that the conflation of Hitlerism with homosexual-ity is illusory: "newspapers of America were strangely compromised by this story," he states, because they could not decide whether to "praise the mur-derer Hitler for suppressing homosexuals" or "credit Roehm and his homo-sexual camorra" for confronting Hitlerism (MFY, 27). In the end, the papers "condemned both and saved their faces," proving Gerber's point: homosex-ual allegations in *Brevities*, *The Nation*, and the *New York Times* were unsup-ported by facts, driven only by profit (MFY, 27).

With these detailed indictments, Gerber dispatched with the two most prominent ways of remembering Roehm, arguing that these spurious inter-pretations were hypocritical, illogical fantasies created by a discredited US press corps. As a result, Gerber warns that press claims about homosexuality should be treated suspiciously across the board. Gerber's essay then moves forward by reimagining Roehm, his men, and homosexuals in general anew—in ways he deems necessary to secure a nascent US homophile movement.

Inventing Valiant and Virile Anti-Fascist Warriors

Having undercut prior memories of Roehm and the SA, Gerber spends the balance of "Hitlerism and Homosexuality" offering readers a dramatic reappraisal that recasts the homosexual captain and his men as masculine, anti-fascist warriors who died while valiantly attempting to overthrow the detestable Hitler. Gerber most explicitly reimagines Roehm as a fallen hero at the essay's end, where he suggests that "Roehm and his valiant men may have been defeated, but the homosexuals will go on fighting to rid the world of tyranny" (MFY, 29). But his powerful peroration builds on several smaller, ascending rhetorical moves from the essay's start.

It begins in the essay's first line, where Gerber defines homosexuals in general (and Roehm in particular) as antityrannical by constitution. Rather than accept Nazi and US press claims that homosexuals are naturally drawn to fascism, Gerber asserts that history shows homosexual relationships have always turned their practitioners against authoritarianism. To support that claim, Gerber introduces readers to an idea from Plato's *Banquet* (more commonly known as the *Symposium*), an ancient text that held powerful cachet in turn-of-the-century homosexual epistemologies for its explicit and favorable discussions of love between men. Here, Gerber quotes Plato's character Pausanias, who argues that male love (which Gerber interprets as homosexuality) cultivates antityrannical impulses between men in civic life: "love relations (between men) . . . are enemies of tyranny," for tyranny thrives when "there be between them (men) no strong bonds of friendship or fellowship" (MFY, 27, Gerber's parenthesis). On the contrary, in societies where these bonds do exist, in which "this (homosexual) love is so well able to tie" one man meaningfully to another, tyranny cannot prosper (MFY, 27). Gerber thus argues, via Plato, that if a society cultivates genuine and lasting love between men—one that can withstand the storms of partisanship and factionalism—it can never be dominated by a tyrant or dictator. Again, Gerber's claim debunks US press discourses that homosexuals were predisposed to fascism; without directly addressing this idea, Gerber defines homosexuality as the antithesis of fascism (i.e., antityrannical), and thereby a natural foe to Hitlerism.

After establishing this new definition, Gerber deduces that this universal principle about homosexuals applies to the particular case of Roehm and his SA comrades. Gerber continues that "there is nothing new under the sun" (MFY, 26) and affirms that Plato's "ancient statement" (MFY, 27) has repeatedly been shown to be true in contemporary times. Only then does Gerber connect homosexuality's antityrannical principle to the "recent happenings in modern Germany," which even the most news-averse US reader would recognize as referring to the June 1934 purge (MFY, 26). Nonetheless, Gerber eliminates any doubts about the "recent happenings" he references, confirming he means Hitler's "bloody murder of his intimate friends [i.e., Roehm]"—a crime that Hitler "in part justified" by invoking their "sexual aberrations" (MFY, 27). In doing so, Gerber compels his reader to make sense of Roehm's demise in a new way. Whereas previously, the US press attempted to cast Roehm as the leader of a homosexual cabal (i.e., the SA), murdered by a competing gang of homosexuals (i.e., Hitler and the remaining Nazis)—all of whom were presented as fascistic—Gerber significantly recasts the roles. In his remembering, the Roehm purge was not the result of infighting among a vast, tyrannical Nazi-homosexual regime, but rather an explicitly anti-fascist homosexual faction battling a heterosexual tyrannical bloc. With this shift, Gerber alters key terms in readers' recollection of the purge from issues of sexual desire to each side's stance on tyranny. In this telling, as Plato insists, homosexuals abhor tyranny by their very nature. Thus, Gerber leaves readers with the inescapable interpretation that Roehm and his men were indeed homosexuals, but also brothers-in-arms determined to cast out a tyrant from their midst.

Gerber adds further rhetorical heft to this reimagining by aligning homosexuals with other segments of German society that similarly struggled against Nazi tyranny: Communists and atheists. Of the two, Gerber spends significantly more time on the Communist comparison. As mentioned above, the German Communist Party waged vicious street battles against the Nazis in its struggle for political power. This well-known fact made Communists a clear rival of the Nazis in some readers' minds, even if the finer points of their dispute were murky. If Gerber could persuade his readers both that Communists were antithetical to Nazis and that homosexuals like Roehm were akin to the Communists, then Roehm, his men, and homosexuals generally should be remembered as anti-Nazi and anti-fascist as well.

Gerber's attempted alignment of Roehm and the SA with the German Communists was odd. One primary reason Hitler valued Roehm and the SA was their involvement in brawling with the German Communist Party in the early 1930s and fostering political violence. Roehm's hands had been stained with the blood of dozens of German Communists, and he was viciously anti-Communist in both word and deed. Whether Gerber was aware of Roehm's anti-Communist bona fides is unclear, but this did not deter him from trying to equate the captain and the SA with Communists in their shared struggle against fascism. This may be why Gerber aligns Communism with homosexuals *generally*, rather than with Roehm as an individual. By doing so, Roehm could be indirectly aligned with Communism without ever being called a Communist himself.

Whereas Gerber earlier used deduction to label Roehm and his men antityrannical, here Gerber uses induction to align homosexuals and Communists. To work this appeal, Gerber applied his own beliefs and experiences regarding Communism to all homosexuals as a group. In 1934, Gerber was an avowed Communist and, in contrast to other Communists who saw homosexuality as a social ill, he believed Communism was a natural ally of the homosexual cause. Gerber even made this point in other essays published in *Chanticleer* prior to "Hitlerism and Homosexuality," particularly one titled "Recent Homosexual Literature" from February 1934. There, Gerber argued that nations often decried as homes to "Bolshevic, Libertine, Swine" were destined to be places of homosexual "Free Love." In particular, Gerber argued that postrevolution Russia, "where the government is no longer capitalistic and is not bound to religious sex superstitions," is where "sex is free" and homosexuals would soon be embraced.[42] While a ludicrous suggestion in retrospect, Gerber was deeply invested in a shared future for Communism and homosexuality, rooted in his own experience.

These beliefs also appear in "Hitlerism and Homosexuality," where Gerber bemoans that the capitalist "persecution of homosexuals goes on," even as historical falsehoods against homosexuality have evaporated (MFY, 28). "No one," Gerber remarks, "has brought forth a plausible reason why homosexuals should be wiped out, except the age old reasoning which is also applied to atheism and communism, that it is contrary to the welfare of the state (the profit and exploitation system of capitalists)." He adds, "With the waning of capitalism . . . the opposition of the governments to homosexuals will also wane" (MFY, 28–29). As a result, Gerber announces that "you cannot, therefore, blame the homosexual, if they throw in their support with the communists and atheists" (MFY, 29). In this previous sentence, the word *support* is key for affirming his larger point: for Gerber, homosexuals and Communists are allies, and each party must be recognized as opposed to Hitler, fascism, and tyranny.

Gerber further demonstrates a shared affinity between Communists and homosexuals in the essay's waning paragraphs. There, Gerber recounts efforts in the German legislature in 1929 to repeal Paragraph 175, highlighting how "the socialists and communists outvoted the nationalist and clerical party, and brought about repeal of the notorious paragraph 175 which punished homosexuals for their acts" (MFY, 29). Gerber is factually wrong here. Significant efforts were made to repeal Paragraph 175 that year, but the law was ultimately retained. In fact, the Nazis strengthened Paragraph 175 a few months after Gerber's essay was published, to the great detriment of male homosexuals—a subject discussed more in the chapter 2. But this fanciful retelling of Paragraph 175's false demise allowed Gerber to again disrupt US memories of homosexuals as Hitlerites, aligning homophiles with Communists in their shared pursuit of homosexual emancipation.

As we have seen, Gerber's primary task in the piece is rejecting the conflation of Hitlerism and homosexuality. But Gerber also does important rhetorical work by providing representationally deficient US homosexuals a praiseworthy figure with whom they might identify. To this end, Gerber expands the depictions of Roehm and his men in *Chanticleer* by assigning three different, affirmative virtues to their actions beyond anti-fascism. First, Gerber uses strategic characterizations to remember Roehm and the SA as warriors. The word *warrior* itself never appears in Gerber's texts, but he uses an array of laudable, alternative terms to cast Roehm in this light. For instance, Gerber uses several military phrases—describing the site of Roehm's capture as a "headquarters" (MFY, 28) rather than a *hotel*, and using his title and rank, "the Chief of Staff of Nazi storm troops" (MFY, 27)—to depict Roehm's actions as those of an ordered and trained unit of military service. Further, Gerber suggests at the essay's end that homosexuals will "go on fighting" against tyranny, much like Roehm and the SA (MFY, 29). Such a wording implies Roehm waged a battle against Hitler and minimizes the narrative that he was caught unaware by the führer. Importantly, all these terms avoid depicting Roehm and his men as either coup plotters or disgruntled mob. Instead, the word *mob* only appears once in the text, to characterize the Nazis' book burning at the Institute for Sexual Science (MFY, 27). Gerber thus distinguishes between the militant, systematic Roehm and the riotous, disorderly Hitlerites.

Second and related, Gerber remembers Roehm and his men in masculinist terminology. Most directly, Gerber wonders if they deserve credit "for being the only men in Germany virile enough to attempt to wipe out the unspeakable Hitler?" (MFY, 27). The masculine word *virile* here frames Roehm as a man of action, with sexual potency and stamina to boot. Similarly, Gerber uses the phrase *wipe out* in the same sentence to suggest the Nazi captain was just as likely to end Hitler's life in a bloody purge as he was to die in his own (MFY, 27). The word *camorra*, while indicating organized criminality, also conveys a sense of old-world chauvinism (MFY, 27). Combined, these depictions amplify the rhetoric of Roehm and his men as warriors by conflating masculinity and warfare. But Gerber's masculinist language also offers his audience a masculine image of homosexuality, which contrasted sharply with the dangerous indictment of male effeminacy that had become rampant during the post–Pansy Craze panic in New York City (AS, 82).

Third and finally, Gerber remembers the actions of Roehm and the men of the SA as honorable while condemning the acts of the Hitlerites as morally bankrupt. The clearest terminological example in "Hitlerism and Homosexuality" occurs when Gerber labels Roehm and his men "valiant" (MFY, 29). A classical war adjective evoking stirring military struggle and the deep honor imbued in battle-tested men, "valiant" helped Gerber depict Roehm and company as role models for an often-maligned US homosexual minority. The term's classical uptake also alludes to Gerber's invocation of Plato earlier in the text, rooting his characterization of homosexuals in ancient values of the Western canon. Gerber adds to Roehm's honorable ethos here by aligning his acts with those of Hirschfeld, who is lauded for "dedicat[ing] his life to the liberation of enslaved homosexuals in all lands" (MFY, 27). Meanwhile, Gerber contrasted the honorable Roehm with the dubious Hitler, whom Gerber variously describes as an "erstwhile . . . friend," a leader who "acquiesced" to others, and finally a plain-old murderer (MFY, 27). Collectively, attributing fine and noteworthy virtues to the actions of Roehm and his murdered men only further provided Gerber rhetorical firepower for shoring up a nascent US homosexual community.

The fullest realization of Gerber's new memory of Roehm and his men—and its utility for Gerber's expressed desire to see US homosexuals get "smart," "get together," and organize (MFY, 28)—appears in the essay's final line, where his preferred memory of Roehm becomes clear. Yet this final line also reveals Gerber's broader aim to envision how a future US homosexual community might look by reshaping the memory of Ernst Roehm. Here, Gerber affirms his vision of Roehm but then pivots away from him, extending Roehm's virile, valiant, and anti-fascist credentials onto homosexuals in general. Acknowledging Roehm's death at the height of his epideictic appeal, Gerber suggests homosexuals "will go on fighting to rid the world of tyranny" in Roehm's absence (MFY, 29). This powerful act of rhetorical induction shifts from the specifics of Roehm to the more general figure of the homosexual. In such a move, Gerber assigns to all male homosexuals the honorable, masculine, antityrannical impulse he cultivated in Roehm—a need to refuse antidemocratic leaders and struggle against them, showing much the same "fight" as the fallen Roehm and his men. Gerber does not specifically state that the tyrant surviving homosexuals must fight is Hitler himself; by the essay's end, this point is self-evident. But Gerber completes his reframing of Roehm powerfully, setting up the dead homosexual captain at the head of an imagined army of virile homophile men, the vanguard in the coming battle for either an American century or an era of German despotism.

Conclusion

Despite Gerber's efforts to disentangle the figure of the homosexual from the rise of Hitler and the Nazi Party, such equations exploded in US public discourse following Germany's declaration of war on the United States in 1941. The years following Gerber's essay would see a dramatic mainstreaming of the homosexuality-and-Hitlerism trope in the States. Now recognized as a confirmed national threat, the Nazis' moral decay circulated well beyond the scandalous anti-Nazi outlets of the early 1930s to countless local, regional, and national outlets of great esteem. For example, weeks after the United States entered the war, the *Tampa Tribune* posited that Hitler might be suffering from a form of "homosexual madness."[43] That angst was heightened further in June 1942, when a former Berlin bureau chief published a series of scandalous, syndicated newspaper articles about Hitler's sexuality that were echoed and amplified by other credible journalists.[44] Eventually, the US press extended Hitler's supposedly disturbed homosexuality to the entire Germany population, calling it a national neurosis endemic to "the most homosexual nation on earth."[45] Each of these claims exemplifies hundreds of other metastasizing conflations of homosexuality and Nazism in the American press between 1935 and 1945, which continued for decades after the war. Given the profusion of such comparisons, it seems clear that any effort by Gerber to stem the tide raging against US homosexuals through re-remembering Roehm failed spectacularly.

Yet, as previously discussed, Gerber's audience was almost certainly not the wider public, but an interested community of homosexual readers. As with many homosexual communities that remembered the Nazi persecution between 1934 and 1981, this memory work during the earliest years of the Nazis' rise to power was almost exclusively aimed at internal audiences to deal with internal challenges. In Gerber's case, the challenges affecting his internal audience were not dissimilar from those facing his external audience: the idea that homosexuals were, as a type, inherently fascistic and, as such, reprehensible. And while this message posed political problems for a nascent homosexual movement in the United States, it also presented inspirational and definitional obstacles for a community only beginning to see itself as such. Who, for instance, would want to claim an identity as an American homosexual if they believed homosexuality was anti-American? What kind of American homosexual community could be imagined if the Nazi homosexuals, whom they were led to see as their kin, were criminally ruth-less not only to other nations but also to each other as homosexuals? And what point did homosexual empowerment serve if it all led to a spectacularly bloody end marked by ridicule, violence, and suffering? For Gerber's read-ers, already experiencing their own growing persecution in the wake of the US post–Pansy Craze panic, his recuperation of Roehm was an important answer. He argued for a vision of homosexual community that was not only far different from the chimeras offered by the Nazis or the US press but also one that American homosexuals could embrace as powerful, virile, honor-able, and implicitly anti-fascist. For this small but growing audience, Gerber presented a homosexual memory that, while lacking victory and optimism, still offered possibility and hope in an increasingly dark world.

In doing so, Gerber was participating in an often unattended to but pow-erful protoqueer reliance on memory as a resource for rhetorical action. As I have written about elsewhere, modern queer people's strategic decision to invoke memory in the face of the HIV/AIDS epidemic in the 1980s was actu-ally part of a much longer lineage of LGBTQ+ predecessors who made mem-ory a central tool in their rhetorical adventures, what I have termed a *queer return to memory*.[46] Gerber's reframing of Roehm, and particularly his reli-ance on the Greeks to help him do so, is emblematic of this longer rhetorical tradition among homosocials, homosexuals, and lesbian and gay activists. It is also notable in this instance because Gerber is doing this past-oriented work *before* the Holocaust—the twentieth-century event many histories of memory studies identify as the inaugurating moment of our wider social turn to memory work. As a result, Gerber's efforts highlighted in this chapter not only elucidates the already-established practices of homosocials, homosex-uals, and lesbians and gays to depend on memory, but also provides compel-ling evidence of how remembering the Nazi persecution of homosexuals in particular did this work before (and therefore outside) the memory tradition centering the Holocaust. From a theoretical perspective, such a move prom-ises larger considerations that I return to in the conclusion. But for now, this chapter shows once again that even at the earliest moment in which American homosexuals were remembering the persecution of their European homo-sexual compatriots, they were doing so as part of a much older, more com-prehensive, and perhaps *distinctive* tradition of queer memory work.

Tracing the effectiveness of Roehm's alternate memory on this limited audience is nearly impossible. The homosexual community Gerber promised his imagined audience would not materialize in archivable discourse until the

1950s, even as at least some homosexual communities grew in size and scope over the intervening decades. Simultaneously, Gerber's text largely fell into oblivion soon after its 1934 publication. His work to organize and defend US homosexuals in the 1920s and '30s was almost completely unknown to early lesbian and gay activists of the 1950s until Gerber reconnected with the community via ONE magazine in 1953. Afterward, "Hitlerism and Homosexuality" would reemerge only in snippets, partially reproduced for the first time in Jonathan Ned Katz's groundbreaking *Gay American History* in 1976. Today, the full text remains available in only a few select archives and databases—largely unread except by LGBTQ+ historians.

Nonetheless, this initial attempt to remember homosexual victims of the Nazi regime has much to tell us about the specific project of using these memories in US homosexual rhetoric at its earliest stages. Gerber's efforts to infuse Roehm's memory with the spirit of a nascent homosexual politics as soon as three months following the captain's execution confirms two of this book's major themes: that US homosexuals and heterosexuals alike knew of the Nazi persecution of homosexuals in real time, and that homosexual activists deployed memories of these events to advance the community's aims almost from the moment they began. Gerber's admittedly limited case shows that early US homosexual activists were quick to see the threat posed by a rising Nazi tyranny and actively worked to align themselves against it. In 1934, this fact was far from certain. The Third Reich was in its infancy, its most horrendous acts of anti-Semitism and violence—events like Kristallnacht, which would ultimately shape many Americans' anti-Nazi perspectives—were years away. Meanwhile, the underlying structures of the Nazi ideology, such as anti-Semitism and racial segregation, were still shared by some Americans and Germans at the time.[47] The full horrors resulting from Nazi power could simply not be seen by most everyday Americans in this moment. But Gerber saw at least some of the Nazi threat for what it could become after Roehm's murder, named it tyranny in print, and sought to align American homosexuals—all homosexuals, in fact—against it, if for no other reason than to ensure a future for a US homosexual community whose growth might be indefinitely impeded otherwise.

Gerber's remembrance of Roehm also illustrates that where other scholars and activists have failed to see any meaningful attempt to advance a memory of the Nazi persecution of homosexuals in the United States before the 1970s, such memories were long present—if we are able to overcome our expectations about who counts as the Nazis' homosexual victims. For too long, activists and scholars in search of such memories looked at the homosexual persecution with anachronistic eyes. On one hand, we searched for homosexual victims who emulated what most Americans today are taught to imagine Nazi victims to have looked like: victims molded in the image of the Jewish experience of the Holocaust and marked by ghettoization, camp internment, and mass extermination. On the other hand, searches for homosexual victims privileged sympathetic homosexual suffering. In a period when so many millions lost their lives to the Nazis, prioritizing the stories of victims whose humanity shines through seemed like the right thing to do. But neither Roehm nor his men massacred in the purge fit these descriptions. In the history of the Nazi regime, June 1934 marked the earliest months of the homosexual persecution. Mass roundups and arrests, fervent anti-homosexual laws, internment in camps—these terrors were months and years away. In fact, some scholars and survivors of the homosexual persecution mark the Roehm purge as the beginning of such targeted oppression.[48] In other words, in a theme I return to again in this book, seeking out homosexual victims of the Nazis for remembrance will always be stymied if we search for homosexual experiences that mirror those of the six million Jews murdered by the Nazis. By the same token, few at the time or in the decades since have characterized Roehm and his men as sympathetic victims of the Nazi regime. In effect, even though at least some of these men were homosexual, their ties to Nazism seem to have justified their persecution, at least for some. As a result, the Roehm purge is too often unrecognizable even today as an act of homosexual repression by the Nazis; nor can Roehm and the Brownshirts be seen as sympathetic victims. Both failings contributed to the false idea that even homosexuals themselves did not remember this persecution until decades later.

But if we widen memory's aperture to include American homosexuals like Gerber in September 1934, the Roehm purge and its remembrances in *Chanticleer* change that narrative. Rather than seeing a despicable homosexual Nazi who got what he deserved, we can see that members of a nascent homosexual community—desperate for representation and adrift in the fog of war about the events of the purge itself—made sense of both Roehm and his death with the facts they had and put them to meaningful rhetorical work on their own behalf. The image of Roehm presented by Gerber—of a consequential homosexual taking up arms against Hitler in a valiant and virile act of anti-fascism—is certainly hard to square today. But considered in its original context, this remembrance of Roehm—one that the in memoriam note published in the *Times* suggests was not unique to Gerber—seems self-serving but also reasonable, plausible, and rooted in contemporary reporting. It also provides a new starting point from which we can trace wider practices of remembering the homosexual persecution by the Nazis by US homosexuals in the decades to come.

What did this image of Roehm and his men offered by Gerber portend for such memory work more generally? Narrow as it was, Gerber's memory of Roehm points to two key facets of remembering homosexual victims of the Nazi regime that reverberate throughout this book. First is the tendency of homosocial, homosexual, and lesbian and gay commemorators over several decades to remember homosexual victims as resisters of Nazi power. In Roehm's case, homosexual resistance to the Nazis is remembered in a form that was both active and militant: an imagined army of homosexuals, reminiscent of the infamous Sacred Band of Thebes, struck down in battle with Hitler's tyrannical forces. As we will see, different homosexual activists also remembered homosexuals persecuted by the Nazis with a similar framing of "resistance" between 1934 and 1981. However, none of these later activists imagined or marshaled this valiant warrior image of persecuted homosexuals in the same way as Gerber. This discrepancy is almost entirely explained by Gerber's partial view of what would become a much wider campaign of anti-homosexual terror in the years after "Hitlerism and Homosexuality" was published. As such, Gerber's remembrance of homosexual resistance emphasizes Roehm's military training, his masculinist disposition, and the Nazis' justification for the purge as preventing a threatened coup. By the next chapter, when these events are again taken up by homosexual activists in the late 1940s and '50s, a much fuller image of Nazi persecution takes precedence, while Roehm and his men's victimization falls almost entirely out of favor. But for Gerber, in September 1934, Roehm's fate embodied the Nazi persecution of homosexuals, and the ethos and actions of the captain and his men leading up to the purge defined the kind of resistance homosexuals of Gerber's time were asked to praise or emulate.

If Gerber's remembrance of Roehm is notable for first infusing memories of homosexuals persecuted by the Nazi regime with the rhetoric of resistance, it is also significant for emphasizing another facet of these events that failed to anticipate future challenges American homosexuals would face: the fearful specter of homosexuals as Communists or Communist targets. As this chapter has shown, this realignment (while factually suspect) was an effective way to depict homosexuals anew as anti-fascist. But as World War II ended and the Cold War began, Gerber's efforts to equate homosexuality with Communism rather than fascism appear, in retrospect, potentially catastrophic. Shortly after the war, the US government, in a frenzy of anti-Communist fervor, turned on American homosexuals in explicit terms. As scholar David K. Johnson notes, this shift resulted in hearings, investigations, dismissals, and arrests of homosexuals in Washington, DC. Soon, the federal government had created a discourse in which "communists and queers" were "indistinguishable threats."[49] The suggestion that homosexuals were sympathetic to Communism or likely to be blackmailed by Communists was a chief barb in such attacks. The Lavender Scare summarizes these events alongside the Cuban internment of homosexuals, which prompted the first march by homosexuals on the White House. This turn against American homosexuals enabled by anti-Communist discourses was impossible for Gerber to imagine in September 1934, when homosexuals were facing very different and more immediate threats at home and abroad. But as I show in the next chapter, the changing nature of these dangers in the immediate postwar period led a new generation of homosexual activists—some of them also avowed Communists—to revisit memories of the Nazi persecution and its victims, using these recollections to attack the emerging anti-homosexual threats of their own era.

Chapter 2

Vagrants and Outlaws

Remembering Nazi Laws to Fight the
American Gestapo, 1949–1965

The Nazi persecution of homosexuals lurked in the memories of five American men as they gathered in Harry Hay's Los Angeles home on November 11, 1950. The meeting's aim was to discuss a new draft of a prospectus, first written by Hay in 1949, calling for the incorporation of an American homosexual organization. By almost any measure, the dangerous and hard-fought meeting was successful, for the men agreed to meet again and proceed with the new endeavor, which would become the Mattachine Foundation. In doing so, these leaders inaugurated a powerful new phase of the US homosexual rights movement. A key facet of the group members' decision was their agreement with the principles and ideas outlined in Hay's prospectus. In at least one telling of the story, the men expressed near unanimity on the document, so much so that they declared each of them could have written it themselves.[1] Among the prospectus's first principles was a simple yet powerful expression of the new organization's raison d'être: that if homosexuals did not organize themselves for political action soon, they would likely suffer the same fate as German homosexuals just a few years prior.

Indeed, Hay argued in point A.1 of the prospectus that homosexuals in the 1950s faced an "encroaching American Fascism" that emulated a "previous . . . International Fascism" (i.e., Nazism) from the recent past. Like the Nazis, this American Fascism sought "to bend unorganized and unpopular minorities" like homosexuals "into isolated fragments of social and emotional instability." He supported this claim by noting how, in the Third Reich, "the socially censured Androgynous Community [i.e., the homosexual community] was suborned, blackmailed, cozened, and stampeded into serving as hoodlums, stool pigeons, volunteer informers, concentration camp trusties, torturers, and hangmen, before it, as a minority, was ruthlessly exterminated." For these and other reasons articulated thereafter, Hay's prospectus argued that the "Andro-gynes of the World" must organize.[2] If not, they risked their own destruction on American shores. What Hay's document only hinted at in text but implic-itly screamed was that this fearful end of US homosexuals would come at the hands of the same entity that stamped out their European forebears: a cruel, corrupt, and legally sanctioned anti-homosexual police force.

As discussed in the introduction, Nazi police forces played a significant role in executing the Third Reich's persecution of homosexuals. This point is often lost in more contemporary public memories of the pink triangles, which emphasize homosexual experiences in Nazi concentration camps to the exclusion of all else. But while camp administration—and the homosex-ual suffering therein—fell under the powers of the Nazi police state (broadly conceived), far more homosexuals were persecuted outside the camps than inside. In those more common situations, it was the police in the guise of the Gestapo (i.e., the secret police) or the Kripo (i.e., the Kriminalpolizei or criminal police) that facilitated the harassment, humiliation, blackmail-ing, blacklisting, arrest, beating, interrogation, castration, and detention of homosexuals. Though the Nazi "police" appeared far different from how most Americans understood law enforcement then and now, the Nazi police appa-ratus was the main tool of homosexual aggravation, persecution, and death described in Hay's prospectus.

As a member of the Communist Party, Popular Front participant, and passing interlocuter with previous homosexual leaders, Hay was keenly aware of the role Nazi policing played in the destruction of the German homosexual movement. But the prospectus and the US organization it called for were not simply about documenting the past—they were also concerned with loom-ing threats to American homosexuality in the present. As the prospectus indicated, the policing of German homosexuals under the Third Reich res-onated strongly with American homosexuals' fears after 1950. The men who joined Hay to discuss his prospectus expressed similar anxieties about law and policing in the months following Mattachine's creation. Among them was Rudi Gernreich, a Jew and Austrian refugee who fled the Nazis as a child. Gernreich was so concerned the young organization would be raided and dismembered that he warned, "If we repeat the errors of Hirschfeld's Ger-man Movement . . . we could set the potential of an American Gay Move-ment back for decades to come."[3] Dale Jennings, another founding member of

Mattachine, who famously emerged victorious from his own anti-homosexual policing case in 1952, believed that the group had been infiltrated by the police or FBI within its first year.[4] For these reasons, as movement historian C. Todd White described, "for the first two years of Mattachine, each time members gathered in private homes, they did so fearfully. Shades were always drawn when they couldn't meet in a basement, and someone always kept a sharp lookout for the police or FBI."[5] The founders of Mattachine were not the only homosexuals who felt this way. US homosexuals knew well that even if the Nazi regime had been eliminated, the anti-homosexual police apparatus they used to crush German homophiles was alive and well in small towns and big cities across the United States.

But these shared anxieties about anti-homosexual laws and policing in the United States and Nazi Germany could also serve as a powerful rhetorical resource for this nascent American community. If used proactively, such comparisons could help the newfangled group define itself as a persecuted minority (as Hay and others believed it was). Such comparisons also had the potential to rally the homosexual community for future action, particularly by turning its sentiments against the institutions of law and policing that many of them had been taught to revere their entire lives. Strategic historical allusions equating Nazi and US laws and policing thus offered a growing American homosexual community the chance to imagine a world in which homosexuals could live free of police terrorism and its horrible consequences.

To that end, members of the newest iteration of the US homosexual movement began to make these comparisons plainly before their community of peers. This work was made possible via an emerging set of homosexual publications beginning in 1953. Chief among the publications to print these kinds of mnemonic comparisons were ONE: *The Homosexual Magazine* and *Mattachine Review*. The two magazines were quite different and adopted conflicting ideas and approaches to US homosexual politics. But in both passing comments and extended broadsides, the homosexuals who created, read, and responded to both publications made powerful connections between an intensifying, postwar anti-homosexual crackdown by US law enforcement and the crimes of the Nazi police, which had occurred less than a decade earlier. In doing so, they again demonstrated how central remembering the Nazi persecution of homosexuals was to the establishment and enactment of a US homosexual rights movement.

This chapter examines how readers and writers of ONE and *Mattachine Review* built opposition in the US homosexual community to American laws and police practices by turning to two inventive remembrances of the Nazi persecution of homosexuals. First, homosexual rhetors in these publications characterized Paragraph 175 as a "Nazi law" and applied this association to anti-homosexual measures in the United States and the United Kingdom. Second, activists used a different but symmetrical memory rhetoric in these publications to argue that anti-homosexual tactics adopted by US law enforcement emulated those of the Nazi Gestapo. As such, indulgent anti-homosexual policing practices rendered US law enforcement an "American Gestapo" that should be repudiated as un-American and morally repugnant. By the end of both publications' runs in the mid-1960s, these practices had not been halted. But both memory rhetorics became essential for building collective resistance in the community against police entrapment and anti-homosexual laws that would bear fruit years later.

Law, Policing, and the Homosexual Press in 1950s America

Dale Jennings's aforementioned arrest and trial for "lewd and dissolute behavior" was part of a campaign targeting suspected homosexuals in the 1950s that was decidedly fiercer, wider, and more pernicious than any preceding it on American shores. US law enforcement had never been friendly to homosexuals. Statutes prohibiting sodomy, buggery, and "crimes against nature" were incorporated into state penal codes from the early days of the nation's history, with law enforcement tasked with upholding them.[6] Yet preventing or punishing homosexual acts was often not a law enforcement priority, and some state and local police forces effectively tolerated a certain degree of homosexuality in places like New York City's Times Square in the 1920s.[7] But key events significantly shifted US perceptions of "sex crimes" in the twentieth century. Domestic newspaper coverage of the trials of Oscar Wilde and the Eulenburg affair rendered homosexual anxieties a potent political weapon at home and abroad. Both the Kinsey Reports and the Lavender Scare further ignited Americans' concerns about the breadth and reach of US homosexual activity after World War II. And Cold War paranoia was used to recharacterize homosexuality as a domestic and national security threat in the American imagination.[8] Amid these changes, citizens, politicians, and religious leaders clamored for crackdowns on homosexual activity—and the police became their tool of choice.

To tackle the homosexual scourge, large cities and hundreds of smaller municipalities nationwide began subjecting twentieth-century homosexuals to a growing panoply of laws intended to vilify and snuff out acts of same-sex desire. These policies criminalized male cruising, banned homosexual depictions on stage, policed cross-dressing, limited homosexuals from congregating in bars, and closed establishments serving or employing homosexuals.[9] But the favored legal mechanism for enforcing US anti-homosexual crackdowns in the 1950s and '60s were vagrancy and lewdness measures, which police and homosexuals alike referred to as *vag-lewd*.[10] Vag-lewd statutes were inherited from earlier legal frameworks to prosecute nuisance crimes like loitering, public drunkenness, and homelessness but could easily be manipulated to police homosexuality. For example, vagrancy laws targeting trespassers were used to sweep up men suspected of cruising for sex, and "lewd conduct" laws for curbing public exposure were often used to fine and imprison men who shared even a glancing touch.[11] As the *Mattachine Review* noted, vag-lewd enforcement was both confounding to understand and destructive in its outcomes: "The uncertainty of acts and facts leaves the offense shrouded in mystery. . . . A business or professional career is easily destroyed if the conviction receives any publicity at all, because 'Vaglewd' . . . looms in such sinister proportions."[12]

Vag-lewd laws were frequently paired with outrageous police tactics to scare, intimidate, and capture alleged homosexuals. While roundups and targeted raids of bars, bathhouses, and parks had been employed in New York as early as 1842, mass arrests became widespread during the 1950s and '60s, with notable examples in Philadelphia, Salt Lake, Boise, New Orleans, Miami, and Los Angeles, among many others.[13] Such tactics ensnared 125 alleged homosexuals in New York in 1959.[14] Similar tactics trapped 220 homosexuals in San Francisco in 1960.[15] US police and law enforcement also created secret and not-so-secret lists of suspected homosexuals. While J. Edgar Hoover most notoriously adopted this practice to track homosexual suspects for the FBI, similar lists were also developed at the state and local levels, either through investigations or by compiling names from previous arrest records and homosexual registries.[16] Police also used name-calling, discriminatory remarks, dismissive treatment, intimidation, and police beatings or violence to disincentivize homosexuality. In at least one 1954 case, dozens of homosexuals were detained but not arrested outside a known homosexual bar in Miami, while officers performed "venereal disease checks."[17] Police departments also leaked the names and home addresses of suspected homosexuals to the men's families, their employers, or the media. In this way, police could significantly harm homosexuals even without arrest.

But of all the police tactics to draw the ire of homosexuals, entrapment was the most nefarious. Entrapment is broadly understood as an act of police subterfuge whereby an officer of the law invites an individual to commit a crime that they would not have committed otherwise. Police entrapment of homosexuals typically entailed surveilling locales frequented by homosexuals (i.e., parks, bars, theaters, bus stops), targeting a suspected homosexual, and deploying an agent provocateur to entice the suspect to reveal, initiate, or agree to homosexual activity. Entrapment was particularly effective when paired with vag-lewd laws that justified arrest with only fleeting touches, looks, gestures, or conversations. Nonetheless, homosexuals regularly alleged that agent provocateurs used persistent and aggressive tactics to facilitate a charge, including pursuing suspects after rejecting an advance, entering homes without permission, demanding suspects say certain things, or forcing bodily contact. Despite homosexual protestations, entrapment practices continued apace in these decades and even advanced with the support of local political and law enforcement leaders, as they produced arrests. For instance, the New York Police Department alone arrested fifty thousand men between 1923 and 1966 using these tactics.[18] This success explains why entrapment became the most fervent priority for men of the newfound US homosexual rights movement in the 1950s.

A persistent US homosexual press soon emerged in the 1950s in response to this aggressive policing. The first two sustained US homosexual publications for homosexual conversations on homosexual topics were ONE (later renamed ONE: The Homosexual Magazine) in January 1953 and Mattachine Review in 1955.[19] ONE and Mattachine Review differed in numerous ways. ONE was a passion project of several early members of Mattachine and another California organization, the Knights of Clock. The Knights of Clock was an explicitly interracial homophile organization based in Los Angeles, focused on social events and fundraising, which "offered employment and housing services to mixed-race homosexual partners."[20] Thanks to this fusion, ONE's earliest efforts included people from various genders, races, and class backgrounds, though it was soon dominated by white men.[21] ONE, which often adopted a passionate, hopeful, incredulous, or angry tone, was intent on pushing the movement forward quickly by throwing sharp elbows and indulging in radical thoughts and stark debates. By contrast, Mattachine Review was the official organ of the Mattachine Society and presented a persona of respectabil-ity. Its tone emphasized American values, virtues, and institutions; heralded medicine and science; and deeply opposed anything hinting of Communism after the expulsions of the organization's five founding members several years earlier. At some points, *Mattachine Review* could not even be called a homo-sexual magazine because it claimed to be for anyone interested in discussing homosexuality, up to and including those who wished to see homosexual-ity be cured. These differences in tone, style, and values led to repeated and often vitriolic tensions between the two publications.[22] Nonetheless, *Matta-chine Review* and ONE had a reciprocal relationship, with homosexuals read-ing, subscribing, and responding to ideas in both publications. This reality made ONE and *Mattachine Review* highly rhetorical documents. Through their editorial boards and contributors—who were often obscured as one and the same through the use of pseudonyms—each magazine asserted its preferred views on homosexuality, its causes, the idea of a homosexual community, and what such a community should do. In their pages, homosexuals argued together about these and other ideas, generating a new era of US queer com-munity in the process.

But for all the differences between ONE and *Mattachine Review*, each pub-lication and its readers held two points in common for this chapter's purposes. First, each publication became a venue for aggrieved homosexuals to docu-ment, debate, and agitate against vag-lewd, police entrapment, and similar anti-homosexual practices in the United States after 1950. Second, in doing so, each publication saw its letters to the editor, articles, and editorial com-mentary both reference and invoke the Nazi persecution of homosexuals to help frame their understanding of domestic US police crackdowns. ONE and *Mattachine Review* thus offer a compelling portrait of how US homosexuals of the mid-twentieth century remembered the Nazi past to collectively influ-ence their shared future.

Remembering Paragraph 175 as a Nazi Law

To challenge the vigorous postwar policing of homosexuals, US homosexual publications took rhetorical aim at laws like vag-lewd that made such pros-ecutions possible. This legal focus emerged in ONE and *Mattachine Review* through profiles of individual state laws, advice from sympathetic lawyers on evading detection and prosecution, and reports from the field on both new crackdowns and pending legislation. But homosexual publications also turned to remembrances of the Nazi persecution of homosexuals between 1933 and 1945 to influence readers' opinions against US anti-homosexual laws portraying them as vile, unjust, and un-American. In doing so, they sought to discredit the laws terrorizing US homosexuals and build a community capable of challenging these statutes in court and state legislatures. Readers and writers of US homosexual publications turned to two related remembrance rhetorics of the Nazi persecution of homosexuals and its legal underpinnings in this task: conflating all German anti-homosexual laws with the Nazis' particular iteration of Paragraph 175 and extending the taint of the Nazis' Paragraph 175 to all anti-homosexual laws, including those in the United States.

Labeling Paragraph 175 a "Nazi law" was a powerful persuasive move and a hefty rhetorical challenge. As the introduction noted, the original German prohibitions against same-sex acts between men were developed in the Prussian penal code in 1851 and stayed on the books, relatively unchanged, through successive German governments. As a result, Paragraph 175 preceded the Third Reich significantly, and the law survived well beyond the Nazi regime's downfall. But this fact did not dissuade readers and writers of US homosexual publications from specifically tying the law to Hitler and the Nazis. In fact, with a few exceptions, nearly every mention of Paragraph 175 in *Mattachine Review* or ONE during their respective runs characterized it as a Nazi law in some way.[23] While this chapter addresses most of these instances, two occurrences deserve extended attention for how they implicate Paragraph 175 as a law of Nazi substance, though not necessarily a Nazi creation.

The first instance appeared at the beginning of the inaugural edition of ONE in January 1953. Titled "Die Insel" (The island), the article was not an original contribution prepared by an American homosexual author, but a reprint from the 1952 German homosexual publication *Die Insel*.[24] Despite an awkward translation, the essay makes three interrelated moves to strongly suggests readers attribute the German persecution of homosexuals both during and after the Third Reich to Paragraph 175, which it deems a Nazi law. The essay first describes German homosexuals' suffering, including historical instances of "gruesome murders committed upon homophiles" and ongoing persecutions like "banishment to prison," "exposure to disgrace," and being "denied the right to live upright lives." Next, the essay blames Paragraph 175 as the foundation of this persecution and demands the law be changed or overturned to bring homosexuals relief: "Forward with paragraphs 175 and 175a of the German penal code . . . ! Rehabilitation of all who have violated this law!" Finally, "Die Insel" attributes Paragraph 175 and the homosexual suffering it facilitated to the Nazis by both explicit and implicit claims. Explicitly, the essay attributes the persecutions and the law to "the era of the late Dictator" (i.e., Hitler). This point is implicitly reasserted when the essay makes no mention of the fact that the law predated Hitler or that Hitler and the Nazis strengthened it to permit the "gruesome murders."[25] Instead, the law is presented as synonymous with Nazism itself. As a result, American homosexual readers of the first issue of ONE are both informed about the Nazi persecution of homosexuals and led to believe this repression was perpetrated by a Nazi law known as Paragraph 175 that was still enforced in Germany.

A similar re-remembering of Paragraph 175 as a "Nazi law" appeared in a poignant and extended letter to the editor in a 1959 issue of ONE. The letter was written by Rudolf Burkhardt, the English-language editor of the German homosexual publication Der Kreis who had been imprisoned for political activity against Hitler during the Third Reich. As a firsthand account from a German homosexual, Burkhardt's memories of Paragraph 175 are uniquely powerful and afford him significant authority to interpret these past events for American readers. So, when Burkhardt asserts that "the infamous #175 of the German Penal Code . . . was made much stronger by Hitler after 1934, causing endless numbers of homosexuals to be sent to concentration camps," he correctly denotes the fact that Paragraph 175 predated the Nazis.[26] Nonetheless, Burkhardt also seems to suggest that it was the Hitler enhancements that made the law the "infamous #175." As such, Burkhardt leaves the door open to remembering Paragraph 175 as both predating the Nazis and only having real force in law once the Nazis deployed it, effectively giving it a Nazi imprimatur.[27] Burkhardt amplified this point later in the same letter when he argues that, given that both the Allies and the new West German government declined to repeal Paragraph 175 after World War II, "homosexuals in Germany are liable to be punished for their 'crime' by a Hitler paragraph in the Penal Code." In saying as much, Burkhardt is correct—the particular provision and force of Paragraph 175 in effect in 1959 relies on Nazi alterations of the old law during their reign of terror. However, the effect of this claim for the novice American reader is much simpler: a credible homosexual survivor of the Nazi persecution states plainly that Paragraph 175 was, in his memory, a "Hitler paragraph."[28]

While these two significant examples demonstrate the extent to which US homosexual publications had begun to remember Paragraph 175 as a Nazi law, such memories also recurred throughout these texts in passing reference. For example, ONE updated readers in 1957 on efforts to reduce the enforcement of German anti-homosexual laws by making explicit reference to "Article 175 (Nazi law against homosexual acts)."[29] In a separate article, 1920s Germany is discussed at length as "very gay and almost licentious" until things changed with "the laws under Hitler."[30] And in 1964, ONE continued to equate Paragraph 175 with the Nazis in an article on obscenity laws that noted "the Nazi legal legacy still remains to oppress them [i.e., homosexuals] both in Germany and in France."[31] Both the regularity and consistency of these references collectively demonstrate just how deeply engrained this particular memory of Paragraph 175 had become in the US homosexual imagination of the 1950s and '60s.

While characterizing Paragraph 175 as a Nazi law was an important piece of the ongoing memory work in US homosexual publications, a second, far more damning move followed: aligning Nazi laws like Paragraph 175 with anti-homosexual laws in the United States, Britain, and other democratic nations. By emphasizing the Nazis' particularly expansive and ruthless deployment of the law beginning in 1935 and suggesting that *all* anti-homosexual laws were of the same merciless type and substance, readers and writers in the homosexual press significantly raised the moral stakes for anti-fascist nations that chose to retain such laws in the postwar period. Homosexual publications thus wagered that if they conflated Nazi-era anti-homosexual laws with those in democratic societies, homosexual readers would quickly begin to see their own contemporary mistreatment under US law as not just a common complaint or nuisance, but both unacceptable and un-American.

How the US government grappled with Paragraph 175 in Germany during its postwar occupation became a prominent way that the taint of Nazi laws was extended to US laws in the homosexual press. When the United States and its allies took control of western Germany after 1945, one of their actions was to revoke laws enacted under Nazism. However, in contrast to the vast majority of laws the Allies sought to overturn, the Americans and British permitted the Nazis' enhanced version of Paragraph 175 to remain in effect. The US logic was simple: since Paragraph 175 predated the Nazi regime, it should remain in the penal code during the post-Nazi era. But US homosexual activists reading and writing in ONE and *Mattachine Review* saw these facts quite differently. They argued that Paragraph 175 became a Nazi law through its enhancements in 1935; when the Americans and Brits ordered the Germans to keep it in the penal code, they effectively affirmed Nazi laws against homosexuality. By doing so, homosexual activists suggested, the Allies implicitly

supported Nazi anti-homosexual laws, as they, too, had laws targeting homosexuals. Thus, homosexual activists extended the taint of the Nazis' Paragraph 175 to American and British anti-homosexual laws.

A key instance of this logic appeared in ONE in Jack Argo's brief 1955 essay
"The Homosexual in Germany Today." In the extended quote below, Argo
lays out the argument described above while also linking the Nazified Paragraph 175 to the Allies' caretaker government:

> When the allied powers had conquered the Nazi ideology of Germany
> and had begun to erect a democracy after 1945, many people in Ger-
> many were filled with a new hope. Among the famished sacrifices of
> the Nazi regime returning from the concentration camps were many
> homosexuals. But this group of the suppressed were to be shamefully
> disappointed: the Western Allies would not revise the laws against
> homosexuality. Only the Russians within their occupation-zone
> changed the laws and reduced them to the status they were before
> 1933. In West-Germany the Germans themselves were responsible for
> changing the laws or not, but nobody expected what happened: the
> laws under Hitler intensified, were more intensified by the Federal
> Republic. A complaint before the supreme court on a constitutional
> question has not been decided or even answered in four years—a
> request which quotes that paragraph 175 . . . disagrees with the new
> German constitution.[32]

Argo clearly places blame for the postwar failure to provide "new hope" to
German homosexuals on the Allies, including the Americans. He also points
out that the West Germans themselves made a similar choice when empowered, further emphasizing the wider critique in homosexual publications that
many democratic nations with anti-homosexual laws chose to equate themselves with the Nazis. However, for a homosexual US reading public, Argo
portrays the US government as complicit in perpetuating Nazi laws, strongly
implying that it is because of the existence of laws akin to Paragraph 175 in
the United States' own penal codes.

Allusions to Paragraph 175 as a Nazi law took on even greater salience
when applied to closely related efforts to change sex crime laws in both the
United Kingdom and the United States in the late 1950s. Both the authors of
those efforts and the homosexual press amplified similarities between American and British law and Paragraph 175 to make the case that the former

needed to be transformed. These campaigns were inaugurated in the United Kingdom in 1954 when the Church of England Moral Welfare Committee released a document titled *The Problem of Homosexuality: An Interim Report*.[33] The church's report, arguing that the UK government should reconsider the severity of the nation's existing sodomy laws and decriminalize same-sex acts between consenting adults, prompted a deluge of commentary on both sides of the Atlantic, including in ONE and *Mattachine Review*.[34] In fact, ONE covered and excerpted it in June 1954, calling it a "bold study" and "surely the most forthright statement on the subject ever to come from a Church body."[35] But each publication also supported the report's recommendations by deploying memories that linked the UK's anti-homosexual laws to Paragraph 175's Nazi fingerprints. For instance, *Mattachine Review* did so by covering and promoting a speech at Oxford University by reform advocate Peter Wildeblood, who made the point that only "Britain, West Germany and Norway" among western European democracies maintained anti-sodomy laws. He added to this point a key addendum about the German law in particular: "In West Germany the law was a Nazi survival introduced from political motives."[36] As seen here, Wildeblood equates Paragraph 175 with a Nazi law and makes a specific connection with the Church of England Moral Welfare Committee's recommendation to repeal the implicitly synonymous British law. Therefore, *Mattachine Review* used coverage and excerpts from Wildeblood's speech to advance for US homosexual readers a specific connection between British anti-homosexual laws and a Nazified Paragraph 175.

A similar move is made in the US context in the homosexual publications' reports on the American Law Institute (ALI). In April 1955, ALI put forward a "Model Penal Code," which sought to revise and modernize US laws, with a notable section tackling jurisprudence on "Sodomy and Related Offenses." *Mattachine Review* took particular interest here and covered the document extensively, including reprinting the proposed revisions in full. In this excerpt, ALI offered several grounds for decriminalizing homosexual acts between consenting adults, including a sketch of the status of similar laws in other nations: "The distinction between civil and religion responsibilities in this area is reflected in the penal codes of such predominantly Catholic countries as France, Italy, Mexico and Uruguay, none of which attempt to punish private misbehavior of this sort. The Penal Codes of Denmark, Sweden and Switzerland also stay out of this area. On the other hand, the German Code of 1871, still in force, contains broad and severe provisions directed particularly against male homosexuality."[37] Unlike Wildeblood's speech, the ALI does not explicitly call out the Nazi connections to the German code in its rationale. Instead, while implicitly invoking Paragraph 175 (i.e., "the German Code of 1871"), it emphasizes that this law's origin predate the Nazis' rise to power. At the same time, by describing the German law as both "still in force" and containing "broad and severe provisions" against male homosexuals, the ALI seems to emphasize the Nazi modifications to Paragraph 175 rather than the law's original parameters. In effect, without making the Nazi connection explicit, the ALI—and the amplification by *Mattachine Review*—tarnishes US sodomy laws for sharing company with German anti-homosexual laws that reeks of Nazi and fascist ideologies.

Whether in extended remembrances or brief allusions, the homosexual press of the 1950s and early 1960s asserted a particular memory of Paragraph 175—not as a generic anti-homosexual law that originated in the late 1800s and had contemporaries in nations across the globe, but as a uniquely horrific law that should be entirely credited to the nefarious and roundly abhorred Nazi regime. In doing so, laws in other nations that permitted the persecution of homosexuality were indicted in homosexual publications in strong terms and cast as antithetical to Western, democratic ideals and values. When these memories of Paragraph 175 were extended directly in comparison to US and British anti-homosexual laws newly under review in the 1950s, they provided a powerful rhetorical tool to advocate for the decriminalization of same-sex acts between consenting adults. Yet efforts to shame anti-homosexual persecutions in the United States were not limited to remembrances of law alone. Rather, the enforcers of these laws—the police, FBI, and postal inspectors of the 1950s and '60s—also became key targets of attacks through a strategic remembering of the Nazi persecution of homosexuals.

Gestapo Tactics: Memories of Snoops and Secret Police

While the US homosexual press rebuked domestic anti-homosexual laws as akin to a Nazified form of Paragraph 175, it also targeted law enforcement officers and their aggressive, sometimes extralegal, tactics against homosexuals by labeling them the "American Gestapo." The Gestapo was the secret police force of the Third Reich and Nazi-occupied Europe, formed in 1933 by Hermann Goering. Later turned over to avowed homophobe Heinrich Himmler, the Gestapo became a weapon for terrorizing, controlling, persecuting, and ultimately destroying the lives of millions of German and European peoples deemed politically problematic, undesirable, or dangerous to the Nazis, including homosexuals. Gestapo officers earned a reputation for their intimidating, violent, and sinister conduct, often deploying particularly devious tactics in their pursuit of homosexuals. This special targeting from the Gestapo and its partners at the Reich Central Office for the Combating of Homosexuality and Abortion included collecting lists of believed or suspected homosexuals for mass raids and targeted arrests; encouraging denunciations by neighbors, family members, friends, and mere acquaintances to root out "perverts"; and torturous interrogations that did not end until the suspected homosexual both confessed and provided a full accounting of every other known homosexual in their circle.[38] In these ways and more, the Gestapo quickly became known as supposed lawmen whose efforts to persecute homosexuals led them to regularly break the spirit of the law itself.

Given the nefarious role the Gestapo played in the persecution of homosexuals, it is unsurprising that the Nazi secret police were commonly invoked in postwar US homosexual communities to warn against the dangers of aggressive policing. While *Mattachine Review* was more likely to opt for "witch hunt" allusions referencing Salem in 1692, readers and writers of ONE made repetitive, vigorous comparisons to the Nazi Gestapo to repudiate anti-homosexual police practices in the 1950s and '60s. These invocations were entirely in line with ONE's more bellicose and confrontational editorial tone, and its reach as the earliest and most widely circulated US homosexual publication made its comparisons highly influential. As a result, framing US homosexual victims of police entrapment and snooping as targets of an American Gestapo became the most common way early activists talked about and understood these issues between 1953 and 1967.

Characterizing US police forces—particularly vice squads—as an American Gestapo began early in ONE's run. Its first explicit invocation appeared in the sixth issue of the magazine's first year in the "Letters" section. There, a New York City letter writer first connected in the homosexual press memories of the Nazi Gestapo with US law enforcement tactics: "I am all for this magazine and for the Mattachine Foundation, for something must be done. The Vice Squad is terrible in Los Angeles, [*sic*] I am from New York City and can't seem to see the difference between the Gestapo of Germany and the Vice Squad of Los Angeles."[39] In this early example, the historical comparison is direct and indisputable: the "Gestapo of Germany" and the "Vice Squad of Los Angeles" are synonymous, and, in an enthymematic appeal that implicates the Nazi crackdown on German homosexuals, the letter writer argues homosexuals must do "something" about it. The presence of such a stark claim in the magazine's first six months raises the question of whether this discourse had already been circulating in US homosexual circles prior to *ONE*'s publication. But regardless of whether *ONE* inaugurates this idea or simply nourishes and circulates it, we see here the seeds of a larger rhetorical tactic that called for US homosexuals to organize against police entrapment by transporting them to Hitlerite Germany.

While similar appeals appeared sporadically over the next three years, comparisons between US vice squads and the Nazi Gestapo exploded in the pages of *ONE* from that point forward. The spark igniting Gestapo memory rhetorics was likely the highly publicized 1956 court case *People v. Martin*, which concerned the arrest of two men sitting in a car at night in a known "lovers' lane." The men were ultimately booked on a minor drug charge, but the impetus for the police officer's stop was the suspicion that they were engaging in homosexual activity. Martin appealed the arrest as an illegal search but lost at the California Supreme Court. However, the case produced a strong dissent from the Honorable Jesse W. Carter, who called the majority opinion "most astounding" given that police claimed "the presence of two men in a parked automobile on a lover's lane at night was itself reasonable cause for police investigation. . . ." Carter continued, "To say the very sight of two men in a parked automobile at night warrants a police investigation reminds one of the Gestapo."[40]

Though *People v. Martin* was not decided on the appropriateness of same-sex acts, Carter's strongly worded critique received significant attention in homosexual publications. His dissent was profiled at length in *ONE*, and a speech by Carter was republished in full in the *Mattachine Review*. *Mattachine Review* even included an enlarged paraphrase in its coverage, which read, "NO GESTAPO TACTICS IN THE U.S., PLEASE."[41] Alongside this editorial flourish, Carter's speech featured a pointed rebuke to the police in even stronger terms than those in the dissent: "We are told that the Nazis, Fascists, and Communists found the above mentioned safeguards [against illegal search and seizure] too onerous for the speedy dispatch of those whose existence they determined would be detrimental to the welfare of their totalitarian state. And I feel disposed to state to those who would break down any of these safeguards that the American system of ordered liberty does not lend itself to methods employed by the Gestapo, the storm trooper or the commissar for the preservation of the totalitarian state under a Nazi, Fascist or Communist regime."[42] Carter thus indicted the conduct of the Los Angeles police, equating its behavior with the Gestapo in a case substantively focused on suspected homosexual acts. Little here suggests that Carter was particularly sympathetic to the homosexual cause; rather, his concern appeared to center on the general principle of protecting Americans from illegal search and seizure. Nonetheless, Carter opened the floodgates for homosexual writers and readers of ONE to interpret comparable anti-homosexual police tactics as belonging to the same Nazi and fascist ilk.

Hereafter, the comparisons between US and Nazi police tactics frequently appeared in ONE. Occasionally, they came from other public officials who, like Carter, were not homosexuals but were repulsed by such civil rights violations against any group.[43] However, the readers and writers of ONE quickly began to make the same historical comparisons in their own words. For example, in an April 1958 article, ONE shared the events of a police raid at the home of a Phoenix divorcee, where the vice squad, state liquor officers, and the "U.S. Customs gestapo" arrested eleven people, including "some admitted homosexuals."[44] In the very next issue, a ONE letter writer critiqued the Los Angeles police chief's belief that "there should be no limits to the methods they are able to use [against homosexuals]. What was good for the gestapo should be good for Los Angeles."[45] In 1959, a letter to ONE profiled an investigation assisted by law enforcement at the University of Florida that ultimately discharged fifteen faculty and employees and prompted the resignations and suicides of several students. The expansive and invasive nature of the operation nudged the letter writer to cry out that "the methods used by the investigators were little short of those used during the World War II reign of terror in Germany."[46] And in 1963, "Mr. E." from New Orleans described how he was "entrapped" by the police and spent five months in prison until he agreed to "chang[e] my plea to guilty." In an account dripping with bile, Mr. E. noted that the "Vice Squad here is everywhere, like the Gestapo was in Germany and just as filthy."[47] Each of these cases represents similar accounts between 1958 and 1967, where readers and writers of ONE reiterated a powerful memory rhetoric depicting a voracious American Gestapo at work against the homosexual.

Many readers and writers of ONE were similarly concerned that Gestapo tactics had wormed their way into the policing of obscenity after World War II. Homosexual anger against an American postal Gestapo became notably vociferous when the postmaster of Los Angeles seized copies of a 1953 issue of ONE from the mail. The postmaster argued that ONE's subject matter as a "Homosexual magazine" rendered it "obscene, lewd, lascivious and filthy," which "constituted non-mailable matter" under law.[48] The courts ultimately over-turned the seizure on free speech grounds in a historic win for the cause. The case nonetheless prompted homosexual readers and writers of ONE to make a wave of comparisons between US postal offices and the Gestapo, which noto-riously searched German citizens' mail for evidence of homosexuality.[49]

In tone and tenor, homosexuals' historical comparisons between the US postal service and the Gestapo varied. Some of these Nazi allusions were derived from fear. A letter writer published in ONE in 1955 shared that he had been "reading it [i.e., ONE] regularly" and hoped to subscribe but was "advised against it" by "a European-born friend of mine, an ex-Nazi refu-gee," who feared "THEY might get a copy of the list" of subscribers.[50] A 1957 letter writer, "writ[ing] . . . for a friend—who in these days of persecutions, wishes to remain nameless," inquired about the postal laws and conceded "it [is] a little bit frightening, and like Nazi Germany and its hatred of Cath-olics and Jews—but—we hope it will not end up like Germany ended."[51] In 1960, a "disturbed citizen" writing in ONE described his belief that the "postal Gestapo" was intercepting his homosexual-themed magazines and letters.[52] Each of these instances conveyed to ONE readers that there was something to this comparison between the US postal service and the Gestapo, so much so that US homosexuals should be extremely careful in their conduct.

But while these fears persisted, Nazi and US postal comparisons shifted strongly toward homosexual anger and resistance after 1960. In a long letter in 1962, a reader described the perversion of the US postal service, partic-ularly the postman who "donned the cloak and insignia of the much-hated Gestapo . . . he now slinks and snoops and pries." The writer added that "this is not the Americanism that we were brought up with. This is a monster of foreign birth."[53] Another writer that year shared the story of an "acquaintance of mine in another city" who "failed to receive his letters, sent first class." The acquaintance "was notified by a postal inspector that he was sending improper matter through the mails and warned to desist forthwith or be prosecuted." The letter writer continued, "Such interception of mail is no doubt illegal, but what does the ordinary citizen do in such a case but pretend to bend the knee to our moral police state? Although my friend of course circumvented the postal Gestapo by very simple means and still gets his mail."[54] In these later years of ONE's run, it is clear homosexuals had become fed up with the postal tactics of the American Gestapo and found ways to resist.

Rhetoric remembering US anti-homosexual policing and postal tactics as akin to the Nazi Gestapo culminated in 1963 with a ONE cover story titled

"The New Nazism." Written by James F. Kearful, the six-page article offered a wide-ranging discussion on the alleged Nazification of the United States, arguing that both local police and the FBI were central to this anti-homosexual process.

Though never employing the term *Gestapo*, Kearful used several rhetorical tactics to indict anti-homosexual policing. Most strikingly, Kearful filled three pages of his essay with vivid descriptions showing how "foul and rotten" US police tactics were reminiscent of the Gestapo (NN, 5). Among these tactics, Kearful described "plain-clothes-men" (i.e., police officers) in New York City who "stalked the fifties and sixties" in a zealous and aggressive search for homosexuals that far exceeded routine policing (NN, 7). Kearful also detailed "frequent and unexpected raids of uniformed police officers" in Central Park and "at the bars in Greenwich Village," which mirrored Gestapo tactics used against homosexuals in 1934 and 1935 (NN, 7). He details "police surveillance" and "pestering activities," up to and including the use of public restrooms with "two-way mirrors," akin to the fascistic practices of "Orwell's *1984*" (NN, 8). Kearful was also aghast at police activities in Miami, where "anyone seen walking on the streets at night was likely to be stopped by police and asked to produce identification" (NN, 8). Along with "the increase in numbers of police throughout the United States" and "a sturdy army of muck-rakers . . . able to conduct its smear campaigns," Kearful argued to ONE's readers that 1959 and 1960 US law enforcement actions represented a "Crack-down Regime" not seen since the Gestapo era (NN, 9).

Similarly, Kearful invoked the image of an American Gestapo by describing police persecutions of homosexuals as a coordinated national campaign rather than a series of local actions. Previous allusions to the Gestapo in ONE or *Mattachine Review* ignored the fact that it was a national police force, permitting skeptical ONE readers to discount these allusions as alarmist or driven by a handful of bad apples in specific US localities. By contrast, Kearful argues that previously dispersed, localized police crackdowns on US homosexuals had become a national effort that warranted the Gestapo comparisons. In this vein, Kearful argues explicitly that the "recent wave of persecutions of homosexuals seems definitely to be nation-wide in scope" (NN, 9). He supports this claim by identifying similar worrying police actions across US regions, including in New York, Los Angeles, Miami, and Ann Arbor. Kearful goes on to invert the localized "bad apple" rhetoric in the remainder of his essay. Instead, Kearful argues that homosexuals are suffering through a "nation-wide crack-down," and only a handful of select cities like Chicago remain "unchanged since the good old days before 1959" (NN, 9). With this rhetorical shift in scale, Kearful's comparisons to the Gestapo—and fears of a repeat of the Nazi drive against homosexuals more generally—feel more salient and ominous.

Last, Kearful makes the case that the upswing in police persecutions of homosexuals is rooted in wider changes in US politics and culture amid the Cold War: "The really serious threat is that the great increase in numbers of the police in American communities is occurring simultaneously with a growing political trend toward the Right" (NN, 9). According to Kearful, this rightward swing is reminiscent of the German move toward Nazism in the early 1930s and threatened to bring about a similar police state apparatus in 1960s America, with one major exception: homosexuals would be substituted for the Jews as the nation's most persecuted minority. Noting that it "cannot be said that the government of the United States treats the Jews in such a manner [as the Nazis did]" (NN, 10), Kearful argues, "In America we persecute not Jews, but homosexuals. In the growing Nazification of thought in this nation homosexuals are finding themselves in much the same position as that of the Jews at the beginning of the Nazi era in Germany. They are despised for being liberal in thought as well as for living what is considered by many to be a reprehensible form of existence. Further, and more important, they have no allies" (NN, 10). This is arguably the earliest and most explicit conflation of the Jewish Holocaust and the persecution of homosexuals to appear in the early US homosexual press. As we will see in later chapters, it was far from the last. There, I closely examine how some activists framed the homosexual persecution by the Nazis—as opposed to US police—as explicitly analogous to the Jewish Holocaust. By contrast, we here see an early example of what sociologist Arlene Stein called the "Holocaust frame," whereby memories of the Holocaust are used to explain contemporary acts of persecution.[55] Nonetheless, this powerful rhetorical substitution near the essay's end furthers the progressive intensification of threat facing homosexuals in the pages of ONE.

Kearful's explicit and implicit arguments connecting US police tactics with the Nazi Gestapo ends with the dire warning that existing police crackdowns on homosexuals would only worsen: "Individual police campaigns do blow over, to be sure. But each successive campaign makes the next one that much easier. And with the trend of thinking that is going on in America at the present time, if the homosexual continues to acquiesce as he has done in the past, his future in this nation will be grim indeed" (NN, 11). But like the 1953 letter writer who invoked comparisons with the Nazi Gestapo to demand "something must be done," Kearful also uses his peroration to demand that homosexuals *act* in their own defense.[56] Specifically, Kearful suggests that their only recourse is to follow the example of Black Americans and "forc[e] society to recognize them and give them their rights" (NN, 11). To do anything less risked succumbing to the dismal fate of their homosexual kin on the continent two decades earlier.

Conclusion

Despite the best efforts by readers and writers of ONE and *Mattachine Review*, neither the laws nor tactics underpinning the postwar policing of US homosexuals receded easily. While some states began repealing sodomy laws in the early 1960s, the 2003 Supreme Court ruling in *Lawrence v. Texas* was required to quash such prohibitions nationwide. Meanwhile, raids, forced outings, smear campaigns, and harassment persisted as police tactics in US states, cities, and municipalities well into the late twentieth century. Today, law enforcement remains a key tool for policing deviations from the cisgender, heterosexual norm. This is especially true for contemporary LGBTQ+ people who are also perceived as people of color. And new antiqueer and antitrans legislation continues to be proposed, passed, and enacted, while old laws targeting homosexuals threaten to be reanimated by a radical right-wing high court. It seems that the specter of the American Gestapo has never been fully banished.

Yet, while we cannot claim victory over anti-homosexual policing in the United States, the memory work performed by the readers and writers of US homosexual publications between 1953 and 1967 helped steer the nation toward greater safety and freedom for gendered and sexual minorities. Indeed, this chapter confirms a central claim of this book: that memories of the Nazi persecution of homosexuals emerged not only before HIV/AIDS, but were also deployed at pivotal moments when homosocial, homosexual, and lesbian and gay communities demanded rhetorical action. Thus, when ONE and *Mattachine Review* launched their precarious publishing adventures in the face of unprecedented attacks on homosexuals from US law enforcement, each publication turned to memories of the Nazi era to help their homosexual audiences understand, assess, and address these accelerating threats and demand that "something must be done."[57]

At the most inspirational level, these memories laid the foundation for an organized struggle against law and police mistreatment that unfurled over the next five decades. But more immediately, ONE and *Mattachine Review* used these memories to drive homosexuals toward a deeper sense of community based on shared oppression, reminded them that they were not the first homosexual community to face these tactics, and urged this community to act, cognizant that if they failed, they risked both their own destruction and the end of a virtuous American ideal. Overall, this discourse was wildly successful, catalyzing a queer world that has remained resilient in the face of ongoing antiqueer onslaughts in decades since.

Why did these homosexuals of the 1940s, '50s, and '60s turn to memory as a key rhetorical resource in this work? As we saw in the previous chapter, the *queer return to memory* continued to be a rich, almost-instinctual gesture within these evolving American homosexual cultures.[58] And like Gerber, these homosexuals found that producing small-scale publications required fewer of the costs that modern commemorative culture often demands in its material markings of the past. But having these familiar appeals circulated in efficient, discrete forms did not mean that such mnemonic acts were without risk. Every memory shared in print in ONE and *Mattachine Review* came with very real threats of exposure, eviction, unemployment, and arrest by an anti-homosexual law enforcement apparatus. These risks are rendered plain by just how often these powerful memories appeared in the guise of pseudonyms, anonymous signatures, and letters submitted for a "friend" or "acquaintance." But what made that risk worthwhile—and what further explains these homosexuals' reliance on memory in this era—was the visceral nature of the dangers they faced. American homosexuals' drive to remember the persecution of European homosexuals at this moment was proximate. These men were not reaching back centuries, but only a few years. The violence, atrocities, and victims noted in each publication were intimately near to these rememberers—far enough to be past, but not so far as to be history. This temporal proximity to the full scale of the Nazis' anti-homosexual campaign was not possible before the immediate postwar period, and it would not be available with this intensity much longer thereafter. As such, in a way not seen elsewhere in this book, this chapter affirms a broader lesson about memory for queer and nonqueer rhetors alike: while it is always a perpetual resource, never allow the exigency of the more recent past to decay untapped. The feeling of the past being "just yesterday" never lasts long.

Yet, while we remain interested in the broader lesson this instance can teach us about memory, this chapter also reveals more specific insights about how the Nazi persecution of homosexuals continued to evolve in the rhetorics of the American homosexual rights movements before HIV/AIDS. We can begin with the individual who is absent from this period's homosexual reminiscences: Captain Ernst Roehm. Roehm had featured significantly in select US homosexual discourses in the 1930s, but those memories had almost entirely abated by 1950 for several reasons. For one, while Roehm's execution was fresh evidence in 1934 of the Nazis anti-homosexual sentiment, by the 1950s and '60s, such memories had grown stale. Much had transpired in the intervening years, including World War II and the persecution of one hundred thousand homosexuals—both events that made Roehm's once-scandalous murder insignificant by comparison. Nor was Roehm ever a particularly sympathetic figure, a point made even more evident after a decade of repudiation by both Nazi propagandists and the American press. By 1953, there were also equally tragic examples of homosexual persecution committed against more genial homosexuals on which to base the community's rhetoric appeals. For all these reasons and more, Roehm's memory was largely forgotten in US homosexual discourses after 1950. In place of Roehm's diminished memory, this chapter shows how the role Nazi police played in the persecution of homosexuals between 1934 and 1945 saw significant growth.

In addition to a shift in subject matter, there was an explosion in the number of US homosexuals remembering the Nazi persecution of homosexuals—even as these discourses remained bounded within the American homosexual community itself. This shift mirrors an earlier growth in memories of the Nazi persecution of homosexuals after 1934, including among both everyday Americans (including homosexuals) and a small but meaningful number of homosexual readers in the pages of *Chanticleer*. But with the advent of a more fulsome US homosexual press in 1953, hard numbers suggest a swell in the number of American homosexuals remembering the Nazi persecution of homosexuals together. For instance, we know that ONE had a distribution of close to 6,000 copies by the fall of 1954, while *Mattachine Review* had a circulation of about 2,200.[59] Each publication likely had even greater reach, since it was common practice to pass the magazines from homosexual person to homosexual person.[60] Given the reiterative appearance of memories of the Nazi persecution of homosexuals in both periodicals, we can say with a high degree of certainty that the number of American homosexuals who remembered the Nazi crackdowns in the 1950s and '60s numbered in the thousands, further repudiating the idea that no meaningful remembering of these events occurred until after Stonewall in 1969.

Consistent with memory rhetorics of the 1930s, this era in remembering the Nazi persecution of homosexuals in the United States is also noteworthy for its general ignorance or disavowal of homosexual experiences in the concentration camps. This absence is particularly notable because so many of the pink triangle memories to appear in the zeitgeist after HIV/AIDS fixated on homosexual incarceration. As we have seen, homosexual concentration camp memories did appear between 1949 and 1965 (i.e., Hay's prospectus, *Die Insel*, and Burkhardt's letter) and would continue with greater regularly thereafter. But more often, when US homosexuals wanted to remember the Nazi persecution in these decades, they highlighted the mistreatment of these sexual minorities by law enforcement outside the camps. One of the clearest reasons why is that the Nazis' mistreatment of homosexuals via the police apparatus—rather than through concentration camp incarceration—permitted American homosexual activists to make useful connections between the Third Reich and the United States in the 1950s and '60s. As such, remembering dimensions of the homosexual persecution external to the camps is where US advocates devoted their time.

Yet, while US homosexuals did not fixate on the Nazi internment of homosexuals in camps in the 1950s and '60s, this period did mark some of the first comparisons between Jewish and homosexual suffering under the Nazis. As we saw in the Kearful essay, the mid-1960s may mark the earliest deployments of the "Holocaust frame" in the homosexual remembrances of the Nazi persecutions.[61] As stated above, this frame is *not* about remembering the Nazi persecution of homosexual as *the Holocaust*—a problematic framing sometimes referred to as *the Homocaust*, which would appear later. But in the 1960s, US homosexuals did use the annihilation of the Jews under Nazi rule as a corollary to warn against the contemporary mistreatment of US homosexuals by American law enforcement officers. The reasons for this turn are unclear, but they may be attributed to the 1961 Adolf Eichmann trial, which brought the Holocaust into sharp focus for American audiences and provided a rich source of sympathetic appeals for certain homosexuals. But this moment marks the beginning of a close alignment between Jewish and homosexual suffering under the Third Reich in the US homosexual imagination—a connection that, as we will see, offered homosexual rhetors both powerful possibilities and deeply problematic pitfalls.

Perhaps most importantly, this chapter once again demonstrates with increasing force that US homosexuals before HIV/AIDS not only remembered the Nazi persecution of homosexuals, but did so repeatedly, with different emphases at different moments, and with a vested interest in serving the community at key rhetorical crossroads. Yet, just as the 1950s and early 1960s marked a shift from earlier homophiles' memory rhetorics to combat a rising tide of police mistreatment in American towns and cities, the late 1960s saw some US homosexual rhetors reanimate these same events from the Third Reich for different purposes. In these cases, the aim of such memories further pushed the envelope of how the US homosexual community came to see itself and chart a collective path forward.

Chapter 3

Habitual Skeptics

Remembering Incarceration and Medical Experiments
in Gay Nazi-Exploitation Pulps, 1966–1969

In May 1972, the acclaimed theater critic Eric Bentley delivered a pointed dia-
tribe in the *New York Times*. His review featured a description of his encounter in "the window of a porno bookstore on 42nd Street" with "the [book]
jacket of what I suppose was a juicy novel about Auschwitz and the high jinks
there." The book jacket, he continued, "showed a Jewish boy kneeling before
an SS guard, and it was entitled *Go Down, Aaron*." The sight of the outland-
ish cover prompted Bentley to momentarily reflect on his "confront[ation] . . .
with *a pretentious pornography of the avant-garde*," something he found loath-
some. Underlining his point, Bentley warned his readers that, whatever their
thoughts about pornography, such texts made clear "there *is* something at
stake" in modern America, "namely our right to be offended and disgusted—
nay, on occasion, our obligation to be so."[1]

Despite invoking the text by name, Bentley's review was not about the
book *Go Down, Aaron*, a 1967 erotic gay pulp novel about a young Jewish and homosexual man's sexual abuse by his Nazi captors during World
War II. Rather, Bentley was reviewing an off-Broadway play, a production
he indicted for its supposedly pointless attempt to shock the audience with
graphic obscenity. But Bentley's objections to creative works juxtaposing
obscenity and the human condition certainly extended to *Go Down, Aaron*
and similar homosexual pulp texts. For Bentley saw *Go Down, Aaron* as a
symptom of a larger cultural decay eating away at earlier American values. As
a gay man himself, Bentley's more moderate, classics-oriented value system
reflected an earlier homosexual era, exemplified by Gerber's Greek allusions
or the *Mattachine Review*.[2] But by the late 1960s and early 1970s, the virtues

underpinning previous homosexual generations were experiencing rapid change, which also altered how and to what ends American gays deployed memories of the Nazi persecution of homosexuals.

This era was particularly marked by a turn away from the respectability and assimilationist politics of some homosexuals decades earlier. In its place emerged a radical gay politics rooted in depictions and discussions of frank sexuality and productive eroticism, which both demanded attention and sought to distinguish itself from American cultural norms. This turn is often marked by the 1969 Stonewall Riots and the in-your-face gay liberation politics, prose, and protests that followed. But this shift was presaged by prior voices and expressions, particularly in the eruption of graphic queer content following several court victories overturning state and national prohibitions on obscene materials, which had silenced homosexuals for decades. It created a new market for explicitly homosexual-themed materials, including erotica and pornographic homosexual magazines, posters, and books. While such texts were now freely distributed, their value continued to be maligned by heterosexual and homosexual critics alike. Nonetheless, a subsection of these texts—like *Go Down, Aaron*—would become vital rhetorical documents, deploying radical reimaginings of the Nazi persecution of homosexuals to advance the erotic needs of a new generation of gay men and cultivate a new gay male habitus essential for post-Stonewall politics.

This chapter attends to rhetorical memory appeals made through a particular subgenre of gay pulp novels of the late 1960s that I label *gay Nazi-exploitation pulps*. These pulps—which fetishized, to varying degrees, the persecution and sexual exploitation of young Jewish men by male Nazi guards, soldiers, and officers in plotlines set during or adjacent to World War II—are a rich but underexamined set of rhetorical texts. Even within the well-developed scholarship on lesbian and gay pulps, gay Nazi-exploitation pulps make few appearances—likely due to the campy and disreputable nature of such texts, positioned at the intersection of sexual pleasure and Nazi persecution.[3] And yet, as we will see, not all pulps in this category relied on graphic sexual content. Some of these texts leaned heavily on themes of homosexual love, devotion, and camaraderie, earning the *pulp* label more for their method of printing and advertising than for their subject matter. The relative scarcity of these texts available for academic study also contributes to their absence in scholarship. Nonetheless, it is exactly because of these diverse Nazi-exploitation plotlines that I argue gay pulps were an effective vehicle for advancing the needs of gay men in the United States in the late 1960s and early 1970s.

I argue that these disreputable texts were essential for the survival, communication, and utility of homosexual persecution memories in the years before Stonewall. Despite these pulps' dubious reputation, they held significant value as an archive of the Nazi persecution of homosexuals. In this vein, Susan Stryker and Martin Meeker have argued that gay, lesbian, or queer pulps in general smuggled vital historical information about the LGBTQ+ past to more contemporary audiences.[4] Gay Nazi-exploitation pulps, in particular, referenced the names of particular camps where homosexuals were interned (like Bergen-Belsen and Buchenwald), the medical experiment conducted on homosexuals in concentration camps by Nazi doctors like Dr. Carl Vaernet, and the fact that, even after liberation by Allied soldiers, homosexuals were not freed but sent to German prisons to serve out their sentences under Paragraph 175.[5] Such vital information alone, trafficked within cheap and campy erotica, demonstrates that these texts were important for shaping how the Nazi persecution of homosexuals came to be understood and used by the US homosexual community before HIV/AIDS.

But this chapter's larger claim is that gay Nazi-exploitation pulps functioned rhetorically by constituting a powerful gay male habitus necessary for an emergent gay male culture starting in the late 1960s. By *gay male habitus*, I mean the cultivation of a specifically gay male American orientation to the world. Drawing from Pierre Bourdieu, this *habitus* is constituted by small, repetitive, often embodied acts that ultimately form a social performance that is not only readable but influential in dictating how people act before others in the world.[6] Katherine Sender previously examined this idea of a gay male habitus by exploring how the magazine *The Advocate* cultivated a gay male style based on certain "tastes, pleasures, and concerns."[7] Here, I argue that something similar is at work in the gay male pulp novels of the late 1960s. Indeed, Michael Bronski argues that gay male pulp novels were essential in constituting a gay male style akin to a habitus, inaugurating novice gay men into a growing urban underground culture rich with performances of speech, dress, decor, and action—elements they could often learn only through the texts themselves.[8] In this chapter, I suggest this same habitus that taught gay men where to live and how to pick up guys also instructed them in important political orientations like whom to distrust. The Nazi persecution of homosexuals was a powerful story for cultivating these skeptical dispositions, which were then extended to help a growing gay male subculture of the late 1960s anticipate and navigate the highly anti-homosexual America they would confront in the post-Stonewall era.

Key to this pre-Stonewall, late 1960s gay male habitus were two political dispositions of skepticism cultivated by gay Nazi-exploitation pulps. First, gay Nazi-exploitation pulps used memories of the Nazi persecution of homosexuals to foster a gay male habitus characterized by skepticism toward science and medicine at a moment when the psychological vilification of homosexuality in the United States was approaching its nadir. Instead, the pulps encouraged gay men of the late 1960s to replace the vestiges of anti-homosexual medicalizing discourses with dispositions toward gay male self-acceptance and expertise. Second and related, gay Nazi-exploitation pulps cultivated a gay male habitus characterized by skepticism toward state power. In doing so, the pulps encouraged gay men to forgo seeking approval from and inclusion in the US nation, instead emphasizing survival through the cultivation of an emerging gay male culture of difference. Collectively, these two rhetorical appeals helped constitute a reservoir of energy and power within the gay male reading public, on which a new 1970s gay liberation politics would draw.

To examine these issues, this chapter focuses on three gay Nazi-exploitation pulps of the late 1960s: *Go Down, Aaron* (1967), *The Concentration of Hans* (1967), and *Middle Ground* (1968). Each text shared several features: a focus on Nazi-related themes during World War II, adherence to the form and content of the gay pulp genre, and the centrality of homosexual love, desire, or erotica in their storylines. Beyond these three points, the texts varied widely, particularly in the extent to which unambiguous sexual descriptions and the fetishization of concentration camps mattered in each plot. In this regard, *The Concentration of Hans* is best described as sadomasochistic erotic literature, *Go Down, Aaron* is a tamer but still sexually explicit erotic novel, and *Middle Ground* is a homosexual romance novel featuring no explicit sexuality whatsoever. Nonetheless, each text emerged simultaneously, was marketed in the same way to the same audience, and has much to tell us about how gay men of the 1960s were invited to distrust two powerful institutions as unconscionably antigay.

Pulps of the Homosexual Past and 1960s Gay Dispositions

While scholars continue to debate what qualifies as *literature*, it is clear that a robust, though not well-known, body of work at the intersection of homosexuality and Nazi persecution (or "gay Holocaust literature") emerged globally with the advent of the earliest homosexual-themed pulp fiction novels in the mid-1950s.[9] The history of gay pulps in general is now well established, with Susan Stryker's *Queer Pulp* (2001) and Michael Bronski's *Pulp Friction* (2003) among the most well-known recent scholars to tackle the subject. Heterosexual and homosexual pulp novels alike grew from an exploding 1930s pulp magazine market. Like pulp magazines, the pulp paperback market succeeded by selling scandalous, attention-grabbing stories with visceral covers at cheap prices through wide circulation.[10] They found initial success during World War II, when the military made pulps widely available to soldiers and the Women's Army Corps, but soon migrated to newsstands, grocery stores, and mail order catalogs after the war.[11] While most pulp plots targeted heterosexual audiences, the industry's reliance on scandal, shock, and sleaze quickly drove publishers to seek storylines that pushed the limits of conduct Americans deemed morally acceptable. In this shift, homosexual themed pulps emerged in force.

Both lesbian and gay male pulps became important subsets of the market. But lesbian pulps were more profitable and popular between 1950 and 1965 because they appealed to a large audience consisting of heterosexual men and lesbian or bisexual women.[12] The most notorious of the postwar lesbian pulp novels, *Women's Barracks* (1950), featured scandalous same-sex acts between members of the Women's Army Corps during wartime. However, *Women's Barracks* and similar pulps soon drew the moralistic gaze of leaders in Washington, DC, and in 1952, the House Select Committee on Current Pornographic Materials, known as the Gathings Committee, held public hearings to investigate pulps and related risqué material. These efforts cooled US production of lesbian pulps for several years—and greatly reduced their explicitness and moral ambiguity, even as obscenity concerns ebbed in the 1960s.[13] Meanwhile, gay male pulps were only beginning to emerge. Compared to the lesbian market, the gay male pulp market was relatively small and unprofitable until 1966, when Richard Amory's *Song of the Loon* earned both popularity and critical praise. By some estimates, *Song of the Loon* sold more than one hundred thousand copies—largely to US gay men—leading to both profits and imitators.[14] Armory's success kickstarted a burst of gay male pulps in the years to follow, including gay-male-themed Nazi-exploitation pulps.

Gay Nazi-exploitation pulps were also greatly influenced by a second thematic lineage: works of Nazi exploitation, or *Nazisploitation*.[15] While many scholars trace the genre to art house films like Luchino Visconti's *The Damned*

(1969) and more pulpy independent films like *Love Camp 7* (1968), a fixation on medium often misses the older history of these themes and plotlines in print. Four different literary trends from the mid-1950s and early 1960s likely influenced gay Nazi-exploitation pulps. First, images and plots fixated on scantily clad women being tortured, abused, or fondled by Nazis were staples of men's adventure magazines (and later novels), popular among heterosexuals starting in the 1930s and into the 1950s. Taking inspiration from these pulp magazines and adding their own twist was, second, Israel's short-lived stalag fiction genre—pulp titles aimed at heterosexuals that emphasized "the female dominance of males" and sexualized Jewish suffering during the Holocaust.[16] Third, Nazi exploitation and homosexual themes intertwined in lesbian pulps, particularly in graphic French titles like *L'Ange de Belsen* (1954) and *Fraulein Gestapo* (1954) as well as much tamer American lesbian pulps, including a 1963 storyline in Valeri Taylor's *Return to Lesbos*, which depicts how a young immigrant woman becomes a lesbian after facing sexual abuse in the Nazi camps.[17] Fourth was the publication of provocative, highbrow Holocaust-themed literature featuring stories of same-sex sexual exploitation of young men and boys. Particularly influential was Ka-Tsetnik 135633's 1961 novel *Piepel*, which focused on young Jewish boys enduring horrific sexual violence and atrocities committed by male Nazi functionaries in often futile attempts to survive in the camps.[18] Thematically, Ka-Tsetnik's novel effectively introduced the real-life experiences of *piepels* (i.e., boy servants or child prostitutes) to a wider US audience, crafting a perverse tone and narrative that fused explicit descriptions of sexual atrocity with Nazi symbolism.[19] *Piepel*'s critical success just prior to the emergence of gay Nazi-exploitation pulps strongly suggests that it provided both the framework and key themes that undergirded many of the pulps to come, including titles like *The Concentration of Hans*, *Middle Ground*, and *Go Down, Aaron*.

But while gay Nazi-exploitation pulps might only be understood as important for their innovative sexual vulgarity, these three representative gay pulps are more complex. Following Bronski, gay pulps should be understood as teaching homosexuals entering the life how to orient themselves toward both gay culture and the often-hostile heterosexual world in which gay men of the 1960s lived. What kinds of topics and ideas did these deceptively simple pulps address for gay male readers? In subject matter, gay pulps covered any number of subjects but tended toward the racier and more sexually explicit—lustful gay sailors, kinky bike gangs, and locker room exploits—the pulpier, the better. But within these storylines, 1960s gay male pulps also grappled with the significant social changes of the era, in both progressive and regressive ways. For instance, some gay pulps featured storylines about race relations and civil rights, giving largely white gay male readers scripts for thinking about race in gay culture. In some gay pulps, these plotlines were wildly racist, both demeaning and fetishizing Black men as sexual objects. Meanwhile, other pulps offered progressive expressions of allyship between Black and gay communities or featured tales of interracial male love. As this example shows, gay pulps were inherently tied to culture, politics, and sexual desires, becoming powerful tools for teaching American gay men how to navigate these issues in their own lives.

Like other lesbian and gay pulps, gay Nazi-exploitation pulps provided readers both sexual gratification and meaningful terrain on which social scripts for gay life could be written. In particular, two significant contextual events of the 1960s are alluded to in the gay Nazi-exploitation pulps analyzed here, each of which strongly resonated with actual events that took place during the Nazis' anti-homosexual crackdowns.

The first significant event was the call by lesbian and gay activists in the 1960s to resist long-standing efforts by doctors and psychiatrists to "treat" or "cure" homosexuality as a mental illness. Since 1952, the American Psychiatric Association's *Diagnostic and Statistical Manual of Mental Disorders* (*DSM*) had asserted that homosexuality was a "sociopathic personality disturbance," a diagnosis that codified the medical establishment's decades-long presumption that homosexuals were "pathological" and "deviant," therefore requiring treatment.[20] Starting in the early twentieth century, doctors, medical professionals, and scientists treated homosexual patients (voluntarily and involuntarily) with all manner of horrific interventions, including forcible commitment, icepick lobotomies, nausea-inducing aversion therapies, electroshock therapy, and surgical or chemical castration.[21] But, beginning in the 1960s, lesbian and gay activists promulgated the idea that homosexuals themselves—*not* doctors—were the experts on the subject of homosexuality and that they were not sick. As such, these activists called for an end to these medieval and often torturous "medical" treatments. They also demanded that the APA and others recognize lesbian and gay desires and self-concepts were valid ways of being in the world by removing homosexuality from the *DSM*. In support of this larger work, gay Nazi-exploitation pulps of this same era drew on memories of Nazi "medical experiments" on homosexuals in the 1930s and '40s to cultivate a gay male skepticism toward science and medicine in line with this political project.

The second contextual event was the 1960s counterculture's growing distrust of authority and institutions writ large, but particularly the state. As seen above, some earlier twentieth-century American homosexual organizations (like Mattachine after the expulsion of Hay and the other founding members) were committed to a vision of homosexual emancipation based on full assimilation into mainstream culture as good citizens. These homosexual messages—and the homosexuals they cultivated—were rooted in traditional American values, opposed Communism, and sought access to the American Dream. But a new generation of homosexuals began to see the gay male experience otherwise, namely as part of a wider 1960s counterculture that wanted none of these things. These lesbian and gay activists of the 1960s were not the first to hold such beliefs; there had always been homosexual activists who were more radical. But as the counterculture strengthened, an army of young gay men and women trained and invested in civil rights, antiwar activism, antipoverty initiatives, and women's issues turned their politics toward topics of gender, sex, and sexuality. This shift eventually became the Gay Liberation Movement, which staked out a defiantly oppositional demeanor. This new attitude was mirrored in many kinds of gay pulps, which embraced and expressed same-sex desires explicitly. But these same pulps also used memories of the Nazi persecution of homosexuals to urge countercultural readers to break with their elders' values and become good gays who were deeply skeptical of the government and the state. As these gay Nazi-exploitation pulps illustrated, any state or nation could turn on homosexuals without warning.

As we will see, issues of countercultural expression and the medicalization of homosexuality both emerge in the gay Nazi-exploitation texts described below. In each case, the novels drew on a larger gay pulp tradition of communicating messages to gay male readers about what they should value, devalue, or desire as part of an emergent US gay male community in the late 1960s. Remembering the Nazi persecution of homosexuals in particular ways was an essential element of how this work was done—and dramatically shaped the face of an increasingly expansive and assertive gay male culture.

Skepticism Toward Science

In the first instance, gay Nazi-exploitation pulps used homosexual storylines set amid the horrors of the Third Reich to encourage 1960s gay male readers to be highly skeptical of so-called scientific experts who claimed authority on the treatment or medicalization of homosexuality. These texts framed efforts to curb homosexuality through science as farcical and dangerous, drawing a direct line to eugenics. Of the three texts highlighted in this chapter, *Middle Ground* remains largely silent on the question of science's and medicine's role in controlling homosexuals. But both *Go Down, Aaron* and *The Concentration of Hans* explicitly mentioned and depicted the Third Reich's experiments on homosexuals, using them to nudge gay male readers to distrust similar scientific figures of authority in their own lives in three prominent ways.

First, the pulps called on gay male readers to be skeptical of antigay science because it was neither rigorous nor sound. Rather, the pulps claimed that the so-called scientists seeking to end homosexuality were not *real* scientists, constrained by methods, ethics, and propriety, but disreputable figures who were performing a medical masquerade. Both texts highlighted the fallacious nature of anti-homosexual science and medicine through their descriptions of this "medicine" and its so-called practitioners.

An early indication of this rhetoric appears on the cover of *The Concentration of Hans*. In addition to an eye-catching image, the cover included a tagline that strongly indicated to potential readers both how to consume the book and how it would predispose them to see antigay science as disreputable: "Yielding to endless 'medical experiments' by day, and agonizing humiliation by night, kept the beauty boy of the horror camp alive."[22] This brief hook makes clear to the perusing newsstand reader that scientific experimentation is the book's primary narrative. Yet, by placing the phrase *medical experiments* in quotation marks in the tagline, the cover also makes clear that the reader should approach this homosexual storyline with deep skepticism. In other words, the book's cover deploys a powerful memory rhetoric that both preserves the forgotten history of homosexual persecution and uses those memories to cultivate scientific skepticism in contemporary readers—those who might find themselves struggling with their own identity in weekly sessions with an analyst.

Alongside such hedging on the pulp's cover, the descriptions of scientists, medical doctors, and their procedures in the text itself also argues to readers that antigay medicine—whether performed by Nazis in the 1930s or Americans in the late 1960s—was simply pseudoscience. This argument is apparent in *The Concentration of Hans* at numerous points. For example, as the book reiteratively describes, no homosexuals in the story ever volunteer themselves to the medical experiments conducted at the camp. On the contrary, different homosexual characters actively seek to avoid or escape from such procedures. Meanwhile, when homosexuals are selected for these experiments, they are immediately given up for dead by their colleagues. No character endures these medical tests and survives, a result that would lead any reputable experimental trial to be shut down immediately. In all these ways, neither the mandatory participation nor the zero percent survival rate of those experimented on communicates to readers that the Nazis' methods conform to the standards of modern science and medicine.

Similarly, how the pulps show Nazi scientists performing their work in unethical and disreputable ways also reveals anti-homosexual science to be a medical masquerade. This is particularly evident in *The Concentration of Hans*, where doctors are shown laughing about their work (*CH*, 40) and nonchalantly harming victims (*CH*, 17). Perhaps most damning of all, the pulps show Nazi doctors and scientists sexually aroused by the perverse horrors they inflicted on their unsuspecting male "patients" (*CH*, 8–13). Collectively, the pulps code Nazi doctors as questionable medical practitioners and faux scientists, casting a pall over all such anti-homosexual experts and supporting the lesbian and gay activist discourses of the 1960s, which argued that antigay medicine was conducted by quacks and sadists.

Second, both *Go Down, Aaron* and *The Concentration of Hans* argue that most of the Nazis' scientific experiments on homosexuals in their storylines are socially sanctioned forms of moral and juridical punishment. In doing so, the texts asked gay male readers of the late 1960s to consider whether their own doctors and analysts were helping or punishing them for their own contemporary same-sex desires. This rhetorical framing of antigay science as torture appears in the first few pages of *Go Down, Aaron*, when after several weeks in Nazi captivity, the titular character decides it is for the best that his younger brother was murdered by the Nazi secret police, rather than captured and experimented on. Aaron explicitly states that he is grateful his brother, who at different turns in the story is alluded to have been potentially homosexual, is already dead because "perhaps he would have escaped the gas chambers, only to suffer a fate worse than that at the hands of an experimenting doctor." Aaron tells himself that a "quick and relatively painless end" for his brother was better.[23] In this admission, the reader hears Aaron rank the horrors of the Nazi persecution of homosexuals. Death by mass execution is horrific, but death by medical experimentation is worse. In unspooling such a claim, Aaron asks his homosexual readers to question whether enduring electroshock therapy, lobotomies, and castrations in contemporary mental hospitals is ever warranted. The pulp uses memories of Nazi medical experiments on homosexuals to nudge contemporary gay readers to consider if the pain and suffering inflicted on homosexuals was, in fact, the point.

Similar ruminations on medicine as a tool for torturing homosexuals appears in a set of visceral and disturbing sequences in *The Concentration of Hans*. Nazi doctors are repeatedly seen threatening to turn a homosexual male prisoner "into a woman" by castration (*CH*, 10). The nature of the procedure makes clear that its only value is to enforce compliance or, failing that, a lifetime of pain and anguish. Numerous threats of medicalized torture across *The Concentration of Hans* are undergirded by a heavily sadomasochistic scene early in the plot, when a rule-violating homosexual prisoner is dragged before an audience of guards and inmates, stripped naked, and forced to test a new drug meant to cure same-sex lust. The experiment fails swiftly, to no one's surprise, and devolves into public torture. Already coated in a pheromone-enhanced ointment, the nonconsenting patient becomes the prey of the Nazi guards' ravenous, chained dogs, who, intoxicated by the scent, feast on him (*CH*, 15). In a similarly disturbing scene later in the pulp, three homosexual escapees are hanged before the collected camp population. But first, they are publicly castrated to study whether the procedure might cure their homosexual desires—and their unwillingness to follow Nazi decrees (*CH*, 73). In both examples, the text argues to gay male readers that homosexual "treatments" under the Third Reich were nothing more than scientific torture. What, then, these men might ask, was the real purpose of the electroshock treatment they regularly endured at the hands of their own doctors?

Finally, the storylines of *Go Down, Aaron* and the *Concentration of Hans* assert a skeptical disposition toward antigay science and medicine by emphasizing that the Nazis undertook this work to benefit heterosexuals—not to aid or assist homosexuals. In doing so, the pulp novels prompt contemporary gay male readers to ask: Who is served by your harsh treatment at the hands of so-called medical and scientific experts? In the text, this question is answered for the homosexuals in the camps in two different ways: one that merits deep attention, and another that is only mentioned in passing. The latter of these two answers is that the castration of young male prisoners serves a perverse Nazi leadership, who go on to consider the men "pseudo-female" and ripe for mass sexual assault. This storyline appears briefly, and only in *The Concentration of Hans*, making it an outlier among the pulps (*CH*, 10–11). Nonetheless, the violent implications in this plotline cannot be ignored. The gay male reader of such a pulp should face no challenge in assessing that, at least in this limited instance, so-called medical procedures performed by the Nazis did not serve homosexuals but only a violent rape culture.

By contrast, a much more common beneficiary from medical experiments on homosexuals in these fictionalized gay pulps is the Nazi war machine. This point holds some significant historical accuracy. Even as these texts take extensive creative license, actual (failed) Nazi experiments to cure homosexuality were indeed conducted by force in Buchenwald.[24] This practice derived from the Nazi belief that homosexual men could be rehabilitated and serve as frontline soldiers and fathers to Aryan children. As the war raged on, this highly eugenic view became more acute as the Germans desperately needed more young Aryan men to serve. As such, it became both a military and a scientific imperative that all capable German men who could fight or produce children did so. These messages appear most directly in the *Concentration of Hans*, where doctors are called on to turn captured homosexuals into militant, powerful, child-producing heterosexuals for the good of the Reich in "Aryan perpetuation experiments" (*CH*, 14). In Hans's words, the doctors' aim was not to cure homosexuals for their own sake, but to select growing boys and to "turn them into young studs" (*CH*, 40)—prodigious populators of the Aryan race, created by the "chemists" (*CH*, 39). More to the point, the Nazis at the camp worked to create a homosexual superman, a hyperactive sexual male capable of spawning a legion of German children. True to what one would expect in a campy, pulp novel of explicit sexuality, these experiments focused on building the *Übermensch*'s physical prowess: long-lasting erections and voluminous semen. But should the Nazi doctors be successful, the text argues, these hated homosexuals would "become decent citizens again" (*CH*, 66).

But the homosexual characters undergoing these trials certainly did not benefit from such experiments. Rather, most homosexuals who underwent these procedures in the story ultimately went insane, died, or were killed due to the overwhelming sexual urges they produced (*CH*, 17). All this comes to a head when the title's protagonist, Hans, is selected for experimentation. Miraculously, Hans not only survives the experiment but defies expectations by retaining his homosexual desires. The story thus imparts another lesson: while science might enhance our bodies, it cannot change our sexual desires because those desires are not wrong. As such, the *Concentration of Hans* builds a skepticism toward scientific solutions to the "homosexual problem" and asks gay men of the 1960s to embrace their sexuality. Not to be forgotten, and in true pulp style, after having created a homosexual superman, the

Nazis reap what they sow. The muscled-bound, sexual specimen that is now Hans not only refuses to help propagate the German race but also rips Nazis limb from limbs until the camp is destroyed and he escapes to the French Riviera. There, he lives out his days as a handsome and virile homosexual cad—everything the Nazi doctors sought to destroy.

Skepticism Toward the State

Gay Nazi-exploitation pulp novels of the late 1960s also cultivated a significant skepticism toward the nation-state. More specifically, these texts presented the state—whether Nazi, American, or Russian—as a danger to the homosexual. In some cases, this threat was circumstantial or implicit; in other cases, the pulps showed the state's hostility directly. In all cases, gay male readers were encouraged to remember the Nazi persecution of homosexuals as a moment crystallizing the peril the state posed—and to integrate these mnemonic fears into their own dispositions toward nations. Three prominent memory rhetorics emerge in *Middle Ground*, *The Concentration of Hans*, and *Go Down, Aaron* to make this claim to readers.

The first rhetoric asserted that the Nazis' anti-homosexual taint should rightly be extended to other nations that also persecuted homosexuals. These pulps argued that there was no meaningful distinction between life under the Nazis and that under the US government, due to their shared anti-homosexual values and practices. This claim required two steps: demonstrating to readers that the Nazis were a menace to homosexuals, and then extending that same demeanor to the Allies. This first task is easily achieved across the collected pulps, which hold up the Nazi regime for particular scrutiny as an emblematic state intent on the destruction of homosexuals. In each text, through dozens of examples, the Nazi state is depicted as repressive, antidemocratic, malignant, and vicious toward sexual minorities. But extending a similar view to the United States was more challenging. Narratively, one might imagine that gay Nazi-exploitation pulps would look favorably on the United States and other Allied nations. To an extent, this assumption is borne out. For instance, at least some homosexual prisoners in the Nazi concentration camps in *The Concentration of Hans* are dismayed by rumors that "America was almost at her knees, begging for peace" (*CH*, 60). In *Middle Ground*, the main character, Tyl, at times presents the Americans in the most amiable form, as when they distribute gifts to the prisoner during the camp's liberation.[25] Similarly, in *Go Down, Aaron*, homosexuals under Nazi rule became excited at the sight of approaching American forces, at least at first (*GDA*, 147–48).

But these same pulps also made the case that the United States and other Allied nations could threaten homosexuals. One stark instance appears during an intimate scene between Hans and another prisoner, named Josef, in *The Concentration of Hans*. Hans considers how his life would change if the Americans arrived and liberated the camp. In response, Josef asserts that he was "not going to try tricks" like another prisoner, who sought to escape, and would instead "just wait until Germany loses the war." When Hans asks Josef, "What will happen to us?" if the Germans won, Josef's response is telling: "Josef bent his head and his mouth gently searched out Hans' eyes, ear lobes; his tongue darted out and encircled the inner ear cavity. His breathing was heavy and belabored. His hands were sweaty as they opened Hans' meagre outfit. His fingers went within and found the trembling boy. 'I am not going to think about it. I just want to have you.' Josef was not the sort to ponder about the deep consequences of the war and its aftermath. He, like many others, lived for the moment. 'Beside[s], I can't do anything about it'" (*CH*, 61–62). Rather than envisioning glorious liberation, Josef conveys a deeply ambivalent message: homosexuals should abandon fantasies of freedom delivered by American saviors. Liberation may never come, and if it did, what would happen was hard to know. For good and justifiable reasons, incarcerated homosexuals freed by American liberators feared that life under a US anti-homosexual agenda might be just as problematic as life under the Nazis. Facing such unknowns, Josef argued that homosexuals should acknowledge they could do little to change their fates; instead, they should embrace their desires in the moment when possible. As a result, gay male readers were encouraged to be suspicious that their lives in the United States in the late 1960s would be better than those of homosexuals in other nations at the time.

Another significant memory rhetoric expressed in these pulps alleged that homosexuals should be skeptical of nation-states because the state apparatus itself was likely to be their undoing. This argument held that in moments of stress and crisis, the state was likely to minimize the needs of homosexuals in pursuit of its larger aims. In such a scenario, homosexuals could become cannon fodder in disputes between nations of the world. In *The Concentration of Hans*, we find a clear example of homosexuals being undone by warring nations. Near the novel's end, encroaching Allied forces appear in the skies above the concentration camp. For the interned homosexual prisoners, these sightings signaled the end of their suffering and suggested "that freedom might be close at hand" (*CH*, 60). But the novel's final pages reveal something far less hopeful. For when the Allied "bombers" do appear again to defeat the Nazis, these aircraft deploy seemingly indiscriminate bombing runs, likely destroying the camp and killing large numbers of homosexual detainees in the process (*CH*, 90). This narrative's key takeaway is ultimately that homosexual lives and well-being are expendable if they stand in the way of a nation-state's forces achieving victory in war.

A not dissimilar outcome befalls homosexuals who place their trust in the Nazi state. Besides featuring homosexual prisoners, each of the texts collected here also depicts notable homosexual characters among Nazi officers and functionaries. Whether this is a plot device or a reflection of the postwar American propaganda that characterized the Third Reich as a homosexual regime is unclear. Regardless, these other homosexual characters provide further support to the pulps' message: homosexuals should be skeptical that the state will protect them. This message appears sporadically over several chapters in *The Concentration of Hans* and *Middle Ground*. In each text, homosexual Nazi soldiers and leaders are alternately threatened (*CH*, 68), demoted, or found strung up by liberated homosexuals at war's end (*MG*, 147, 173). In each case, Nazi homosexuals who place their faith in their own authoritarian regime are shown to be the ultimate fools. The novels argue that, like any nation-state, the Nazi regime should have been more deeply distrusted by homosexuals living within it.

Perhaps the most powerful instance of this rhetoric emerges in the final pages of *Go Down, Aaron*, where we find the main protagonists, Aaron and Peter, having freed themselves from their Nazi captors, enjoying a romantic respite in the war's waning days. However, as American and French soldiers converge on their location, the small city that hides them becomes riven with fear. Amid the falling Allied bombs and Nazis' failing lines, Aaron and Peter become separated. A known homosexual, Aaron is soon stalked by the city's citizens as the cause of their loss, ultimately (and unbelievably) driving Aaron to suicide before he can be torn apart by his neighbors. Meanwhile, Peter races to find his lover, only to be driven to his knees when he discovers Aaron's limp, dead body. At that moment, an American GI kicks down the door and, absorbing the scene, declares Peter Aaron's murderer and inundates them both in a spray of bullets. Aaron and Peter's tragic conclusion makes a point of showing that it is the American liberators who end the lives of the story's homosexual protagonists. *Go Down, Aaron* illustrates that regardless of whether it is Nazi or American, the state apparatus cannot help but see homosexuals as objects for destruction—and that homosexuals must therefore distrust the state as a guarantor of their freedom and safety.

The final memory rhetoric advanced in these three texts argues that homosexuals who are skeptical of the nation-state are likely to be rewarded. The pulps claim that distrusting and deceiving the nation-state should be the homosexual's modus operandi. In *Go Down, Aaron*, this distrust is marked when Aaron chooses to evade and resist Nazi storm troopers when they first appear at his front door. This decision is based on Aaron's earlier skepticism, drawn from the "many stories—weird and horrible tales of gore and death" and "accounts of murder and destruction" he overheard "late at night, when his parents had thought that he was sleeping" (*GDA*, 12). In this way, Aaron is depicted as a wise and observant homosexual, clear-eyed about Nazi brutality and the need to resist. For Aaron and his family, their defiance initially focused on escape: "If the war ever began to probe into the forest depths, they would flee" (*GDA*, 12–13). But Aaron's family is never afforded that opportunity; his father, mother, and younger brother are all gunned down by the Gestapo at his door because a Nazi officer claimed they refused "not to resist" (*GDA*, 8). Walking in on the scene, Aaron does not hesitate; he grabs a kitchen knife and "slic[es] into the [Nazi] officer's groin, grinding and ripping his flesh" (*GDA*, 9). The balance of the chapter features Aaron evading Nazi search parties in the forest for "week[s]" (*GDA*, 13) that sometimes felt like "months" (*GDA*, 11). By narrative necessity, Aaron is eventually captured; however, this fictional account of a homosexual defying the Nazi state is celebrated. Indeed, throughout the text, Aaron's evasion, deceit, and acts of resistance are portrayed as his means of survival, even as other homosexuals fall.

Themes of escape are also lauded in the gay Nazi-exploitation pulps when homosexual characters plan, organize, and work against the odds to free themselves from their oppressors. In *The Concentration of Hans*, three young homosexual prisoners plan to escape camp Belsen by overtaking a young soldier and commandeering his truck. According to the narrative, "The boys who worked in various parts of the concentration camp had made notes with crude chunks of flint and coal upon wooden shavings. A map was thusly fashioned from such 'notes' and a plan was devised" (*CH*, 60). The three succeed for a time before they are recaptured and forced to endure horrific torture. In relating the events, Hans describes the boys' escape as both "foolish" and "crudely planned" (*CH*, 60). Yet he also begrudgingly acknowledges his own desire to break free from his incarceration and suffering. A quite different scene unfolds in *Go Down, Aaron* when Aaron escapes Nazi entrapment numerous times—first, by engendering himself to a sadomasochistic officer to gain freedom from the camps, and later by seducing a guard to escape to a blissful, if short, reprieve from persecution and pain (*GDA*, 123). As such, both the *Concentration of Hans* and *Go Down, Aaron* assert that homosexuals persecuted by the Nazis earned vindication through their acts of resistance.

While other pulps emphasize homosexual characters defying the Nazi state apparatus, *Middle Ground* depicts homosexuals as skeptics of American state power and suggests that contemporary homosexuals should follow suit if they wish to survive. This characterization appears prominently when Tyl is kept in an American refugee house after his liberation from the camp. There, Tyl relates how he often lies to and distrusts his American hosts. Early in the text, Tyl notes the numerous inaccuracies in the files kept by his American minders, including lies about his age, hometown, parentage, and family's welfare (*MG*, 5). The only truth he claims to share with the Americans is his name: "I don't bother to lie about it. It is my most meaningless possession" (*MG*, 5). As he plots his postwar life, Tyl also considers seducing his male American guardian for leverage or blackmail at the urging of a freed acquaintance, who states, "You know what these Americans are. He will feel obliged to suicide himself" (*MG*, 41). In addition, Tyl shares that he was unwilling to provide the Americans with testimony against his Nazi guards after the war (*MG*, 46). Thereafter, Tyl and his compatriots build a lucrative business by gouging American GIs, selling them Nazi paraphernalia as souvenirs (*MG*, 175).

However, the most striking moment celebrating homosexuals for their distrust of the American state occurs in *Middle Ground*, when Tyl and his mates decide to flee the camp after its liberation by the Americans, driven by a profound sense of mistrust: "It turned out we were not so free as all that. The young [American] lieutenant, who spoke German fairly well, called us together and told us we would have to remain at the camp for a few days longer. We would be fed and looked after, of course, and would presently be taken in charge by appropriate agencies for the purposes of repatriation et cetera. He was sure we appreciated the fact that we could not suddenly be let loose on the countryside without papers and identification" (*MG*, 172). While Tyl's storyline is fictional, the process described above is largely based on fact. Tellingly, this process resulted in hundreds, perhaps thousands, of homosexuals interned in the camps being remanded back into incarceration, as both the Americans and Brits viewed them as criminals, regardless of their mistreatment at the hands of the Nazis. With that known fact, the subsequent events carry significant weight. Immediately after this announcement, Tyl notes, "I called a conference by Karel's grave. We met there, outside the circle of light cast by the bonfire, sick from eating too much food. I said, 'We're going to fuck off, tonight. I'm not staying here another night, Yanks or no Yanks'" (*MG*, 172). No explanation is given for Tyl's decision. But the fact remains that our homosexual protagonist flees American supervision after liberation, and, we are led to believe, only finds freedom by doing so. The moral of this story is clear: homosexuals must never be naive enough to entrust their fate to supposed liberators, regardless of the state they represent.

Conclusion

Most casual readers of gay pulps take for granted that the homosexual characters will meet their demise in the novel's final pages after suffering some horrible fate. As the idea goes, these deaths are unavoidable, demanded either by the reader's moral expectations or the era's production demands. But Bronski correctly asserts that the presumption that homosexuals faced "tragic endings" in all gay pulp novels "is one of the most deeply inscribed myths of the last three decades."[26] Not all endings for homosexual characters in gay pulps were tragic, and even the tragic ones were nuanced. The conclusions of the 1960s gay Nazi-exploitation pulps examined in this chapter demonstrate just this point. In each case, the pulp ended with a fitting catharsis—Nazi persecutors facing justice for their crimes, thanks to the wily, committed resistance of the story's leading homosexuals.

The ending of *this* chapter occasions us to consider these Nazi-exploitation pulps' impact in the context of the United States in the 1960s. As with other rhetorics examined in this book, it is difficult to know whether the rhetorical remembrances discussed in this chapter were effective in their aims. The men consuming these texts likely read them in private or shared them among trusted intimates. Nor are the pulps' rhetorical agitation for gay male readers to adopt a different disposition toward medicine and the state readily trackable. If such a shift occurred, there may be little to no evidence to demonstrate it. By contrast, what might appear to be a small change in disposition at one moment might ultimately have had enormous effects, such as pushing individual readers into gay political activism or giving them confidence to reject their analyst's attempts to alter their sexual desires. In short, the impact of these rhetorics and the role that remembering the Nazi persecution of homosexuals in these texts may have played for the gay male reading audience of the late 1960s is simply unknowable.

Nonetheless, we do know that major themes articulated between the lusty lines of these gay Nazi-exploitation pulps would become tangible demands of the Gay Liberation Movement after June 1969. The post-Stonewall movement differed significantly from its predecessor, including coordinated and explicit attacks on the institutions of medicine and the state that underpinned the repression of homosexuals in the United States. By 1973, the Gay Liberation Movement would succeed in forcing the APA to remove homosexuality from the *DSM* as a codified mental illness. In that same period, new organizations like the Gay Liberation Front demonstrably aligned the struggle for gay liberation with the counterculture and the New Left with calls to resist the state by "revolutionary" means.[27] There is insufficient evidence here to claim these gay pulps drove the movement toward these positions. But it seems likely that the gay Nazi-exploitation pulps of the late 1960s anticipated and captured the spirit of the movement to come by issuing a clarion call in the form of remembering the homosexuals persecuted by the Nazi regime.

In our broader consideration of memory, these three representative gay Nazi-exploitation pulps confirm a previously established aspect about the reliance on memory among homosexual, lesbian, and gay male activists during this time in US history: that in the absence of a rich and well-preserved lesbian and gay archive, lesbian and gay activists were ready to supplement what was known with an array of fictional discursive infill to generate a usable past for the contemporary struggle. Fiction is a new genre in which the Nazi persecution of homosexuals emerges in this book—but it is far from the first homosexual-aligned past to be rendered in fictional form. Historian James Steakley has noted that most of what was understood about the homosexual past prior to 1973 took the form of fiction.[28] Christopher Nealon refers to this practice within sexual and gendered minorities communities as a tendency toward the creation of "foundling" memories.[29] Foundling memories represent a deeply rooted need for the past among homosexual communities, a need that can be traced back to even earlier homophile literatures, performances, attire, and related discourses. Uninhibited by strict demands for rigor, evidence, and objectivity found in other past-oriented practices, foundling memories have contributed significantly to forwarding the community's business. Indeed, their utilization reflects both an *absence* of a homosexual archive and its *erasure* through a complex apparatus of silences, forgettings, and destructions intentionally engaged by our heteronormative society. As such, foundling memories like those expressed in pre-Stonewall "Holocaust literature" become not just a rhetorical choice but a necessary rejoinder in the face of a multifaceted, multigenerational campaign of mnemonicide.

In this vein, there are numerous reasons why expressing these foundling memories of the Nazi persecution of homosexuals in pulp fiction novels proved valuable as an argumentative resource. Chief among them, as we already discussed, was the genre's ability to take previously brief and limited allusions to the Nazi oppression in earlier texts and expand them in ways that afforded the persecution greater degrees of consideration. In particular, by giving narrative form to facts about the persecution—characters, settings, and plotlines—homosexual activists could bring substance to the events in ways that passing mentions in a newspaper or homosexual publication could not. Similarly, the fusion of fact and fiction in the pulp genre afforded activist authors greater freedom to tell the story of the persecution in new ways. While previous memories highlighted the numbers of homosexuals rounded up and incarcerated, the allegations over who was a homosexual, the work they were forced to perform, and the meaning of the persecution itself, the pulp novel permitted homosexual activists the opportunity to highlight—if only fictionally—the feelings, thoughts, motivations, concerns, and perspectives of the homosexuals subjected to these larger forces. Admittedly, this work was often done with a campy demeanor, and the quality of the writing could be lacking. But these foundling memories were nonetheless significant in shaping what dimensions of the persecution were featured. Last, sharing these memories in pulp form greatly enhanced the size and diversity of the audiences engaged in remembering the Nazi persecution. As this book shows, previous remembrances circulating in the United States before the late 1960s had limited reach and traveled in confined forms. By contrast, the pulp form significantly broadened the availability of these kinds of remembrances to grocery store aisles, newspaper stands, mail order catalogs, and pornographic bookstores, reaching mostly male readers who may not yet have been active in gay politics or culture. In all these ways, the emergence of pulps as a vehicle for these remembrances demonstrates how valuable shifts in the media through which memories are expressed can be crucial for achieving a community's rhetorical aims.

As we have done in other chapters, it is also important to consider what this new instantiation of remembering the Nazi persecution of homosexuals meant in the larger story of these appeals in the US lesbian and gay movement, and how these remembrances differed from what came before. The clearest shift in this appearance of the Nazi persecution of homosexuals is the dramatic emergence of a new affective dimension: desire. Up to this point, when homosexuals recalled the Nazi oppression, it was done so with defiance, resistance, anger, and outrage. But due to the combined constraints of obscenity laws, an underdeveloped market for sexual exploration, and the realities of the persecution as a human catastrophe, desire was inaccessible to the homosexuals who might have wished to explore these overlaps in previous decades. But the 1960s brought swift changes toward sexual freedom, encouraging more and more gay men to explore their deepest wants and desires, up to and including the fetishization of fascism. The social, cultural, and psychological forces that shape and drive this fetishization are beyond the scope of this book. But from this moment on, desire became a possible—if still the least common—entry point from which to learn more about the Nazi persecution of homosexuals. And as these pulps demonstrate, the inclusion of desire in this affective registry made possible new audiences for these memories and provided an entirely new way to communicate the realities and complexities of the Nazi persecution of homosexuals to American readers.

Remembrances of the Nazi campaign against homosexuality in the late 1960s are also marked by a dramatic shift toward including explicit considerations of the Third Reich's medical experiments. Given the egregiousness of the crime, it is somewhat surprising that the facts surrounding this mistreatment had not emerged in any previous homosexual text prior to 1967 that I have examined. But before the late 1960s, the American psychiatric and medical establishment had largely seen homosexuality as an ill to be cured, and no sufficiently large homosexual community existed that was willing and able to push back with real force on doctors and scientists. But activism against the APA, starting in the 1960s, shifted this reality and gave homosexuals a perspective through which they could remember these events—and actually consider the experiments as *criminal* rather than typical. Interestingly, while the late 1960s marked the first emergence of this part of the persecution, it was also one of the last. Given changes in the *DSM* in 1973, the urgency of the question for homosexuals—and its threat of perpetuation—dropped considerably. Today, few narratives that recall the Nazi persecution of homosexuals emphasize this aspect of the story, suggesting that the prominence of certain historical dimensions often aligns with the evolving needs of the contemporary movement.

The pulps of the late 1960s also reveal a certain fearlessness in confronting earlier conflations of homosexuals with Nazis. As we saw in chapter 1,

Gerber developed a powerful reimagining of the Roehm purge in large part to challenge a pernicious discourse in US heterosexual publications of the time: the myth of the homosexual Nazi. For Gerber, this stereotype posed an existential threat to a nascent American homosexual movement, demanding strong statements that distanced homosexuals from the Nazis. While such fears are less apparent in chapter 2, homosexual publications' silence on the Roehm purge during the 1950s seemed designed to continue distancing the US homosexual movement from allegations of a Nazi taint. In stark contrast, the gay Nazi-exploitation pulps in this chapter feature both non-Nazi and Nazi homosexuals by the dozens, fully engaging and playing with this pernicious myth of an earlier era. Why? On one level, these pulps' primary sexual appeal lay in their ability to flirt with scandal—and what greater lines of propriety existed for homosexual readers to cross than to sexually covet a Nazi, whose ideology sought their subjugation? At another level, these indulgent representations showed a willingness to remember Nazi crimes against homosexuals with a complexity that previous texts did not. Rather than reproducing earlier black-and-white depictions of "good homosexuals" and "bad Nazis," these pulps bared the murky reality: that some homosexuals had been Nazis, some homosexuals had loved or desired Nazis, and some homosexuals were themselves "bad guys." This acknowledgment—that homosexuals appear in all human groups, associations, and communities, including the vilest—rarely appears in other public remembrances in the decades to follow. In fact, it might be that only a genre like pulp, which can conceal hard truths beneath highly sexual and sometimes campy plotlines, is capable of doing so. But such acknowledgments are necessary for scholars to discuss fascism's pernicious appeal and consider how to keep it at bay.

Finally, this chapter highlights the first sustained appearance of concentration camps for homosexuals in the memories of the Nazi persecution. To this point, pink triangle memories have appeared with limited but increasing frequency across all remembrances of the Nazi persecution since 1934, a trend that reaches a climax in 1987, at this book's end. But in gay Nazi-exploitation pulps of the late 1960s, concentration camps memories first emerge in a fully formed and consistent way. As we have now seen, the bulk of these storylines take place within concentration camps interning homosexuals. This new, expanded element of Nazi persecution memories is valuable for communicating to readers that this internment happened and needs to be remembered. It is also useful for complicating previous depictions of the Nazi oppression that focus on the wider persecution of homosexuals unfolding outside the camps themselves. In the chapters to come, I note how this tendency to fixate on the camp experience in remembering the persecution of homosexuals both accelerates and becomes problematic in the decades after the 1960s. Yet here, at the middle point in our historical trajectory, a noticeable shift to emphasize the camps appears in force for the very first time.

By the end of the 1960s, the remembrances of the Nazi mistreatment of homosexuals had developed in several dramatic ways. By turning to gay pulps and the erotic, these memories ventured into places they had never reached before—and produced rhetorical effects that previous incarnations of this past could not. In doing so, these pulps presaged an intense shift in the tone and tenor of lesbian and gay discourses in the United States in the 1970s. But before that swing could reach its full acceleration, the community and the wider world would have to face a reckoning, brought on by decades of unanswered attacks, abuses, and belittlements of American sexual and gender minorities. That reckoning would take the form of the Stonewall Riots, an event that would have cascading effects for how the Nazi persecution of homosexuals would be remembered thereafter.

Chapter 4

Spectral Siblings

Remembering Our Ghostly Brothers and Sisters
as Martyrs for Gay Power, 1970–1977

Despite an incessant discourse to the contrary, the June 1969 Stonewall Riots were not the beginning of US lesbian and gay activism.[1] Rather, as numerous scholarly and community discourses over the last fifty years demonstrate, Americans of diverse sexes, genders, sexual expressions, and intersectional needs long struggled in their own ways and times to build a better life for themselves across the nation's history. But while Stonewall did not start this activism, it did mark a turning point in how people who previously considered themselves inverts, homophiles, and homosexuals understood and organized themselves. As the previous chapter details, some of these shifts were anticipated in texts of the 1960s. But the post-Stonewall Gay Liberation Movement introduced other dimensions into this emergent lesbian and gay sensibility, including the persuasiveness of pride, the importance of being out, and, in the realm of politics, a demand for gay power. Calls for "gay power" existed before Stonewall, too, most clearly in assertive acts of resistance like the 1966 Compton's Cafeteria riot. But the incendiary events of Stonewall—and their circulation in both heterosexual and homosexual media at the time—supercharged these calls, making the expansion of gay power a central plank of the movement for the next decade.

A key title in which calls for "gay power" surfaced following the riots was a small but fierce publication launched in Berkeley in 1970 called *Gay Sunshine*. It was also in *Gay Sunshine*'s inaugural issue that the first post-Stonewall US remembrance of the Nazi persecution of homosexuals emerged in print, in a relatively short essay titled "A Question Written in Blood." As the title indicated, the Nazis' persecution of homosexuals was central to the essay's aim, and it was not addressed timidly. Rather, in strident language and an accusatory tone emblematic of the post-Stonewall movement, the piece asked whether the wider world would continue to ignore past and present harms inflicted on homosexuals in this new era of gay liberation. In frank terms, it demanded accountability for the homosexual lives lost to the Third Reich and, implicitly, from all those regimes, institutions, and nations that followed in their footsteps in the decades since.[2] This remembrance of the Nazi persecution of homosexuals was far different from what had come before and deeply entwined in broader demands for gay power.

The author of this terse, angry essay was a thirty-four-year-old itinerant priest by the name of Rev. Mikhail Itkin. Itkin was a dedicated lesbian and gay activist in the 1960s and '70s, one with a reputation as a radical and a troublemaker. But Itkin was also deeply philosophical, drawing on his strong spiritual understanding of gay liberation to animate his thinking and drive change through acts of service, support, and instigation. His 1970 essay in *Gay Sunshine* would be his first venture in remembering the Nazi persecution of homosexuals, turning that memory to calls for gay power from a new generation of US lesbians and gays. But it would not be his last. From this essay onward, Itkin would devote significant time advancing a new framework for remembering these victims in his speeches and writings, making him one of the most important American voices in remembering the Nazi persecution of homosexuals at this time.

Within this discourse, Itkin argued that contemporary US lesbians and gays of the 1970s should remember the Nazis' homosexual victims as part of an ongoing fellowship, a community of transhistorical "brothers and sisters" (QWB, 17). More specifically, Itkin framed these earlier victims as both defiant martyrs who died for today's lesbians and gays and spectral agitators who haunted contemporary homosexual lives and cried out for action. Collectively, Itkin deployed this unique rhetoric of fellowship to remember the Nazis' victims—not to defend their reputations, encourage organizing, or cultivate a queer sensibility, but to demand gay power. By the middle of the 1970s, Itkin's memory rhetoric would not be the only one in circulation, for that decade marked a moment of significant change in this discourse, both within and beyond the lesbian and gay community. But starting in 1970 and into 1977, Itkin's discourse became essential for empowering a newly emboldened Gay Liberation Movement after Stonewall.

This chapter highlights and reconstructs the largely uninvestigated rhetoric of Reverend Itkin and the particularly important ways he remembered the Nazis' homosexual victims in the pivotal years during which the US Gay Liberation Movement was forged. But examining Itkin's rhetorical history is challenging, which perhaps explains why scholars have conducted so few examinations of his works. These difficulties include the frenetic forms of his activism, the transitory nature of his work and movements, his ideas' complex and sometimes obscure references, and his radical tone and subject matter. Itkin also published under more than a half dozen iterations of his name, and it did not help that he was disliked by many of his contemporaries. Perhaps most problematic of all: Itkin's death from AIDS in 1989 meant that much of his voluminous work went unarchived.[3] Despite these challenges, Itkin's memories of the Nazi persecution of homosexuals are partially reconstructed here through his 1970 essay in *Gay Sunshine*, his 1975 poem "Visitors from the Holocaust," and his 1977 pamphlet *Silent No More*. There is considerable reason to believe that these texts do not represent a full and complete rhetorical corpus of Itkin's work relating to the Nazi persecution of homosexuals. But collectively, these surviving documents consistently demonstrate how Itkin shaped a particular image of these victims that aimed, above all else, to obligate lesbians and gays of the 1970s to activate their own power and set gay people free.

Itkin and the Rhetoric of Fellowship

The Reverend Bishop Mikhail Itkin is a ghost haunting the American lesbian and gay rights movement. Like all ghosts, he was certainly once flesh and blood yet today largely exists only in a fleeting and ephemeral fashion. His impacts on the movement are ever present; yet, as a man, he remains quite unknowable. This all points to a figure whose place in the past is decidedly unresolved, spectral to be sure. But his unsettledness should not suggest that Itkin's impact was insignificant. Rather, Itkin's engagement with the memory of homosexuals persecuted by the Nazi regime is central to crafting the understanding of this history at the turning point between the late 1960s and early 1980s.

Befitting Itkin's ghostly figure, many of the details of his life went unverified and unconfirmed, even to those who apparently knew him. What has been said about him is much warmed over, but these disparate stories reveal a novel personality. For instance, the gay historian and Itkin's friend Jim Kepner once described him as a "stormy petrel of the gay movement in New York,

San Francisco, and Los Angeles."[4] Joseph Plaster's book mentioning Itkin says he often "presented himself as a trickster: foolish and weak given his affinity with storytelling and fantasizing; and yet rebellious, syncretic, and potentially undermining of larger cultural structures."[5] Historian James T. Sears described Itkin as "impish"—a troublemaker—a sentiment shared by writer and associate Ian Young, who remembered Itkin as a "general, all-purpose shit-disturber."[6] He was also a well-known "hypochondriac"—so much so that when Itkin died of complications from AIDS in 1989, some people were surprised he had actually contracted the disease.[7] At times, one cannot read characterizations of Itkin without getting the sense that many simply did not like him. Indeed, Young noted his "lack of personal charisma," and more than a few men in other parts of the gay spirituality movement actively despised him, claiming Itkin was a liar, prostitute, and convict.[8] But like him or not, everyone in the US lesbian and gay movement in the 1960s and '70s seemed to know him—and knew he could not be ignored.

Itkin's confusing brew of energy, anxiety, and chaos sometimes masked his considerable skill as a rhetorical actor. At eighteen, Itkin was drawn into both gay rights activism and missionary work, where his rhetorical proficiency was honed by both predisposition and practice. He had been tutored in activism from an early age when his parents introduced him to the Progressive Party of Henry Wallace, Franklin Roosevelt's former vice president.[9] By 1954, Itkin was both "an underage street radical" and a founding member of the precursor to the New York Mattachine Society.[10] Once in the movement, Itkin was a nearly constant presence in early lesbian and gay politics on both coasts. Young notes that Itkin "often acted as the spark connecting all these disparate groups and individuals, the artists and the activists, the old homophiles and the young gay radicals, the spiritual and the political."[11] As such, Itkin had a wide and diverse audience for his ideas, even if his devotees and spiritual followers were few in number. Itkin's rhetorical prowess itself was highly theatrical and performative. He was reported to have performed a street exorcism of the San Francisco Federal Building in 1969 to cast out its "demons of violence and exploitation."[12] Itkin was also an important part of the Gay Liberation Front's now-famous "zaps" of the American Psychiatric Association in 1970 that helped remove homosexuality from the *DSM*. In remembering the zap—highly unruly demonstrations and displays that aimed to embarrass public figures—Karla Jay characterized Itkin and other members as "haunt[ing] the APA sessions, disrupting them with displays of guerilla theater and angry protests from the floor."[13]

But Itkin also excelled in more traditional genres of rhetorical action, even if he did so with a sassy and vicious tongue. Kepner remembered him as "produc[ing] militant resolutions by the score."[14] Itkin also demonstrated against segregated lunch counters in the American South in 1960, led protest marches against nuclear proliferation, and was arrested for his street activism.[15] In addition, he claimed to have gone undercover to root out neo-Nazis.[16] By at least one account, he was present at the Stonewall Riots.[17] Itkin also published a book, *The Radical Jesus and Gay Consciousness*, a text Ian Young characterized as "a political document very much of its time" that described Itkin's "struggle to reconcile the complexities of Christian theology with the spiritual, social, and sexual needs of his own people."[18] In short, when Itkin saw an opportunity to discourse for change, he snatched it, often to great success.

While Itkin has been understudied, those who have studied him tend to approach his work from one of two perspectives—as a revolutionary who questioned the foundations of US spirituality, or as a gay radical involved in numerous facets of the cause. Where his spirituality and homosexuality intersected or clashed has also interested several writers.[19] But Itkin's contributions to the US lesbian and gay movement's remembrances of the Nazi persecution of homosexuals has, until now, gone entirely unexamined. This absence is surprising, given how animated Itkin became about these events that took place years before he was born. But his interest in these homosexual men's suffering is wholly consistent with his devotion to the world's "alienated" and forsaken populations.[20] As a homosexual, a Communist, a person with mental illness and an arrest record, and possibly a sex worker, Itkin understood the experience of being discarded by all facets of society. Yet this isolation only fueled his zealotry in service of similarly dispossessed people. From his canonization, Itkin's work focused on providing care, service, ministry, and mutual aid to people experiencing homelessness, "street kids" in "gay ghettos," hustlers and sex workers, migrants, draft dodgers, people of color, and homosexuals.[21] The one hundred thousand homosexuals persecuted by the Nazi regime a generation earlier were just another group of his people.

What Itkin knew of the events in Germany between 1933 and 1945 before he became an evangelist for the cause is unclear. Born in 1936, he would have been too young to encounter the reports in the US press. But he was an active participant in the homosexual rights movement as early as 1954, when many of the memories described in chapter 2 became more prominent among engaged homosexuals. By at least one account, Itkin may also have been affiliated with John Lauritsen, who, along with David Thorstad, wrote

The Early Homosexual Rights Movement in 1973—one of the first in-depth English-language texts on the Nazi persecution of homosexuals.[22] Importantly, Itkin was also born and raised Jewish, and his family was of Eastern European descent. Though there is little evidence that he ever renounced his Judaism—it is perhaps more realistic that he added Christianity to his own dynamic spiritual brew—it is entirely likely that he acquired a deep cultural knowledge of the Holocaust from his family of birth, perhaps including the adjacent experiences of homosexuals. But Itkin narrated his own discovery of these events in print. In the summer of 1970, Itkin reported meeting "two young men from Alaska, Russian Orthodox" who were on pilgrimage in San Francisco when they attended mass at his church. He continued, "During the Nazi occupation of Czechoslovakia, these (at the time young boys, lovers then and still lovers) were prisoners at the Dachau concentration camp" (QWB, 17). This interaction is little detailed; yet Itkin would continue to tell this story repeatedly in his advocacy for remembering these homosexual victims. Regardless of what he knew about the Nazi persecutions beforehand, meeting these two men ignited Itkin's interest. As a caretaker and advocate for the alienated, how could it not?

Yet Itkin's interest went beyond the pastoral. This chance encounter ignited a rhetorical spark that Itkin would nurture into a raging fire of memory for the remainder of his life. Between 1970 and 1977, Itkin would make telling as many people as possible about the Nazi persecution a key tenant of his activist and spiritual work. As we will see, these (likely incomplete) discourses were rich and varied in form, but each text contributed to Itkin's message for 1970s lesbian and gay audiences: that they owed a debt to the homosexual victims of the Nazi regime—and in repaying it, they might find a new freedom of their own.

To this end, Itkin deployed what we might call a *rhetoric of fellowship*. By this, I mean Itkin constituted within contemporary lesbians and gays a memory of earlier homosexual victims that saw them as part of a shared community, rooted in mutual obligations and linked to a conjoined transcendental aim. Such an approach was consistent with Itkin's rhetorical and spiritual background. Rhetorics of fellowship are commonly used in Christian discourses to build a community of shared belief, invested in faith in God. However, such discourses were uncommon in previous homosexual, lesbian, or gay rhetoric of the era, even before the emergence of the Religious Right. But Itkin stood firmly in this breach, aiming to merge the message of fellowship with a long-alienated homosexual community. Indeed, in the years following

Stonewall, building an explicit community of lesbians and gays was an obligation to which Itkin was all too happy to contribute.

But community itself—while laudable—was insufficient for Itkin's aims and for the needs of the early 1970s lesbian and gay community. What was required was lesbian and gay community *action*, more commonly described at the time as *gay power*. The lesbian and gay community of the post-Stonewall era was fixated on widescale social change through participatory actions: marches, protests, voting, agitating, zapping, and, perhaps most importantly, coming out. As a result, the socially conscious Itkin framed his remembrances of the Nazis' homosexual victims through this lens: a call to action aimed at honoring and continuing the activism and resistance of a previous homosexual generation. As a result, Itkin's complex memory rhetoric was deeply shot through with an aura of *motivation*.

This demand for action was facilitated by joining Itkin's rhetoric of fellowship and martyrdom with what we might think of as a queer rhetoric of hauntology. Queer scholars have recently devoted an impressive number of pages to the radical queer possibilities of ghosts and hauntings.[23] Yet spectral capacities to generate queer possibilities are not rooted in queer theory but earlier literary and rhetorical eras like the gothic, where the appearance of uncanny others denoted something queer at work. More modern scholars have laid out the value of ghosts explicitly. For instance, Jacques Derrida describes hauntology as a way of engaging "time and, the untimeliness of its present," among others.[24] Carla Freccero elaborates that Derrida imagines spectrality as a "mode of historical attentiveness that the living might have to what is not present but somehow appears as a figure or a voice, a 'non-living present in the living present,' that is no longer or not yet with us."[25] In almost all cases, we might then say the emergence of these ghosts is rhetorical, for ghosts wish something from their haunted audiences. Or to borrow from Freccero, the spectral invokes "the way the past . . . presses upon us with a kind of insistence or demand, a demand to which we must somehow respond," an insistence she earlier calls an "ethical imperative in and across time."[26] These demands can vary widely depending on the person visited. In many cases, the response of the haunted is to "displace" or "bury" such ghosts—to acknowledge them to forget them, and potentially to replace them with the voice, text, or discourse of the haunted.[27] But queers often take a different tack: to invite the haunting rather than turn away from it, and to figure worlds in which we grapple to live with our ghosts. Of course, who is haunting and who is ghosted affects this calculus, for a ghost "does not . . . necessarily belong to those who are haunted by it."[28] A queer ghost might not, for instance, haunt a modern queer. But that is exactly what Itkin figures in his remembrances of the homosexuals persecuted by the Nazi regime. As such, the haunted queers of the 1970s faced an insistence to see their ghosts as doppelgängers to whom they owed a debt that must be repaid by action. How Itkin frames his ghosts through a tripartite rhetorical appeal is central to this investigation.

Bonds of Brotherhood and Sisterhood

The first piece of Itkin's rhetoric of fellowship cast homosexual victims of Nazism as "brothers and sisters" of contemporary gay and lesbian audiences. In this work, Itkin ensured that lesbians and gays of the 1970s—some of whom were learning of the Nazi persecution for the first time—did not see the European homosexuals of the 1930s and '40s as foreign "others," experiencing persecution substantially different from their own. Rather, Itkin wanted contemporary lesbian and gay audiences in the United States to closely identify with these earlier homosexuals an ocean away, asserting that they shared lasting bonds across queer generations that demanded action in the present, on the part of living. To this end, Itkin adopted several assorted rhetorical strategies.

Most immediately, Itkin deployed vivid descriptions of the Nazis' victims in his texts to depict them as three-dimensional homosexual people, rather than abstract references from long-forgotten lists of the dead. This approach was not revolutionary in itself; humanizing victims by providing audiences key details about their lives is a common tactic across varied rhetorical endeavors. But this move was especially consequential in Itkin's memory discourse because, until the 1970s, most remembrances of the Nazis' homosexual victims lacked specifics. Previous chapters confirm just how vaguely sketched these victims' experiences were when glimpsed through the fog of war and across the Iron Curtain over the previous thirty years. This lack of detail afforded homosexual rhetors opportunities to mold victims' stories to their needs. But these vagaries also created exaggerations, false equivalencies, and significant misunderstandings about the German homosexual victims' experiences both inside and outside the more contemporary US community. However, early credible research on the facts of the homosexual persecution under the Third Reich emerged in English in the United States in the 1970s, and Itkin readily used these details to provide his audiences a fuller view of just who these earlier homosexual brothers and sisters were.

Itkin was particularly fortunate to have engaged in a face-to-face conversation with two actual homosexual survivors of the Nazi regime, which provided him with valuable insights into this earlier generation. His visit with two homosexual Dachau survivors around 1970 had a powerful influence on him, and he would mine this brief interaction often in his works to humanize these victims. This synecdoche posed representational risks: the experiences of these two men could never fully stand in for those of the thousands of persecuted homosexuals across Europe. But given the rarity of this interaction, when Itkin shared the *real* experiences of these two men in his memory work, it added a degree of force to this history that had not been seen since Burkhardt shared his experiences of homosexual persecution in ONE magazine in 1959.

Itkin uses vivid descriptions of these two homosexual survivors and their suffering in each of his extant texts to bring them to life for his audience. For instance, he keenly emphasizes that the two men were young boys during their internment in Dachau. His first published account of their meeting in *Gay Sunshine* characterizes the men as "at that time young boys" who were "lovers then and still lovers" (QWB, 17). In his 1977 pamphlet *Silent No More*, he would describe them as "lovers since their early teens when they met at Dachau" (*SNM*, 5). Itkin's poem "Visitors from the Holocaust" describes the pair as "visitors I did not know," but when he continues to emphasize what they endured in Dachau as young people, Itkin effectively plays on his audience's emotions to build connective threads of identification.[29] Itkin adds to this emotional appeal by detailing the affective tenor of their conversation. One story stresses that the men "were reduced to tears" by telling their tale, particularly when they shared how the suffering and deaths of homosexuals went unremembered in Dachau's official memorials (*SNM*, 5). Other iterations emphasize the men's recounting as rife with anger (QWB, 17). In each case, the men's emotions add a human dimension to their experience for lesbian and gay audiences of the 1970s. Last, Itkin includes key details of the men's lives after the war to further define them (and other homosexual victims) as unique individuals. Exemplary of this move, Itkin shares that the two men resided in Alaska, were "Russian Orthodox," and had been traveling in San Francisco when they encountered Itkin. In true Itkin style, in his first account in *Gay Sunshine*, he also includes detailed information about the date, time, and location of his weekly service where he encountered the men, intent on never missing an opportunity to advertise his work (QWB, 17). Similar postwar details about the men's return visit to Dachau years later also appear across texts. Collectively, Itkin's vivid description of these two men transforms them into genuine incarnations of a previously vague past, enriching his memory rhetoric for modern lesbian and gay audiences.

In a not dissimilar way, Itkin uses vivid descriptions of the suffering of homosexuals as a distinct category of victims under the Third Reich to engage the general lesbian and gay reader. Itkin is not the original source of these essential details; rather, he effectively researches earlier accounts detailing homosexual suffering and curates them in *Silent No More*. Among these descriptions, he provides estimates for how many homosexuals faced persecution by the Third Reich to make their suffering feel tangible to his readers. These estimates, however, range from wildly divergent and inaccurate figures such as "many thousands and hundreds of thousands" to "220,000 to 250,000" (*SNM*, 2). Itkin also cites Janet Cooper to relate how "the Nazis burned the library of the Homosexual Rights Movement" and "herded Gays into the various concentration camps and forced them to wear the pink triangle" (*SNM*, 3). In addition, Itkin quotes the autobiography of Rudolf Hoess, who oversaw several Nazi camps with large homosexual populations and described specific aspects of the homosexual persecution. Itkin paraphrases Hoess to explain how homosexuals "were given the heaviest labor, pushing the great metal rollers used to level the unpaved camp streets or sent to work in the clay pit of a large brick works" (*SNM*, 4). Itkin also shares Hoess's characterization of the suffering: "Those who were sufficiently strong minded to renounce their vice were able to stand up to the hardest work. The others died like flies. The true homosexuals, knowing they would never be set free, suffered extra stress" (*SNM*, 4). Elsewhere, Itkin cites an unnamed survivor who related how the "homosexuals were grouped into liquidation commandos. . . . That meant less food, more work, stricter supervision. If a prisoner with a pink triangle became sick, it spelled his doom" (*SNM*, 5). These few examples from Itkin's text each painted a more specific picture of homosexual suffering under the Nazis.

Across his various works, Itkin adds to his efforts to portray these victims as brothers and sisters by emphasizing that they were not only real people but also fundamentally similar to contemporary lesbians and gays. The most obvious example of this effort was his explicit and repeated use of slightly different permutations of the phrase *homosexual brothers and sisters* (QWB, 17) to describe Nazi victims so that modern lesbians and gays would be motivated to see themselves in their forebears' suffering. In making this point, it is worth emphasizing that Itkin actively invited remembrances of lesbians under the Third Reich in his discourses—a first in the examples I highlight since 1934—even if his evidence and examples rely near exclusively on men's experiences. That said, Itkin draws on powerful lesbian voices in *Silent No More* to underline this gender-spanning persecution. In particular, he cites lesbian and Jewish professor Janet Cooper's commentary about her experience at the 1974 Conference on Auschwitz, where she introduced herself as a "Jewish Gay" who "became angry . . . because they had not represented all the other groups that the Nazis had systematically exterminated. . . . I especially resented the lack of concern . . . for the people whom the Nazis had exterminated specifically because they were Gay" (*SNM*, 2). In relating Cooper's experiences and words, Itkin demonstrated how contemporary lesbians could identify with the struggles of both Jews and homosexuals targeted by the Nazis decades earlier.

But Itkin also augmented this kinship appeal with other simple, identificatory moves in his rhetoric. For example, he specifies that the two survivors he met were from Alaska to emphasize their American citizenship, even if their earlier suffering took place in Europe during World War II. Itkin also connects the suffering of earlier homosexuals and the experiences of contemporary lesbians and gays, noting at one point that the Nazis' efforts to make incarcerated homosexuals "normal again" were "not so different than what one experiences in the psychiatric hospitals today" (*SNM*, 4). And in a rather provocative comparison that flattens the homosexual and Jewish persecution under the Nazis in some uncomfortable ways, Itkin asserts:

> The spirit of the Warsaw Ghetto inspires us Gays to courage and determination so that no one will silence us. The spirit of the Warsaw Ghetto lives on in the spirit of the Stonewall [Riot], for those of us who have come out of the closets, and for those of us about to come out. . . . The kind of courage it took to stand up in the Warsaw Ghetto and offer resistance is the kind of courage it takes to be Gay in our society. As long as this same society remains silent about the psychic and physical violence which this society does to Gays every day, we Gays are all martyrs. (*SNM*, 3)

Itkin's conflation of the 1943 Warsaw Ghetto Uprising and everyday lesbian and gay life in 1970s America is overstated for dramatic effect. Nevertheless, it provides another powerful and direct linkage between the earlier generation and the lesbians and gays of the time.

While this connection is forged in all of Itkin's texts, it is done so most fervently in his poem "Visitors from the Holocaust." The poem's explicit aim is to encourage contemporary lesbians and gays to see themselves as kin to the Nazis' homosexual victims. This effort is evident in several compelling examples. In one powerful line, Itkin asserts that homosexual victims of the Nazis "wear your mask, we are your surrogates." Earlier in the poem, he suggests that both generations of homosexuals are merging and "becoming one entity." Itkin also reminds modern readers that "the oppressor is the same today as then." In a particularly visceral metaphor, Itkin claims that remembrance links like "lighting flashes from east to west," connecting homosexuals across time and geography amid the Cold War. Again, these are just a few examples from the poem. But each instance compounds Itkin's efforts to forge connections between homosexual generations (VH, 1).

The last way that Itkin builds identification between these generations is by employing intimate body metaphors in some of his rhetorical works. By this, I mean Itkin presents both past and present homosexuals as engaged in a conversation, in which their bodies interact intimately to signify a powerful affinity. While these metaphors crop up often in Itkin's texts, his poem is by far the most explicit in this regard. The poem begins by describing the arrival of two guests, "visitors I did not know." At first, they stay at a distance: "they neither talked nor ate but visibly watched us." But even from a distance, these visitors access the inner sanctums of contemporary lesbian and gay lives by observing them "at our barhopping and socializing, at our lovemaking and our interminable movement meetings." This distance quickly dissipates as the past and present engage in conversation. In this imagined dialogue, the voice of contemporary lesbians and gays gradually recedes, and the reader begins to hear the voices of the past, while a physical intimacy develops between both sides. For instance, "the guests . . . take our hands and make us trace each other's features on their pain-scarred faces." The poem suggests that the two bodies staring at each other face-to-face are engaged in a deep, deliberate talk (VH, 1).

As the guests continue their benediction, the embodied metaphors shift, drawing attention to comparisons between then and now, rooted in the homosexual body:

Remember each time you turn on lights at night,
that tattooed human skin stretched thin
gave our oppressors a more diffused glow.
Remember as you lie on cool white sheets
making love awake and sweating,
or as you go into your troubled sleep,
how gentle nuclear families kept their linen clean
with soap of human origin.

Here, the juxtaposition of past and present bodies makes it clear that, while each generation's experience is different, these homosexual bodies are shared. They are separated "by birth and time and place alone" (VH, 1).

As the guests finally turn to urging their homosexual contemporaries of the 1970s to resist, the visitor's voice suggests that nourishment is required—nourishment provided by will and effort, "which only the brave will feed" (VH, 1). Still unconvinced of their obligations, the guests from the past once again place their hands on the contemporary homosexuals of the 1970s: "Their hands probe, find, probe again then open wide our still unhealed and festering wound" (VH, 1). In this example, forgetting and inaction are depicted as an open sore, one that lesbians and gays in the 1970s can heal only through remembrance and action. Meanwhile, a few lines below, these intimate metaphors culminate in hushed words and direct eye contact: "staring into our eyes now denuded of lies" (VH, 1). In this final interaction, the guests urge the contemporary homosexuals not to "escape into sleep" but to recognize that "when you hear our screams, you must know that you do not merely dream" (VH, 1). With this, both the conversation and the poem end. But the reader cannot escape the call from the past—a connection rooted in symbols and words, now felt in the very bone.

Defiant Martyrs for Future Generations

On top of the identification built between the Nazis' homosexual victims of the 1930s and '40s and lesbians and gay men of the 1970s, Itkin adds to his memory rhetorics the characterization of these victims as defiant martyrs for homosexual rights. Martyrdom is a powerful rhetorical framework that highlights actions of past individuals to motivate others to act in the present. Of the three pieces of Itkin's memory discourse, this call to remember the

Nazis' victims as martyrs most closely resembles those highlighted in other chapters of this book. But by reframing these earlier homosexual men's past actions from a struggle *against* individual destruction to a fight *for* future homosexual generations, Itkin introduces a new and consequential dimension into remembrances of the Nazi persecution of homosexuals in US gay liberation discourses.

To advance this next step, Itkin needed to complete two corresponding rhetorical tasks: remembering these men as martyrs and characterizing that martyrdom as defiant in tone. Of the two, the rhetorical construction of martyrs in public memory discourses is more complicated because the Third Reich's homosexual victims do not fit the standard model of martyrdom. As victims of mass arrest and national persecution, these men were not "martyrs of choice" who gave themselves over willingly to death for a greater cause.[30] Rather, these men who suffered or died at the hands of the Nazis are better considered "accidental martyrs."[31] This rhetorical category of martyrdom is constructed from three interanimating features: vividly marking the dead and their embodied suffering, transmitting the dead from the earthly to the sacred or secular realm beyond, and building identification between the martyrs and a wider people or community.[32] Ironically, Itkin easily clears the bar in constructing the Nazis' homosexual victims as accidental martyrs. Itkin's discourses work to humanize these victims by emphasizing their embodied suffering and connecting them with the contemporary lesbian and gay community. As the next section of this chapter shows, Itkin's depiction of these homosexual victims as haunting present-day lesbians and gays also clearly frames them as transcending the terrestrial plain. Itkin also explicitly uses the language of "gay martyrs" throughout his texts. By referencing "our Gay martyrs" and the "martyrdom of Gay people," and asserting that "we do have our Gay martyrs," Itkin effectively calls the memory of these homosexuals as martyrs into being in *Silent No More* (*SNM*, 5, 2, 3). As such, between Itkin's various generic moves and his explicit invocations of the term, Itkin's memory rhetoric provides ample evidence to render these homosexuals martyrs in the making.

Itkin next proceeds to characterizing these "Gay martyrs" as having a defiant character. This step was essential because Itkin could not achieve his larger rhetorical aims by casting these men as martyrs alone. To motivate lesbians and gays of the 1970s to claim their gay power and *act* in the world on their predecessor's behalf, he needed to depict these homosexual victims specifically as "defiant martyrs," since the term *martyr* by itself tells us little about the manner of such a person's life or death. Accidental martyrs, in particular, need not have resisted their own deaths to be of rhetorical value for the community that survives them.[33] But Itkin both needed to and chose to remember the homosexual victims of the Third Reich as defiant martyrs who went down fighting. For in the early 1970s, at the dawn of a newly radical and confrontational Gay Liberation Movement, the Nazis' homosexual victims needed to be remembered not just for their suffering and death, but also enacting their own power in the process if they were to offer any rhetorical benefit.

Itkin again turns to specifics instances and compelling metaphors—some more dubious than others—to tell modern readers that these earlier homosexual martyrs died militantly and boldly. He achieves much of this by simply using defiant language to refer to these homosexuals in his various texts. In *Silent No More*, Itkin characterizes homosexuals in the camps as full of "defiance and resistance" (*SNM*, 4). He also uses the adjective *defiant* to describe these same homosexuals in "Visitors from the Holocaust" (VH, 1). Elsewhere in his poem, Itkin refers to homosexuals' toil in the camps as "Promethean," suggesting they stole proverbial fire from the gods in an act of defiance in service of others (VH, 1). And Itkin borrows from the powerful words of the Reverend Jo McVay, when she states we must remember these victims "with love for them and for their sacrifice for us . . . with gratitude for the inspiration and power they have given us" (*SNM*, 2). Through these and similar examples, Itkin directly names these earlier homosexuals as militant martyrs for his contemporary audiences, making the connection unmistakable.

But Itkin also bestowed a defiant character on the Nazis' homosexual victims in other ways. Some of his techniques are understated, like when he subtly refers to earlier memories of the "valiant" Nazi captain Ernst Roehm's supposed resistance to the Nazis by demanding that readers "Remember the Night of the Long Knives!" (VH, 1). But Itkin is rarely restrained, preferring instead strong and explicit declarations of earlier homosexuals' militant bona fides. Among these, Itkin argues that surviving day-to-day in the concentration camps was an act of defiance. In one specific example, Itkin talks about how homosexuals "were given the heaviest labor" in the camps, yet many were able to "stand up to the hardest work," even as most would eventually succumb to death (*SNM*, 4). Itkin also highlighted homosexual survival as resistance in a long discussion of "bluffing" in the camps. By "bluffing," Itkin meant tricking "the camp directorates into thinking they [i.e., homosexuals] had been 'cured' . . . that they had nothing in common with those 'real homosexuals'" (*SNM*, 4). In Itkin's telling, such deception came naturally to the "street-wise hustlers," who, as repeat offenders of homosexual crimes, were likely to be among the first to be imprisoned. Itkin argues that "bluffing clients had been a necessary part of the profession . . . and they were able to apply this earlier 'on-the-job training'" in the camps (*SNM*, 4). To support this view, Itkin suggests that Hoess, who relates in his memoirs how he successfully altered homosexual behavior through work, sent these homosexuals "back into the world" (*SNM*, 4). But where Hoess saw behavioral modification, Itkin saw another example of homosexual defiance.

Itkin's further examples for remembering homosexuals as defiant martyrs relied on describing the character of these interned individuals. As a group, Itkin claims homosexual personalities in the camps varied widely, including "gays" who were arrested because they were out of the closet, "were part of the Early Homophile Movement; because they were 'obvious'; because they were known by police informers; or because they were . . . promiscuous Gays or *strichjugen* hustlers" (*SNM*, 4). The camps also included "hidden Gays in the ranks of non-Gay groups," but Itkin clearly preferred to emphasize the former because, in his telling, this group sowed seeds of resistance in the early homophile community. To this point, Itkin describes how Hoess "bitterly complain[ed]" about these "blatant and upfront Gays" and their "open defiance and resistance" (*SNM*, 4). Itkin quoted Hoess as saying, "It was often not easy to drive them to the gas chambers" (*SNM*, 4). Itkin's assertions here are probably overstated; yet the image of defiant homosexuals who resisted to the end is exactly what he wanted to convey to his contemporary lesbian and gay audience. Itkin even emphasized this point with a modern analogy, noting that just as in "the Stonewall Rebellion, in the concentration camps it was not the respectable, but the upfront and even outrageous Gays who provided the resistance!" (*SNM*, 4).

Itkin's characterizations of defiant homosexual martyrs interned in Nazi concentration camps reach a stirring crescendo in "Visitors from the Holocaust." Like Itkin's other texts, the poem plays up themes of resistance, defiance, and martyrdom. But given literal poetic license, Itkin makes the point even more stridently in his poem that these homosexuals should be remembered as insolent in the face of Nazi atrocities:

remember those who defied the crematories,
who in the last few seconds of life raised a clenched fist
and like a defiant giant rising from its slumber

screamed out to the murderers:
"Your structures yet will choke to death on our smoke!"
Remember them: remember all of us! (VH, 1)

The rhetoric exemplified in the stirring scene excerpted above is only further enhanced by its captivating visuals and metaphors of resistance. The image of the "clenched fist," for example, was a well-known representation of defiance in several 1970s American social movements and clearly conveyed to the audience how to make sense of this story. Likewise, the metaphor of the "slumber[ing]" giant suggests not only waking up but a reckoning yet to come. And the excerpt's penultimate line succinctly sums up the idea that homosexual bodies might clog the Nazi killing machine, even in death, in an eloquent and tragic turn of phrase. Itkin's imagining of a group of homosexuals' final moments before entering the gas chambers is certainly highly dramatized in the poem. His aim, though, is not to relate facts but to inspire gay power through a fervent spirit of resilience. In that regard, the passage depicts a highly effective homosexual epideictic of defiant martyrdom.

Unquestionably, Itkin's rhetorical portrayal of defiant homosexual martyrs in the camps must be taken with a grain of salt. Given the time in which he was writing and his own lived experience, he simply did not have sufficient facts to articulate such a robust visualization of the Nazis' homosexual victims without overstepping the bounds of evidence and rational circumspection. And yet each of the examples highlighted helped Itkin advance his tripartite remembrance strategy—this particular piece being particularly important in offering his lesbian and gay audience of the 1970s a new image of their homosexual forebears, one that was starkly different from those encountered before.

Gay Hauntings

The final step of Itkin's rhetorical appeal lies in portraying the hauntological connections that linked the Nazis' homosexual victims with American lesbians and gays of the 1970s. Without this essential step, Itkin's rhetoric of fellowship is merely celebratory and his recognition of homosexual victims of the Third Reich's martyrdom simply laudable. But by calling forth ghosts into this same memory rhetoric, Itkin uses the spectral to obligate present-day lesbians and gays to their martyred homosexual "brothers and sisters" of the past (QWB, 17). As such, Itkin's invitation to his readers of the 1970s to be haunted by homosexuals of the Nazi era is necessary for driving the modern community to act for gay power.

Itkin's intention to cast contemporary lesbians and gays as haunted by their homosexual predecessors is undoubted in "Visitors from the Holocaust," which depicts these earlier homosexual dead not as ghostlike but as *actual* ghosts. However, more nuanced hauntological themes also permeate his entire rhetorical corpus on the subject. In Itkin's other works, the visitations by aggrieved homosexuals of the past are more "spectral" than figural, in the manner of Carla Freccero's "attentiveness" to the past."[34] For example, Itkin relies extensively on ventriloquizing the Nazis' homosexual victims, allowing them to make their demands through him as their vessel. A notable instance of this ventriloquizing rhetoric appears in *Gay Sunshine*, when Itkin adopts the persona of his two visiting survivors and asks readers their titular "question written in blood" (QWB, 17). Similarly, *Silent No More* is almost entirely devoted to (re)stating facts about the Nazi oppression of homosexuals that survivors themselves would have shared were they "free to speak out about genocide" rather than "fearful of further bigotry" (*SNM*, 5). *Silent No More* is also haunted by remnants—stray stories and admissions about the Nazi persecution of homosexuals found in the writings of Third Reich leaders that had previously been unshared or unpublicized. The constant return of these homosexual ghosts, and their reemergent trauma in the guise of fascism's perpetually threatened reoccurrence, likewise raises the hauntological in these essays where ghosts, per se, do not appear.

But "Visitors from the Holocaust" is the rhetor's most forceful expression of these memories' hauntological potential. The poem's title, describing 1970s lesbians and gays being "visited" by their homosexual forebears, alludes to the point. Readers might not find it clear at first because Itkin clearly establishes in *Gay Sunshine* and *Silent No More* that he has, in fact, been visited by two living survivors of Nazi persecution. Yet the "visitors" whom readers might mistake as living homosexuals at first are quickly revealed in the poem to be of a strangely spectral sort. Over several lines, Itkin described how the visitors "came early, and stayed with us," "neither talked nor ate," and "invisibly watched us at our barhopping and socializing, at our lovemaking and interminable movement meetings" (VH, 1). That a haunting was afoot is also clarified in the poem as time becomes nonlinear—or, as Derrida and Freccero say via *Hamlet*, "out of joint."[35] This fact is demonstrated in a back-and-forth between the poem's narrator and the ghosts:

The visitors paused—and in that pause, I cried:
"But I was not there! I was not there!"
"You knew and you know now," was their reply:
"and in that knowing you did not stop it." (VH, 1)

The ghostly visitors reject chronological time and its attendant claim that contemporary lesbians or gay men can evade responsibility for the past. Rather, the ghosts assert that past and present coexist, and our "knowing" transcends them both. In doing so, the poem makes plain to readers that these visitors are not illusory—and these spectral forces have arrived to drive present-day lesbians and gays to action.

To empower these ghosts to demand action from their contemporary peers requires further rhetorical work. Itkin thus turns to two related, animating rhetorical techniques to connect this haunting with calls for gay power. One is the rhetorical power of watching. Scholars have long recognized that being or feeling watched by others is a powerful driver of action.[36] Whether choosing to do or not to do something, our actions in response to being watched are largely dictated by the configuration of the procedures of being observed by others. While we imagine these procedures in modern life through closed circuit television, surveillance, or the panopticon, ghosts have for centuries been considered a powerful technology of watching that shaped people's actions. Indeed, given ghosts' figurations as invisible, omnipresent, and sometimes omniscient, they can be highly effective drivers of change in human behavior. For these reasons, Itkin's invitation to lesbians and gays of the 1970s to be haunted by watchful homosexual ghosts of the Third Reich in his memory rhetorics is a powerful motivator. These "visitors from the Holocaust" create an ethical imperative among his audience that they must seek gay power or fail this trial of justice. This dynamic is marked often in Itkin's texts, including by simply alerting readers that these homosexual visitors "watched us" in the present (VH, 1). Later in the poem, Itkin asserts that these ghosts "star[e] into our eyes now denuded of lies" (VH, 1). Similarly, Itkin declares metaphorically that "The witness who fails to halt the murder is never freed from the crime—it must stay there in consciousness until death relieves" (VH, 1). In other words, Itkin asserts that contemporary lesbians and gays' haunting continues unabated. Should they wish to free themselves—and to free their ghostly kin—they must act in their name. Otherwise, as Itkin declares, "those who were absent can never escape the pleas and agonies of all!" (VH, 1).

The other way Itkin uses these ghostly homosexual visitors as an impetus to act is through a series of obligating metaphors in his memory discourse. These vary widely in subject, but they are united in enhancing the haunting ghosts' demands for action. One of the most powerful considers modern lesbian and gay activists as debtors to their homosexual predecessors. Itkin uses this metaphor in his poem remembering homosexual victims of the Nazi regime when he argues that "all must pay the cost of each one lost" (VH, 1). He describes how every modern lesbian and gay has accrued a "cost" that must be remitted for each homosexual who suffered at the hands of the Nazis. Itkin reiterates this point a few lines below, stating that "humanity's beingness" will never be "free of debt, until you bring our people's liberation" (VH, 1). The connection in this line is plain: "you"—the reader—are the debtor, and the "liberation" of modern lesbians and gays is the price to be paid. Seeds are another obligating metaphor in Itkin's texts. The persecution by the Nazis planted a seed in the past that today's generations are obligated to tend, reap, or uproot. Itkin argues that earlier homosexual deeds in the camps were sown like seeds, and that "brave" lesbians and gays today must nourish themselves on them, as captured by the following line: "gay deeds now seeds, on which only the brave will feed" (VH, 1). In a different vein, Itkin uses the seed metaphor later to argue that "Auschwitz and Dachau and Buchenwald are ever within us, their seeds sown in patriarchy" (VH, 1). Rather than representing a potential for good, seeds are the persecution itself, rooted in patriarchy, which the current generation must rip out.

A final obligating metaphor featured prominently in Itkin's discourses revolves around sleep. He claims that lesbians and gays of the 1970s must "awake" from a slumber of forgetfulness and complacency. Here, Itkin cautions contemporary homosexuals against going "into your troubled sleep" and urges them, like earlier homosexuals in the camps, to become "giant[s] rising from slumber" (VH, 1). Similarly, he implores today's activists "do not escape into sleep" and "know that you do not merely dream." Instead, he urges, "Awake and sing . . . *Awake for our freedom!*" (VH, 1). Each of these metaphors instills a sense of a duty in 1970s lesbians and gays to act for gay freedom.

In his final rhetorical act, Itkin leaves readers with a question: What do these homosexual ghosts of the past want? If his peroration aims to drive gay power, what actions do Itkin's remembrances demand of contemporary lesbians and gays? This question is not rhetorical, because Itkin provides in response a veritable list of actions—specifics for any and all homosexuals to take in the moment. The most concrete of these tasks is to demand that homosexual victims be remembered in the official memory of the Holocaust, particularly the plaques and memorials installed at the various concentration camp sites. Itkin frames this demand as an act of "symbolic 'retribution,'" one that is needed "outside the gates of the infamous death camp, Dachau" (QWB, 17), and all other "stone monuments outside the camps of death" that "do not remember the Gay victims with the others" (VH, 1). In fighting for these memories, he argues that contemporary lesbians and gays can "stand up and be counted!" (*SNM*, 5). Itkin also demands that lesbians and gays of the 1970s become educated about their past more broadly. He asserts that "there's a widespread ignorance" (*SNM*, 2) about homosexuals in the past and that "the stories of our unknown history" must now "be discovered by a new Gay people" (VH, 1), including by "scholars doing research on the number of Gays the Nazis killed" (*SNM*, 3). This historical knowledge is important, for it can give peace to the thousands of homosexuals who suffered or died under the Third Reich and ensure that something similar never happens again. For Itkin, learning the "legacy" of this earlier persecution matters; it "still may save you all" (VH, 1). He also claims these lessons learned demand that modern lesbians and gays champion the safety and security of others. This includes safeguarding other homosexuals: "Let every Gay life be [an] *unyielding shield* for every other!" (VH, 1). But remembering the Nazi persecution of homosexuals also demands acting to prevent other minoritized communities from facing the same fate. In this spirit, Itkin argues that lesbians and gays must "Seek out the outcast and the despised and the rejected . . . those who are weak and suffering and with them build a common bond of strength" (VH, 1). Only in this way, Itkin believed, could lesbians and gays "*prevent the torment of the innocent!*" (VH, 1).

But perhaps most pointedly, Itkin argues that the essential way his lesbian and gay audience of the 1970s can repay its debt is to act politically. This activity could take many forms. At some moments in his text, Itkin characterizes a modern lesbian and gay politics as emulating the tone of their homosexual forebears by employing calls to "*revolt! defy and dignify!*" or to "*Resist! Defy!*" (VH, 1). Elsewhere, Itkin's texts argue that this new politics requires that his audience become "angry" (*SNM*, 2) and "forsake your fears!" (VH, 1). Such work requires putting contemporary lesbian and gay bodies on the line. Itkin says that lesbians and gays of the 1970s can't "shrink back from the reality of Gay oppression," "pretend it doesn't happen," or "leave the fight for liberation to others" (*SNM*, 2). Instead, lesbians and gays themselves must act to "expose . . . this genocidal oppression of our Gay people" by showing "total resistance to Nazism regardless of what guise it wears" (*SNM*, 5). Most pointedly of all, Itkin claims that modern lesbians and gays owe their progenitors a full commitment to "bring our people's liberation" or "bring Gay Freedom" (VH, 1). In the absence of that, Itkin concludes that earlier generations "will have died in vain and your lives will be lived in vain" (VH, 1). In sum, it is only through seeking gay power that the modern US Gay Liberation Movement could "redeem ourselves" for the suffering inflicted on our homosexual forebears (*SNM*, 5).

By the end of 1977, over a series of independent but thematically connected texts, Itkin advanced a radically different way of remembering the homosexuals persecuted by the Nazi regime. In framing them as brothers and sisters, extolling their acts of defiant martyrdom, and demanding action on their behalf by ghostly visitation, Itkin connected these long-suffering homosexuals to new calls for gay power in the 1970s United States. In doing so, Itkin helped move the lesbian and gay movement to imagine new ways of using the past for contemporary political struggle.

Conclusion

Itkin's tripartite memory rhetoric commemorating the Nazis' homosexual victims emerged less than four decades after the Third Reich had claimed its first victims. Yet this discourse marked a significant shift in how lesbian and gay Americans saw themselves in relation to the persecution previously. While some differences between Itkin's remembrances and those performed by Gerber, early homosexual publications, or gay pulps seem obvious, others are more nuanced. Overall, Itkin's commemorations, spanning multiple genres and different lesbian and gay audiences in a sustained, multiyear campaign, wrought very different outcomes, signaling consequential shifts from what came before.

From a wider perspective, Itkin's turn to memory writ large as a tool of rhetorical action in the early 1970s was not particularly different from what we have seen in other chapters of this book. But Itkin's rationale for placing faith in memory reflects a uniquely personal approach. As shown in the next chapter, the shift to a post-Stonewall politics did not necessitate a *return to queer memory*; in fact, powerful forces sought to displace memory as a meaningful resource for the suasory work of the movement in the 1970s.[37] But Itkin in particular argued that memory was an essential tool for the movement's next phase, in ways notably different from his predecessors. Unlike Gerber's use of personal and recent memory, the homosexual press's reliance on recent historical allusion, or the pulps' "foundling memory," in Itkin, we see a turn toward memory that is deeply ensconced for one powerful reason: Itkin believed that a new lesbian and gay community could not succeed without knowing its past. He says repeatedly that lesbians and gays must know their history if they are to triumph. Itkin claimed that remembering the Nazi persecution necessitated a greater commitment to lesbian and gay history. This belief is underscored in Itkin's worldview—one later shared by prominent historians and scholars alike—that lesbian and gay people not only had a past (and something worth remembering), but that an anti-homosexual society was actively working to take it away from them. As such, remembering the lesbian and gay past became an act of gay power, which Itkin regarded as essential for two reasons. On the one hand, Itkin believed that the Nazi persecution was not a one-off; rather, homosexuals of the 1970s were always on the cusp of yet again being subjected to this level of danger. On the other hand, Itkin firmly believed the persecution should be remembered as a trial, one that homosexuals survived through defiance, martyrdom, and action—and that such values could save us in the future. But these values at the core of the new gay liberation did not appear out of nowhere. Instead, the lesbian and gay past reveals that they were part of a tradition of resistance. To maintain that tradition and infuse the current struggle with greater meaning, a return to memory was essential. And Itkin found no part of the past more informative about gay power than the Nazi persecution of homosexuals.

As a particular expression of how we should remember such Nazi oppression, Itkin's rhetorical corpus is marked by significant evolutions as well. Perhaps the most noticeable shift in Itkin's remembrances of the Nazi persecution of homosexuals is the adoption of an aggressive, radical, and political tone, reflecting the US Gay Liberation Movement after Stonewall. While this movement and its posture did not begin with the Stonewall Riots, the event focused and redirected much of the energy for subsequent gay liberation, presenting a very different appearance from some of its predecessors. Rejecting a quiet, patriotic, assimilationist approach, gay liberation embraced pride, publicity, and *power*—and if the Nazi persecution of homosexuals was to factor into that movement, its memory would need to align with these values. Such a realignment was not preordained. Frankly, many young lesbian and gay activists saw little value in decades-old stories of the community's victimization, an idea explored in the next chapter. But Itkin recognized the raw rhetorical firepower in remembering the Nazi persecution for this next phase of the wider lesbian and gay cause. As such, he claimed it as a touch-stone memory of the movement almost immediately after Stonewall, refor-matted it with the defiant ethos of gay liberation, and injected these memories in his voluminous rhetorics. In this way, both Itkin's rhetorical acumen and his assessment of the post-Stonewall rhetorical situation were essential fac-tors in shifting the memory of the persecution into potent calls for action.

Alongside this shift in tenor, Itkin's remembrances of the Nazi persecution of homosexuals also embraced a degree of specificity, depth, and detail that earlier iterations of these memories lacked. As explored above, Itkin's memory rhetoric benefited significantly from two factors in this regard: more details published in English about the persecution and the chance to speak with two homosexual survivors of the Nazi persecution. Both occurrences became founts of rhetorical invention, permitting Itkin's memories to feature greater elaboration of how homosexuals suffered in the camps, resulting in longer and deeper rhetorical texts on the subject than almost any that came before. By a count of words and examples, Itkin's memory works stand as some of the most extensive remembrances on this subject in English in the 1970s, provid-ing him with powerful rhetorical tools, like vivid description and identifica-tion, that were unavailable to earlier rhetors. Nonetheless, Itkin's breadth of evidence in his collected accounts did not mean his claims could always be substantiated. Twenty-first-century readers of Itkin's texts should be mind-ful that many so-called facts he deployed have been discounted, adjusted, or proven inaccurate by more recent scholarly investigation. That being said, Itkin's accounting of the Nazi persecution of homosexuals drew significant power from its ability to avoid the generalities, passing references, or short retorts common to earlier invocations of this past. With some significant exceptions that greatly reduced these memories' breadth for rhetorical effect, this turn toward greater detail and consideration would only accelerate over the next few decades, as LGBTQ+ people continued to remember the Nazis' systematic targeting of homosexuals.

Another notable shift in Itkin's remembrances of the Nazi persecution of homosexuals was his reliance on a deeply spiritual sensibility to honor and commemorate what he saw as the community's martyred dead. From the start of this book, no hint of spirituality has been present in American homosexuals' remembrances of these atrocities. In fact, despite these mem-ories being situated in spiritually familiar zones like gravesides, obituaries, and epideictic speeches, atheism—introduced by Gerber—has been more likely to frame the fallen homosexuals than any appeal to faith, religion, or God. But the Reverend Mikhail Itkin offered, if not an explicit endorsement, at least a broader framework for audiences to remember the Nazis' homosexual victims through a spiritual lens. In particular, Itkin's casting of these men as "defiant martyrs" drew heavily on the idea that homosexual souls lived on after their bodies were decimated by the Nazis; in communing with them at the boundary between life and death, contemporary lesbians and gays might discover new ways to make meaning of this past and gird one another for future action. In addition, Itkin used his own complex faith and spiritual position to frame the Nazi persecution of homosexuals as a moral outrage. While the Nazi campaign of oppression certainly was morally repugnant, previous homosexual activists rarely framed it as such, instead relying on condemnations rooted in capitalistic failings, inequitable systems of justice, and the dangers of scientific excesses. But Itkin saw faith as a tool for gay power and the struggle against fascism as a moral crusade. In this way, Itkin's view reflected a brief US lesbian and gay spiritual boom in the 1970s, a faith-based gay liberation theology movement that would remain a minority view within the community and soon be tested by the rise of the Religious Right. Nonetheless, Itkin's remembrances of these homosexual victims of the Nazis, framed through powerful appeals to spiritual fellowship, marked a notable departure from past rhetorics, one not repeated to the same extent thereafter.

Itkin's memory work is also remarkable for its explicit invitation to lesbians and other women-loving-women to be embraced by the tragic events that befell mostly male homosexuals in Germany three decades earlier. Before the late 1970s, lesbians, bisexual women, and other women in the movement appeared to have done little with the memories of the Nazi persecution of homosexuals in the rhetorical arena. Above, I proposed that much of this refusal may be linked to the explicit ways men were persecuted by the Nazis; the different, less direct, and often ignored ways that the Third Reich targeted women who desired women; and the large divides within the male and female iterations of the US homosexual community for much of the twentieth century. Given these challenges, Itkin's explicit invitation to homosexual women to see themselves as part of a lesbian and gay community, and therefore implicated in this European persecution years earlier, is notable. Itkin does this work primarily through the simple and consequential phrase *gay sisters and brothers*, which reflects his ministry that served people of all genders (VH, 1). It is similarly marked by Itkin's quoting and citing of women movement leaders in his texts, particularly those who spoke to the persecution as affecting both homosexual men and women, then and now. Even so, it is hard to see Itkin's invitation as anything other than strained, lacking as it does in any meaningful reference to the thousands of women persecuted by the Nazis for desiring other women, just not under Paragraph 175.[38] These women's experiences in camps like Ravensbrück have long been contested, but they cannot be ignored. Still, Itkin's efforts to evolve our memories of the Nazi persecution of homosexuals both to recognize and consider the experiences of lesbians and other women portends both shifts that emerged in the 1980s about these pasts and a wider debate within the community over how gay men and lesbians would, or would not, matter to one another in the emergent gay liberation politics that followed.

Similarly, Itkin's remembrances of the Third Reich's homosexual victims are noticeably rife with calls for a coalitional politics, which was lacking in earlier memory rhetorics. While by the 1970s, homosexual movements in the United States had long marshaled stories of the Nazis' homosexual victims in their own struggles, Itkin's commemorations of these victims represent one of the first times these memories are used to link the cause of gay power and freedom to something bigger. As we have discussed, earlier rhetorics of these victims have invoked shared struggles experienced by Jews, people of color, atheists, and Communists. But in most of those cases, these invocations were comparative political allusions that required no common cause. Itkin, by contrast, draws on both his ministry and his sophisticated understanding of social justice to see the struggle for gay freedom indelibly interlocked with those of similarly oppressed peoples. In his texts, he repeatedly argued that remembering the Nazi persecution of homosexuals obligated lesbians and gays to free others—such as people experiencing homelessness, sex workers, young people, and people of color—from the "*torment of the innocent*" (VH, 1). Nor was this call performative; rather, Itkin both practiced and advocated for coordination, support, and an integrated coalitional politics between the Gay Liberation Movement and other communities—an idea that was pursued with promise during the 1970s but continues to challenge LGBTQ+ movements and organizations today. Nonetheless, Itkin's recognition of the power of interanimating political action is a poignant legacy of the Nazi persecution of homosexuals, which itself implicated numerous categories of people the Nazis considered dangerous, difficult, or worthy of destruction.

Despite these unique contributions in Itkin's memory rhetoric, not all his efforts served the lesbian and gay community's long-term interests. In particular, Itkin's memories likely played an important role in moving the community's attention away from earlier, broader memories of the persecution to an almost exclusive focus on homosexual experiences in the concentration camps. To be fair, Itkin did not start this shift. Such a move was already at work in the gay Nazi-exploitation pulps of the late 1960s and was less extensively invoked in scattered memories from the 1940s and '50s. Nor was Itkin alone in making this shift in the 1970s: German homosexual activists were making similar moves on the continent, and lesbian and gay scholars and activists following Itkin in the United States would do much the same. Such shifts made sense rhetorically. By the 1970s, the memory of the Holocaust—particularly the Jewish experience of the concentration camps—had gained significant influence in the American public imagination. As such, linking homosexual suffering to Jewish suffering under the guise of the Third Reich proved a tantalizing rhetorical possibility for a movement seeking any paths to recognition it could find. But the homosexual experience of the Nazi regime often differed greatly from that of the Jews; moreover, individuals embroiled in the homosexual persecution outside the camps far outnumbered those who suffered within them. As a result, remembering the Nazi mistreatment of homosexuals as primarily the story of the pink triangles significantly diminished the lesbian and gay memoryscapes after Stonewall, with Itkin playing a key role.

While Itkin's 1970 essay in *Gay Sunshine* marked an important shift in the memory rhetorics surrounding the homosexual victims of the Nazi regime in the post-Stonewall era, it would not occupy this space for long. The 1970s saw multiple important and diverse remembrances of these victims emerge by the middle of the decade. This period marks the moment when scholars and activists supposedly rediscovered the Nazis' anti-homosexual past. This book explicitly contests this characterization, demonstrating that US homophile, homosexual, and lesbian and gay communities had taken up these memories in significant ways from almost the moment the persecution began. Nonetheless, the 1970s saw a shift in both *how* and *who* remembered the Nazis' homosexual victims: lesbians and gays, for the first time in a sustained way, began to share memories of these pasts *outside* the community to serve their rhetorical aims. Two publications would be essential in this shift: John Lauritsen and David Thorstad's 1973 pamphlet *The Early Homosexual Rights Movement, 1864–1935* and historian James Steakley's series of articles on the "Gay Movement in Germany" in the influential gay magazine *Body Politic*. Both works were soon developed into book-length projects, each garnering significant interest within the US lesbian and gay community and further expanding the number of lesbians and gays who knew of and could remember these victims. Yet what really set these texts apart was how quickly they contributed to circulating the Nazis' crimes against homosexuals to heterosexual audiences. By the middle of the 1970s, post-Stonewall political organizers across the nation would seize on these events to argue for gay liberation. David Thorstad perhaps most famously did this when he was elected president of the New York Chapter of the Gay Activist Alliance in 1974. In that role, Thorstad leaned heavily into the pink triangle—the symbol worn by homosexuals in some Nazi concentration camps—as a symbol of gay persecution in the 1970s. From this point on, US remembrances of the Nazi persecution of homosexuals saw a dramatic increase in both the quantity and variety of expressions, a trend that would continue well into the HIV/AIDS era.

But *inside* the US lesbian and gay community, memories of the Nazi persecution continued to be put to different purposes—and in this regard, Itkin's remembrances were a powerful and influential framing for much of the 1970s. However, by decade's end, invocations of this persecution from within the lesbian and gay community took on a radically different and significantly darker interpretation—one that would forever alter its ability to understand these men as empathetic, let alone inspirational victims.

Chapter 5

Lambs to the Slaughter

Harvey Milk, Memories of Shame, and the
Myth of Homosexual Passivity, 1977–1979

A little more than a decade after the end of the Nazi regime, *Mattachine Review*
published a peculiar two-page essay titled "The Mutiny" by Classen Von Neudegg.[1] What made the essay peculiar was not how it detailed the Nazis' execution of three homosexuals in an unnamed concentration camp—a subject
already well circulated in US homosexual publications. Neither was *Mattachine Review*'s decision to republish "The Mutiny" after it first appeared in a
West German homosexual publication noteworthy. Indeed, American homosexual publications regularly relied on clipping and repurposing other publications at the time.[2] Nor was the piece odd for its foreign genesis. By 1957, both
Mattachine Review and ONE circulated homosexual news from abroad as a key
part of their editorial strategies. What made the essay's appearance in *Mattachine Review* puzzling was that it represented the Nazis' homosexual victims
in a way that differed sharply from any other instance in the United States,
both before and for the next two decades. For "The Mutiny" argued that the
homosexual victims of the Nazi regime should best be remembered as pow-
erless and ineffectual dupes—homosexual men led like lambs to the slaughter.

The excerpted essay begins with an interned homosexual man and his
confined compatriots roused from their slumber by a disturbing clanging.
Gathered in the courtyard before the completed gallows soon thereafter, the
jarred men conjecture about the coming execution. Soon, Nazi guards lead
three docile young prisoners, their clothing emblazoned with the word *homo*,
into the courtyard. Readers are told that these men were caught by their Nazi
oppressors "salvag[ing] a moment of brotherhood, of love." The three men
"march[ed] in locked step" to their doom on the platform, while the "hangman

followed at leisure." There, the men "stood quietly, staring, not seeing," each resembling the others with "haggard faces and stooped bodies." Before a gathered audience of Nazi guards and prisoners, the men are severely beaten, then summarily hanged. The author notes that the men "died quietly, indifferently, too broken to know death." Afterward, the rest of the homosexual prisoners shuffle back to their barracks, "but as though deeply ashamed, neither speaking nor looking one another in the face."[3] The excerpt concludes there, leaving its homosexual readers with the strong suggestion that the Nazis' homosexual victims—executed and audience alike—were meek, compliant, and shameful figures, pitiful people whose only value to the modern US movement was as a cautionary tale.

In this regard, "The Mutiny" was a significant outlier in American remembrances of homosexuals victimized by the Nazis.[4] As this book demonstrates, these same men were remembered in diverse ways between 1934 and 1981. In nearly every case, these homosexual victims were shown as actively resisting, fighting, or surviving against the Nazi machinery. But by the mid-1970s, a noticeable change developed. From that point forward, the previously unusual remembrance of passive homosexual victims dying without a fight in Nazi concentration camps seen in "The Mutiny" became commonplace in US lesbian and gay discourses. Despite Itkin's multiyear campaign to remember these men as defiant martyrs who advanced the cause of lesbian and gay rights in the years immediately after Stonewall, by the end of the 1970s, the homosexuals who suffered and died under the Third Reich were discredited by contemporary US movement leaders.

These starkly different memory rhetorics reflected a changed political landscape for US homosexuals in the years following the 1969 Stonewall Riots. Subsequent to Stonewall, a newly assertive US Gay Liberation Movement had propelled itself into the public sphere and, by moving "out of the closets and into the streets," won a number of high-profile, if relatively limited, victories across the nation.[5] These triumphs demonstrated the utility of gay power and gay politics, and the potential for future lesbian and gay victories seemed boundless. But by 1977, the movement had been laid low, and backlash was everywhere. That year, a newly organized and highly aggressive, religiously inspired political movement in the United States actively worked not only to oppose lesbian and gay rights, but to roll back whatever minor victories had already been achieved. Epitomized in the figure of Anita Bryant, the former beauty queen and orange juice pitchwoman who inaugurated some of the earliest of these antigay attacks in Miami-Dade County, Florida, this movement was a jarring rejoinder to gay liberation that presaged the fully formed Religious Right that arrived with Ronald Reagan's election to the presidency in 1980. With strident anti-homosexual rhetoric and a deeply engaged network of thousands of Christian and conservative Americans at their beck and call, these antigay forces toppled lesbian and gay rights protections in state after state, sending a chill down the spines of every homosexual in the nation.[6]

In the wake of this onslaught, US lesbian and gay activists called for the widest community action since Stonewall. But previous mobilization efforts had benefited from driving people toward positive change with the wind at their backs. This new effort to unite a community under direct and personal threat was different and would require something more. That something more, as we will see, was yet another radical re-remembering of the Nazi persecution of homosexuals. Like previous memories, this new remembrance asserted that the Nazi repression was a shameful era of the lesbian and gay past. But it differed significantly by placing the blame for this shame on the victims themselves. In short, this new phase of memory asserted that these homosexual victims of the past should be repudiated in the here and now to inspire a new wave of lesbian and gay political action.

Within months, denouncements of the Nazis' homosexual victims were commonplace in lesbian and gay political rhetoric across the nation. The constraints of this chapter prevent a full accounting of all the various iterations of these remembrances. But while each of these rhetorics were inflected with their own variegated takes on this repudiation, most focused explicitly on the highly circumscribed memory of homosexuals' supposed failure to rebel or take up arms when interned in the concentration camps. As such, we can focus on one of the earliest—and certainly most influential—of these articulations, a framing that serves as a representative anecdote for this wider memory rhetoric and also dramatically shaped how thousands of other lesbians and gays in the decades to follow would recall their persecuted forebears.

That particular remembrance was coined by San Francisco Supervisor Harvey Milk, most prominently in his famous Gay Freedom Day speech in June 1978. In his remarks and other affiliated discourses, Milk indicted German homosexuals of the 1930s and '40s for refusing to fight back, resist, or save themselves while standing face-to-face with the horrors of the Nazi concentration camps. Milk drew on the long, idiomatic history of the phrase *lambs to the slaughter* and conflated the Jewish and homosexual experiences of Nazi persecution to rhetorically reinvent these events and stir lesbian and gay mobilization. By doing so, Milk—one of the most prominent gay male leaders in the nation and a key figure in the movement to defeat the Briggs Initiative in California in 1978—renounced the homosexual past in hopes of forging a more active and confrontational lesbian and gay community capable of withstanding the coming onslaught of the US Religious Right. Through a close reading of Milk's words and remembrances, this chapter explores this new memory rhetoric and considers its significant impact on the memory of the Nazi persecution of homosexuals. As we will see below, this new approach forever changed how the lesbian and gay community remembered the Nazis' homosexual victims.

Bryant, Briggs, Milk, and Prop 6

The shifting political fortunes of lesbian and gay rights were among the most important drivers of this change in how American lesbians and gays remembered the Nazis' homosexual victims in the late 1970s. While no single incident fully explains this change, the precipitating event may have been the vote in Florida to repeal the Miami-Dade County gay rights ordinance on June 7, 1977. The referendum, which passed with 69 percent in favor and 31 percent opposed, rescinded a countywide law protecting individuals from discrimination based on sexual preference. The law was not the first of its kind, but the ferocity of opposition it spawned among a coalition of religious groups was heretofore unseen.[7]

The public face of the repeal effort, Anita Bryant—an ambitious entertainer, spokeswoman, and conservative Christian—became a highly effective advocate against the measure. With the support of a nationwide network of religious groups that would later become the Moral Majority, Bryant formed the political coalition Save Our Children and launched a smear campaign against homosexuals, framing them as "sick perverts, child molesters, and seducers of the innocent" to win the ordinance's repeal.[8] The scale and fierceness of Bryant's victory shocked lesbian and gay advocates but further galvanized their opponents. Taking Miami-Dade as inspiration, intolerant religious leaders used vicious antigay rhetorics and popular referendums to overturn similar lesbian and gay rights laws in Wichita, Kansas; Saint Paul, Minnesota; and Eugene, Oregon, within a matter of months. Not to be outdone, California State Senator John Briggs proposed a ballot initiative for the 1978 election to further suppress the rights of lesbians and gays in his home state. Dubbed the Briggs Initiative, Proposition 6 targeted lesbians and gays in public schools and called for the firing of teachers found to engage in "public homosexual activity" or approve of "public homosexual conduct."[9] All these events set the stage for a strong shift in how Americans came to remember the Nazis' homosexual victims.

Harvey Milk was key to authoring the lesbian and gay community's response to Briggs and the wider dangers encroaching on their way of life. Milk was born and raised in a Jewish family in a New York suburb in the years before World War II. As a young man, he explored his sexuality but struggled to find his place in a world hostile to lesbian and gay people.[10] He would eventually follow tens of thousands of other homosexual men and move to San Francisco, which had become a teeming "gay Mecca" by the time of his arrival in 1972.[11] Within a short time, Milk established both a business and a community and emerged a perennial candidate for public office. He lost repeatedly. But with each race, he earned more credibility with city leaders and became an increasingly influential voice for gay men and the city.[12]

While Milk made a name for himself in San Francisco, the defeat of Miami's lesbian and gay rights ordinance in June 1977 made him a national figure. In the wake of Bryant's victory, despondent lesbians and gays worldwide nursed their wounds in glum gatherings marked by fearful conversations. But the lesbians and gays of San Francisco quickly turned their dejection to righteous anger. As the results were announced that evening, hundreds of aggrieved homosexuals began to gather in the streets of the Castro, one of the country's first gay neighborhoods. As news spread, hundreds more joined them, including dozens who were pulled out of the bars by friends and lovers shouting, "Out of the bars and into the streets!" The crowd swelled to at least three thousand, including not just gay men but lesbians and transgender people.[13] Fearing a riot, gay organizers and city leaders turned to a credible gay leader whom they knew could control the crowd. Milk proceeded to lead the angry, chanting multitude on a five-mile march late into the night, focusing their unorganized anger into highly directed political activism. More marches would follow, and, as more conventional gay leaders floundered, Milk declared his intention to run for a seat on the San Francisco Board of Supervisors. In November 1977, Supervisor Milk became the first gay man elected to public office in California, an achievement that would catapult him directly into the growing national struggle over lesbian and gay rights.

Along with other movement leaders, Milk formed a multifaceted campaign to defeat the Briggs Initiative the following November. Named "No on 6," the campaign included a diverse cross section of the city's and state's often-conflicted lesbian and gay scene. Among the few things uniting this haphazard community of resistance was an increasingly evident knowledge of the Nazi persecution of homosexuals in the 1930s and '40s. While activists like Itkin had spent much of the early 1970s agitating to bring these memories more fully into the post-Stonewall movement's political consciousness, the supposed rediscovery of this "newfound history" of the persecution starting in 1973 supercharged that effort.[14] By the evening of Bryant's victory in 1977, the pink triangle was already recognizable among lesbians and gays. But within a matter of weeks, the pink triangle "became the most prominent symbol of the San Francisco gay rights movement." Pink triangles appeared in lesbian and gay publications, were emblazoned on pins and clothing, and graced posters at anti-Briggs and anti-Bryant events.[15] A column in the *Los Angeles Times* declared, "Bryant's Brigade Uses Hitler's Tactics."[16] Milk biographer Randy Shilts described San Francisco gays at this time as "constantly harp[ing] about Hitler and concentration camps" and being quick to define Briggs as "a contemporary incarnation of Hitler."[17] Other movement leaders weaved similar appeals into their speeches, like when Cleve Jones reminded angry lesbians and gays at a rally that Nazi crackdowns on homosexual rights rhymed with Anita Bryant's contemporary antigay agenda.[18] But while this moment evidenced a burst in remembrances among American lesbians and gays of the Nazis' anti-homosexual campaign, none of these invocations broke new ground. In broad terms, these memory rhetorics mirrored the messages produced by people like Itkin: this persecution had happened before, and those who faced it died as heroic martyrs for the cause. Beyond that, this wave of new attention to the Nazi persecution of homosexuals remained largely agnostic about drawing any wider conclusions.

Milk's public statements before 1977 on the Nazi persecution of homosexuals were largely consistent with this conventional framing. What distinguished him from other gay male leaders at first was how quick he was to wrap his lesbian and gay rights rhetoric in the memory of the Nazi repression campaign. On this point, Jason Edward Black and Charles E. Morris III note that Milk was fond of using allusions to the Holocaust "as analogies and rhetorical frames in denouncing his political enemies."[19] Much of this tendency can be explained by how formative the events of the Holocaust were to a young Harvey Milk. His friends recalled that Milk rarely talked about his upbringing but routinely shared the story about the day in 1943 when his parents sat him down to share the news that the Jews of Warsaw had staged an uprising. Milk's biographers have long attributed the politics of hope that guided his career as an adult to this influential memory of resisting against all odds in the face of annihilation.[20] As a result, Milk saw dangerous synergies between the Jewish Holocaust and the plight of modern American homosexuals. Accordingly, Milk was often seen invoking Hitler, the Nazis, and concentration camps in his rhetorical works.

But by 1978, Milk's interpretation of the Nazi persecution of homosexuals took a turn. Facing down the immediate threats of the Briggs Initiative and sensing the opportunity to spark a truly national lesbian and gay rights movement in the United States, Milk amended his familiar framing, which linked the prospects for lesbians and gays in the United States with the fate of the Third Reich's homosexual victims. To this conventional perspective, Milk added his own innovation, reframing these earlier homosexuals not as "defiant martyrs" but as pathetic figures who refused to fight for their own survival. This shift was not derived from new historical evidence or some special insight; rather, it served an immediate rhetorical end. By framing earlier homosexuals as weak, scared, and feckless—a community of whom homosexuals should be ashamed—Milk created a counterpoint against which he could define the modern struggle. In other words, instead of advocating that present-day lesbians and gays follow in the footsteps of their European forebears, Milk demanded that contemporary lesbians and gays repudiate them as failures. This rejection would become the first step toward crafting a newly empowered, energized, and active lesbian and gay community that would fight its own evil aggressors to the bitter end.

Of several notable invocations of these memories, Milk's most influential discourse repudiating the homosexuals persecuted by the Nazi regime appears in his famous Gay Freedom Day speech, delivered at a rally outside San Francisco City Hall on June 25, 1978. Milk made numerous passing references to the Nazis and the Holocaust, but his retort against the Third Reich's homosexual victims appeared in the second paragraph, constituting the most quoted part of the address: "We are not going to sit back in silence as 300,000 of our gay brothers and sisters did in Nazi Germany. We are not going to allow our rights to be taken away and then march with bowed heads into the gas chambers."[21] Estimates of the size of Milk's audience that day begin at 375,000, and he was known to amplify his messages after a speech by passing out copies of the text to any reporter he could find.[22] As a result, and given the high stakes of the speech in the lead-up to Election Day, it is undoubted that Milk's decision to impugn the memories of the Nazis' homosexual victims in the first few lines of his speech was impactful. In fact, as one of Milk's most famous

addresses, his Gay Freedom Day speech in 1978 is among the most consequential rhetorical texts to address the Nazis' crackdown on homosexuality.

Milk also gave media interviews in which he made similar memory
claims. Perhaps his most significant appeared in the *San Francisco Examiner* on November 29, 1978. Milk continued his invocation against German
homosexuals' failures in the face of Nazi oppression, even after the defeat of
the Briggs Initiative three weeks earlier: "Do you think gay people are going
with their heads bowed into the gay chambers? I mean, I'll go kicking and
screaming before I go with my head bowed. I've read history: 300,000 gays
went into the gas chambers in Germany, and then six million Jews. I don't
think the Jews are going to go quietly the next time, so why should gay people?"[23] In the interview, Milk does not radically add to his memory work from
the Gay Freedom Day address. But his remembrance in the *Examiner* took on
extra resonance, given that it appeared two days after Milk was assassinated
on November 27, 1978. Recorded just a few weeks prior to Milk's killing, the
interview was reworked by staff at the *Examiner* to meet the context of his
murder. As a result, Milk's posthumous warning against anti-homosexual
forces evoked a deep sense of sorrow, resonated with foresight, and reached
an unusually large reading audience.

In this speech, interview, and similar statements, Milk cast the homosexuals who suffered and perished under the thumb of the Nazis as disreputable figures whom the US lesbian and gay movement of the late 1970s should
define itself against. This denouncement was potent, but such a dramatic shift
in memory could not be achieved by assertion alone. As we have seen, Milk's
revision of these men as shameful figures departed from a memory discourse
of defiant martyrdom that had begun to take root across San Francisco's
lesbian and gay community and the wider world. Renovating these victims
into "lambs to the slaughter" required rhetorical modification. In his public
remarks on the Nazi persecution of homosexuals, Milk made these modifications through a series of interconnected but consequential rhetorical acts.

Subtracting Homosexual Experiences of Persecution

One of the most notable dimensions of Milk's remembrances of the Nazis'
homosexual victims in 1978 was the highly circumscribed way he defined
that persecution. Unlike other movement leaders of the decade, who leaned
into the supposed rediscovery of the Nazi actions in 1973 and its expansive

insights into the particularities of the repression (i.e., specific names, key dates, and particular details of suffering), Milk did not provide his audiences voluminous, detailed information in his remembrances. Instead, Milk—whether by shrewd calculation or natural instinct—greatly simplified and limited the memory he told of these homosexual victims, an act of rhetorical subtraction. By subtraction, I mean a choice by a speaker or writer to omit or reduce a point in text for some desirable rhetorical effect.[24] As we will see, by narrowing his interpretation of the scope of the Nazi campaign against homosexuality in several ways, Milk constituted an enthymematic-rich appeal, one that relied significantly on his lesbian and gay audiences to fill in the details in this memory's gaps and conflate the Jewish and homosexual experiences of the Nazi regime for his desired rhetorical outcome.

Three acts of rhetorical subtraction are at work in Milk's brief remembrances of the Nazis' crusade against homosexuals. The first was a form of temporal subtraction. In this act, Milk significantly omits portions of the period that others used to define the Nazi persecution. More specifically, Milk discursively narrowed the Nazi persecution of homosexuals to the relatively short and specific era of the Third Reich itself (1933–45). Such a scope significantly contrasts with the choices of other activists, whose own memory work relied on a broader temporal framework that reached back to the struggle against Paragraph 175 in the 1860s, extended to struggles against the Nazis as they rose to power, and continued into the postwar era.[25] In contrast, Milk's framing lops off those decades and resituates his remembrances exclusively in the period of the persecution itself.

Alongside and in conjunction with this temporal reduction, Milk utilizes a geographic subtraction, condensing the spaces, places, and locales in which he understood the Nazis' homosexual persecution to have occurred. Once again, Milk's remembrances do this in ways that differ from other elaborations that sought to expand the audience's understanding of the geography of the persecution, extending beyond the border of modern Germany to lands conquered during the Third Reich's military expansion. Instead, Milk opts for a more circumscribed set of choices, all within the boundaries of the German nation. By emphasizing a narrow and targeted set of places in which his remembrances are reconstituted, he further delineates the terrain of memory on which audiences judge the homosexual victims' actions.

Interestingly, both the temporal and geographic forms of rhetorical subtraction that Milk deploys in his memory work are found in a small set of key words and phrases in his speech and interview. Exemplary of this point is Milk's explicit reference to *Nazi Germany* in his Gay Freedom Day address. This otherwise simple phrase contains two clear delimiters. On one hand, it tells the audience that Milk's reminiscences of the Nazi persecution of homosexuals will be contained to the geographic boundaries of the German nation (even as homosexuals faced persecution and internment during the war in occupied France, Poland, and other nations). On the other hand, that same invocation of Nazi Germany limits Milk's consideration to the temporal zones of the Third Reich, signaling his interest only in the period between 1933 and 1945. By using the term in his discussions of the persecution, Milk explicitly omits any judgments about homosexuals' actions during the Nazi crackdown, particularly those extending back to the era of the Weimar Republic or to any events inside or outside the camps after the war ended.

Another important and related term that appears in both Milk's speech and interview and further subtracts from his audience's remembrances of the Nazi persecution in time and place is *gas chambers*. Again, invoking those words has both temporal and geographic effects on remembering the Nazi persecution of homosexuals. On the one hand, it limits the audience's consideration to the period when gas chambers were used in Nazi Germany. Historians may differ on the specifics of how we mark that moment, but most would agree this entreaty limits our consideration to no earlier than 1939, when the Nazis' authorized the child euthanasia program that would later be adapted for the Final Solution against the Jews.[26] At the same time, *gas chambers* largely defines the geography of his audience's remembrance of the Nazi persecution to the killing centers and concentration camps. For while it is certainly true that gas and poisons were used outside the camps to facilitate mass extermination, it seems safe to assume that when Milk uses the term when he is invoking the permanent facilities embedded in certain concentration camps after 1939.

By using these two terms—*Nazi Germany* and *gas chambers*—Milk provides by far the narrowest framing of the persecution encountered in this book. In effect, he argues that when his audience remembers the Nazi persecution of homosexuals, they should only consider the events that took place within concentration camps (particularly those with gas chambers) from 1939 forward (i.e., only during the war). Thus, Milk uses these acts of temporal and geographic subtraction to narrow his audience's imaginings of the homosexual persecution to the experiences of a relatively small subset of those persecuted under Paragraph 175: the pink triangles. Such a move, as mentioned above, is not unusual in these memory rhetorics in the lesbian and gay community from the 1970s onward. But Milk's focus is particularly definitive in claiming that the homosexual persecution can and should be understood by modern lesbians and gays of the late 1970s as synonymous with the experience of homosexuals incarcerated in the concentration camps.

In combination with these two important forms of rhetorical subtraction, Milk uses one more subtraction strategy of a slightly different sort: allusion. Of course, allusion—the brief reference to a prior historical person or event that has the capacity to shape the audience's understanding of the present situation—is not unique to Milk. Indeed, many of the various memory works involving the Nazi persecution of homosexuals featured in this book can be described as allusions. But Milk's use of allusion is particularly notable because of its reliance on brevity. Allusions, in other words, are supposed to be *brief* gestures or passing mentions, not long or sustained recountings. Milk's references to the persecutions in both his interview and speech are clear examples of using allusion's expectation of brevity. In sum, Milk only references the persecution in four lines of a seven-page speech and four lines in an interview that fills a full newspaper page.[27] This brevity, of course, has the effect of greatly circumscribing the rich and complex history of the actual persecution, reducing what the audience can remember by the sheer force of word count. It is not, in other words, that Milk could not have said more—it is that he chose not to.

This leads to the question of why, when there was so much more capability after 1973 to connect the suffering of homosexuals before 1945 with the dangers facing 1978 America, Milk said so little. The answer, I suspect, lies in the reason successful allusions are brief: their deep reliance on the hope that the audience members will get the reference and fill in the details with their own memories and experiences. This enthymematic appeal is true of most rhetoric in a classical sense, yet its power is crystallized in the use of allusion. By making a transitory reference to the past, the speaker tells those in the audience to connect past and present but anticipates (or perhaps invites) them to fill in that connection with details from somewhere else. It is this move—the rhetorical "somewhere else"—that is a key facet of Milk's rhetorical appeal. For as we will see, rather than offer a rich and variegated history of past homosexual oppression to drive their anger, Milk invites his audience to complete the claim with a different experience: the suffering of the Jewish people in Nazi extermination camps.

Pink Triangle, Yellow Star: Rhetorics of Substitution and Transposition

Having reduced the complex struggle of European homosexuals against the rising tide of fascism to the limited period of the Third Reich and the highly circumscribed and unrepresentative zone of the concentration camp, Milk's remembrances of these earlier homosexuals are well prepared to be substituted in mass for a different form of suffering: the Jewish experience under the Nazi regime. This rhetorical substitution is an act of transfiguration, a turning of the homosexual experience—here almost undefined—into the Jewish experience of the Holocaust.

To be clear, the experiences of Jews during the Holocaust and homosexuals facing persecution under the Third Reich were not the same. The timing and intensity of their oppression, the ideologies underpinning their torment, the mechanisms by which their persecution was conducted, the kinds of subjugation they faced, and the manner in which their lives were ended (or not)—all of these and others reflected significant variability between the two minority communities. And each community's intersectional identities (i.e., race, class, gender, age, and nationality, among others) introduced even more capriciousness into the experiences of individual Jews and homosexuals. Even individuals who were Jewish *and* homosexual might have very different experiences of oppression under the Nazis, their fates determined by a series of unknowable and inconsistent decision points within the Third Reich's complex systems of human destruction. Nonetheless, scores of lesbian, gay, and Jewish activists have at different times and for various reasons merged these two experiences of Nazi hate, with varying levels of understanding of the consequences of such actions.

Milk was certainly among those activists who found rhetorical value in conflating the pink triangle and the yellow star. His strategy in asking his audiences to remember the homosexual persecution as substantially similar to—and perhaps even indistinct from—the Jewish Holocaust is threefold. For one, most Americans had a far richer and deeper understanding of the Jewish Holocaust than the homosexual persecution—even within the lesbian and gay community. This was particularly true in 1978 after NBC aired a nine-hour miniseries titled *Holocaust*, which followed a fictionalized Jewish family enduring the full force of Nazism from Kristallnacht to the Final Solution.[28] With Americans' growing familiarity with the experiences of the Jews depicted in *Holocaust*, it was simply easier for Milk to have his audience imagine homosexual suffering as akin to Jewish suffering under the Third Reich.

Second, the allusion to the Jewish experience was faster. A full accounting of the complex and distinctive suffering of homosexuals would have invariably required time and space in Milk's texts, which was better devoted to explaining the threats posed by the Briggs Initiative in the present and his audience's appropriate response. Third, substituting the Jewish experience for the homosexual experience was useful because the Holocaust's dark realities raised the threat facing homosexuals to the highest affective register, leading to a corresponding rise in lesbian and gay motivation. But regardless of the reason, *how* Milk uses these allusions to substitute the yellow star for the pink triangle is what matters most.

In the texts, two explicit tactics are employed to do this work. One, as we have already discussed, is his use of the term *gas chambers*. While Milk used the image earlier to place geographic and temporal constraints on the subjects of his remembrances, this same term also permitted Milk to merge the experiences of millions of European Jews exterminated in Nazi killing centers with the tens of thousands of homosexuals persecuted in variegated ways, both inside and outside the camps. This conflation is factually incorrect. While millions of Jews were exterminated by gas chambers and similar devices in death camps and mobile killing units, it is likely that comparatively few homosexuals faced this fate for their desires alone. Despite the Nazis' dislike of homosexuals, they largely saw them as recoverable creatures who could be put to use on the front lines or worked to death in the camps. As a result, while some homosexuals certainly met their end in gas chambers, it was likely due to their intersectional Jewish or Roma identity, or, at the very least, the numbers were far fewer than what Milk suggests. Nonetheless, Milk's invocation of gas chambers serves to substitute Jewish mass extermination for the gay male experience.

He also uses a temporal logic in the form of transposition to flatten the Jewish and homosexual experiences. Like substitution, transposition is a classic rhetorical strategy of change that works by transmuting one thing into something else. In Milk's case, transposition is applied to the order of events during the Third Reich to further collapse the Jewish and homosexual cases. This tactic is particularly clear in his final interview, where he outlines the order in which the supposed executions of homosexuals and Jews took place. In Milk's telling, "three hundred thousand gays went into the gas chambers in Germany and then six million Jews." Or to put it chronologically, the Nazis murdered three hundred thousand homosexuals and *then* proceeded to murder millions of Jews. Such an assertion has numerous factual errors but sets up a powerful, if inaccurate, memory of these events. In particular, Milk suggests that the murder of homosexuals and Jews in the camps were not different or unrelated experiences but rather part of the same undertaking. Indeed, through a use of the rhetorical trope hysteron proteron, Milk reorders these events to transmute the largely simultaneous and overlapping persecutions into a shared order of operations, placing the murder of homosexuals as a first step in the destruction of the Jews.[29] In doing so, Milk combines Jewish and homosexual experiences under the Nazis into a single shared Holocaust, in which he argues that the murder of homosexuals should hold first position.

Establishing the Myth of Homosexual Passivity

The final piece of Milk's memory rhetoric, after conflating the homosexual and Jewish experiences, was defining the former in a particular way: as one of passive submission. In other words, Milk's brief allusions to the persecution aimed not just to substitute the yellow star for the pink triangle; it also worked to substitute the myth of Jewish passivity with a myth of homosexual passivity. In doing so, Milk raises the stakes for modern lesbians and gays while condemning past homosexuals for failing to act in defense of their own lives.

The myth of Jewish passivity is a stereotypical, false, but rhetorically rich resource that Milk used in this work. In short, the myth promotes the idea that Jews, in general, but particularly in the context of World War II, refused to fight the Nazis and simply accepted their own annihilation. As Richard Middleton-Kaplan has argued, this is a dangerous discourse that ignores the complex and multifaceted ways that Jews actively struggled against the Nazis during the war.[30] Yet, as a rhetorical device, it has been used by both Jews and non-Jews to forge calls for action in more contemporary circumstances. Middleton-Kaplan and other scholars trace the myth to the Hebrew Bible, which recounts the story of a young man who, mistakenly accused of misdoing, accepts his punishment nonetheless: "He was oppressed, though he humbled himself and opened not his mouth; as a lamb that is led to the slaughter, and as a sheep that before her shearers is dumb; yea, he opened not his mouth."[31] For centuries, Jewish philosophy praised this verse, interpreting it as a depiction of a Jew accepting mistreatment to demand that God act to right a prior wrong.[32]

However, during World War II, many Jews shifted their interpretation to drive Jewish resistance against the Nazi regime. This change has been noted explicitly in the rhetoric of Abba Kovner, a Jewish resistance fighter in Vilna, who released a communiqué to fellow Jews in European ghettos, urging them to take up arms and resist the Nazis: "We will not be led like sheep to slaughter. True we are weak and helpless, but the only response to the murders is revolt. Brethren, it is better to die fighting like free men than to live at the mercy of the murderers. Arise, Arise with last breath. Take courage!"[33] Kovner's interpretation became instrumental in encouraging the Vilna Ghetto Uprising and similar insurrections elsewhere, capturing a spirit of defiance that quickly became tied to the phrase throughout the war.[34] After the war, similar interpretations appeared in Zionist literature and later Israeli national discourse.[35] The rhetorical value of this claim was apparent but complex: it proved a powerful way to shatter apathy and marshal action, but it required Jews to accept the myth that previously they had been passive victims and failed to put up a "good" fight.

It is this dynamic that Milk helps cultivate in his limited remembrance of the Nazi persecution of homosexuals for the same reasons. In his speech and interview, Milk works to recraft the homosexual persecution as befalling a community of passive victims—a shameful past that must be rejected by acting in the present. In doing so, Milk not only oversimplifies the homosexual persecution, substituting its facts with those of the Jewish persecution—he also applies the myth of Jewish passivity onto the homosexual experience under the Third Reich.

Of all the aspects of Milk's rhetorical invocation of homosexual persecution, it is this connection that he makes most explicitly. In both his interview and speech, the myth of homosexual passivity is rendered plain, even though he does not use that exact term. In his speech, Milk does this by articulating what he understands to be the various ways that homosexuals, like Jews facing annihilation, did nothing. For instance, in his speech, Milk uses the phrase *sit back* to suggest that homosexuals saw the campaign against them coming and chose inaction. These homosexuals, he argues, avoided direct intervention when it could have mattered. When Milk says homosexuals "allow[ed] their rights to be taken away," he again suggests passivity; homosexuals did not lift a finger, in his telling, to fight for their rights. Finally, in an affective burst, Milk claims these homosexual men "march[ed] with bowed heads to the gas chambers." The imagery of the bowed head is powerful here, for it signifies submission, an acceptance of death without a fight. Likewise, the imagery of the march—one so well depicted in Jewish art around the Holocaust—indicates agreeable and orderly participation, not revolutionary resistance.

Similar imagery and terminology appear in Milk's interview. Again, Milk uses the term *heads bowed* to indicate submission by homosexuals en route to the gas chambers. This depiction is juxtaposed with Milk's description of how he would handle a similar situation in the present: "I'll go kicking and screaming before I go with my head bowed." The number of homosexual dead appears again here, amplifying his moral condemnation of these supposedly spineless homosexuals, whom he claims were executed in staggeringly large numbers without a fight. But Milk also adds something new to his remembrance repertoire in the interview with his use of the subjunctive. It appears in Milk's interview implicitly, evoking the phrase *what if.* Here, Milk states that the next time oppression comes, "I don't think the Jews are going to go quietly." Milk follows up by asking, "Why would gay people?" But unlike the earlier Jewish example, this is an open question, the only place in which Milk severs the Jew from the homosexual in his texts. For Milk, it is clear in this description that the age of Jewish passivity has ended. But he asks rhetorically whether homosexuals will also rise to the occasion and act when death comes to their door?

With this three-part appeal, Milk challenged lesbians and gays in 1978 to act by repudiating the homosexuals of 1939–45 for their mythologized passivity. By the broadest possible measure, this rhetorical gambit worked, in that it contributed to the resounding defeat of the Briggs Initiative. And Milk's Gay Freedom Day speech, featuring this powerful allusion, is regarded as one of the most consequential moments of his short time in office.

Although Milk's innovation in framing the memory of the Nazi persecution of homosexuals was effective, it also sparked controversy and, in some cases, drew criticism. For instance, in a 1978 open letter in the newsletter *Sister*, a gay-Jewish collective harangued Milk among several other homosexual leaders for using the memory of the Holocaust "opportunistically." In particular, the letter pointed to "a statement widely used these days at gay political events," namely, that "we [i.e., homosexuals] will not be led off like lambs to the slaughter." This phrase, alluding to Milk's speech, is highlighted alongside another quote credited to Milk from that day, which the author attributes to his unexamined, internalized anti-Semitism. Such discourse, according to the letter, "perpetuat[es] the myth that we [Jews] did not resist the Nazis and therefore we allowed our own extermination." The letter ends by calling such claims a "distortion of the facts to fit a stereotype," and asks that the lesbian and gay community reeducate themselves so that "facts, not myths," are used to defeat their shared opponents pushing the Briggs Initiative.[36]

But such condemnations did little to stop Milk from leaning into this memory rhetoric and its apocalyptic judgments against the Nazis' homosexual victims. When an assassin's bullet pierced Milk's brain and killed him a few short weeks after the movement's victory over the Briggs Initiative, it only confirmed his point in the minds of many of his lesbian and gay supporters. Lesbians and gays in the United Stated were under existential threat, and only action—the kind earlier homosexuals had refused to take—would save them.

Conclusion

A year after the lesbian and gay rights movement in California beat back the Briggs Initiative, a new religious threat again demanded the repudiation of German homosexuals from the 1930s and '40s. Pope John Paul II began his papacy in October 1978, a mere two weeks before the Briggs Initiative was rejected by California voters. One year later, during his inaugural US visit, the pope made his very first public remarks about homosexuality. In his comments, the pontiff affirmed the church's long-standing anti-homosexual stance, describing homosexual acts as a moral abomination.[37] For millions of homosexuals across the globe, those statements were a searing rejection that represented an ongoing commitment to the destruction of lesbian and gay culture.

In response to the pope's remarks, the International Gay Association blanketed US lesbian, gay, and heterosexual publications alike with an open letter. While respectful and expressing openness to dialogue, the letter relied extensively on recent, denunciatory memories of the pink triangles—a message with significant subtext for the Catholic Church's first Polish pontiff, who himself lived through the Nazi occupation. In the letter, the authors reminded the pope that "it was not only Jews who died in Auschwitz" and that "the [T]hird Reich performed their grisly work on hundreds of thousands of homosexuals also." They added that it was the "pious platitudes of Church authorities" that paved the way for the mistreatment, experimentation, and murder of homosexuals. And in a powerful warning, the letter writers "serve[d] notice" to the new pope that "the days when homosexuals allowed themselves to be led like lambs to the slaughter ended in 1969 with Stonewall."[38] The letter was a powerful statement that reflected the tumultuous relationship between lesbians and gays and this pope. But it also signaled, in the final month of the 1970s, that remembering the homosexuals persecuted by the Nazi regime as part of a shameful past to be repudiated by modern lesbians and gays had been deemed a highly effective rhetorical strategy—one that would be normalized in the US lesbian and gay struggle for years to come.

That the story of how American lesbians and gays remembered the Nazis' homosexual victims in US public discourse ends with wide agreement that these individuals were from now on to be repudiated marks a radical departure from this book's journey up to this point. From 1934 onward, these homosexuals were almost always recalled with sympathy, pride, or grace by their US contemporaries. But in 1978, that consideration turned to scorn and shame. In doing so, it demonstrated a key argument of this book: that memories of these men were used in wildly different and sometimes contradictory ways between 1934 and 1981.

In this regard, the jarring disjuncture between laudatory and condemnatory memories of the homosexuals persecuted in the Nazi regime in this chapter reminds us why memory in general has been and continues to be such a powerful tool in public argument. Memory, as a particular orientation to invoking the past for present purposes, is nothing if not forgiving as it relates to this kind of whiplash. It is hard to imagine any other tool of recollection—history, memoir, et cetera—accommodating, within the span of ten years, an entire community's shift from celebration to shameful rejection. This is especially true considering that the shift in the late 1970s was not marked by the influx of new information or a revelation that turned the meaning of the past on its head. For even while the mid-1970s featured a cascade of new details about the persecution itself, little in that discovery justified the shameful frame-up the pink triangles received in Milk's and other lesbian and gay leaders' public statements. By some measures, the facts about the persecution of homosexuals presented in texts authored by Steakley, Lauritsen, and Thorstad should have reasonably made lesbian and gay audiences more sympathetic to these victims, not less. But as has already long been established in memory studies, the facts of the case are not the measure of a memory's worth. Rather, it is the responsiveness of memory to the needs of a given moment that makes this past-oriented process shine brightest. By this measure, Milk's exemplary repudiation of the Nazis' homosexual victims is eminently effective. It permitted a community facing an unprecedented threat to marshal its mnemonic resources in whatever way suited its impulse for survival. That this memory shifted to such a degree and manages to cohere is a testament to the compelling resourcefulness that memory provides. It is also an exemplary reminder more broadly: in the purview of memory, there is no shift or change too great to imagine, so long as it meets the needs of its audience.

The specific case of Milk's repudiation of his homosexual forebears raises the question of why this dramatic shift in memory occurred so quickly, particularly after forty years of a different affective assessment of these men. Several possible answers to this question are worth considering. Chief among these suppositions is that the state of lesbian and gay rights and politics in the United States changed drastically in the late 1970s. While the movements worked apace in difficult times in earlier decades, at least two factors were radically altered as we approached the 1980s. First, unlike almost any other example in this book, this moment featured a lesbian and gay community facing loss. As opposed to earlier moments, when homophile, homosexual, and lesbian and gay communities used these memories to build and grow, the community in the late 1970s had notched real-world victories that were at risk of collapsing. In these changed circumstances, tried-and-true memories of earlier eras needed to change—and with them, how the community remembered its European kin. Second, unlike in earlier instances, the 1970s represented a time in which mass lesbian and gay action offered a conceivable solution to defeat its enemies. The Miami-Dade County and Briggs votes were among the first lesbian and gay rights issues to be decided by popular referendum in the United States. Unlike in previous eras, when lesbian and gay salvation could be found in asking individuals to alter their personal lives, question their analyst, or take pride in themselves, lesbians and gays in the 1970s could effect positive change by going to the ballot box directly. Justice for homosexuals, in other words, required mass participation—and mass participation required deeply felt and highly recognizable stakes that could mobilize millions of individual electoral choices. The story of the persecution of homosexuals by the Nazis provided that crystallizing drive, but only to the extent that it could be retold as a story of failure to act. In each instance, the unique nature of the moment and the community shaped what remembrances of the Nazis' homosexual victims needed to be effective. And effect was tied directly to repudiation.

Relatedly, the impact of Stonewall—particularly the approaching ten-year anniversary of the riot in 1979—cannot be ignored as we try to make sense of this sudden shift in memory in the late 1970s. Stonewall was a pivotal event in lesbian and gay American history, one that deeply reshuffled the meaning of the Nazi persecution and its role in the community's collective remembrances thereafter. Prior to Stonewall, the Nazi persecution was among the only large, unifying events of homosexual community in lesbian and gay public memory. As such, lesbians and gays did with it what they could to make their lives better in the present. But after 1969, the Nazi persecution was displaced by Stonewall, particularly in the United States—and for good reason. The Stonewall Riots could be remembered as a moment in which the community came together and won. By contrast, the persecution of the 1930s and '40s was rendered even more clearly a memory of loss, victimization, and death, and also as befalling foreigners. In this post-Stonewall world, the annihilation of homosexuals by the Nazis lost significant rhetorical cachet. What value it had left was as a negative comparison. Lesbians and gays were told that they should follow the example of Stonewall; in doing so, the path of German homosexuals between 1933 and 1945 offered a stark contrast. With the advent of Stonewall memories, American homosexuals no longer needed to understand lesbian and gay politics through this past framework. Instead, they could advance a framework closer to home, one that ended in victory.

Undoubtedly, these reasons do not fully encapsulate the turn away from the Nazis' homosexual victims as epideictic heroes in the late 1970s. In fact, a "turn away" is an incorrect description, as the negative and shameful remembrance of those mistreated by the Nazis was circulated more frequently after the 1970s, not less. Regardless, the perpetuation of these rejections—some more factual than others—continued for one powerful reason: they worked. In ways we cannot measure for previous examples, remembering the Nazi persecution of homosexuals as an opportunity to denigrate these victims and reject their supposed apathy in the face of death was believed to have driven a powerful electoral shift. This is almost certainly why lesbians and gays in 1979 again turned to this memory to confront the renewed threat of the Catholic Church. In the face of snatching victory from the jaws of defeat, remembrances of the Nazis' homosexual victims appeared locked for at least a generation to come.

Yet, for all the potential victories and opportunities some members of the US lesbian and gay community saw in radically remembering the Nazi persecution of homosexuals as disreputable forebears, little unfolded over the next few years as prognosticators would have predicted. For 1980 would see the same forces that gave rise to Anita Bryant and the Religious Right ascend to the White House and adopt a national vantage point from which to target and harass US lesbian and gay communities. Such religiously inflected forms of antigay persecution would soon become a mainstay of US partisan political struggles for the next decade, and its vestiges continue with us today in only slightly altered forms.

Yet the nefarious threat posed by the Religious Right would represent only part of the story. For the 1980s threatened, in ways no one could anticipate, the very real possibility of gay male annihilation by a very different means.

Conclusion

Never Again, Never Forget, 1981–1987

When the six men responsible for "Silence = Death" agreed to feature the pink triangle as the central image in their now-iconic AIDS poster, they did so begrudgingly. In fact, when the *Village Voice* asked the five surviving members of the "Silence = Death" design collective to recount the poster's origin, they revealed that the group originally rejected the pink triangle symbol, in part because they did not want to imbue their activist message to fight AIDS "with a sense of victimhood." However, after previously discarding more representational imagery as unworkable and scorning other gay iconography as inappropriate, they ultimately returned to the pink triangle simply because "they hated it less than the other options."[1]

The pink triangle's foibles in "Silence = Death" did not end there. As the creators articulated, they felt they needed to update the color of the triangle to further distance it from its bleak origins. And the creators themselves acknowledged that they had not sufficiently researched the original pink triangle before committing to a design and mistakenly printed the image upside down. Nonetheless, the shortcomings that ultimately contributed to the poster's final design did not inhibit its success. Within days, it had been wheatpasted across major New York City neighborhoods. Within a year, the poster was taken up as perhaps the most visceral and recognizable image of the HIV/AIDS activist organization ACT UP. Today, the artwork is recalled alongside other iconic imagery, both for the power of its design and for the role it played in leveraging social change.[2] As such, recounting the origins of the "Silence = Death" at the end of this book is a useful reminder of how central human needs are to the force of rhetorical memory and just how malleable the past is when we need it to be.

But "Silence = Death" also marks perhaps the most significant moment of transition in the remembrance of the pink triangle—and the homosexuals persecuted by the Nazi regime it was meant to symbolize—in American memory to date. By 1987, this emblem of the horrific mistreatment of European homosexuals between 1933 and 1945 became inexorably linked to the struggle against HIV/AIDS, which the US Centers for Disease Control first identified in the United States in June 1981.[3] As with all public memories, there was nothing predestined about yoking Nazi atrocities committed against homosexuals to the deaths of millions caused by a microscopic virus. But the rhetorical synergies between both catastrophes—the large number of homosexual dead, the wasting and decline each inflicted on its victims, and the role of national governments in facilitating the horror—were prominent. To put it another way, if Stonewall memories were a rhetorical balm that permitted modern lesbians and gays to define themselves against the indignities homosexuals suffered under the Third Reich, the HIV/AIDS epidemic was a painful scab torn off to reveal the all too familiar narratives of dehumanization and death that marked the homosexual experience a half century earlier. Given these synergies, it is easy to see how the redeployment of the pink triangle to battle the scourge of HIV/AIDS felt inevitable.

Yet, as every other chapter of this book shows, what at times appears to be a natural resonance between past and present is almost always the work of committed activists who recognize opportunities in such moments and work to make those resonances clear for their desired audience. In the case of "Silence = Death," the above collective originated this process in the 1980s, creating through choice and chance a new rendition of the pink triangle to confront a new age and a new problem. But the poster's creators only started this work. In time, thousands of people across the globe—LGBTQ+ and heterosexual alike—played a part in urging the world to see HIV/AIDS as a portion of a much older, revanchist anti-homosexual agenda. With each ACT UP chant, speech, debate, pamphlet, button, documentary, drag show, protest, and die-in exclaiming "Silence = Death" or flashing the pink triangle, activists reiterated a powerful rhetorical performance of memory that continues today. Not all these performances of memory have been consistent or aligned; like others in this book, they sometimes conflict. But with the inauguration of "Silence = Death," the memory of the Nazi persecution of homosexuals took off as a widespread social force, a rhetorically potent remembrance detached from its much tighter lineage of decades past. In that unmooring, this 1980s version of remembering the Nazi persecution of homosexuals made possible the deeply changed world we inhabit today.

However, the power of the pink triangle as a symbol for fighting HIV/AIDS did not lay in its visual reconfiguration alone. Rather, the *meaning* of the Nazi persecution of homosexuals needed to be altered yet again to make these memories work—a rhetorical necessity faced by many homosocial, homosexual, and lesbian and gay activists before. Unlike such instances described in the previous chapters, these rhetorical transformations after 1981 have been well studied by scholars and do not need a full accounting here.[4] But at least one of the alterations to these memories warrants consideration to bookend this project: the almost complete conflation of the entire Nazi persecution with the pink triangle. This full-scale shift was the culmination of dozens of smaller modifications in this direction outlined in this book's earlier chapters. From decade to decade, US rememberers of the Nazi persecution relied more and more expressly on images and descriptions of homosexual men interned in concentration camps to achieve their rhetorical ends. In the 1980s, with a large assist from "Silence = Death," this creep became comprehensive. In the totalizing struggle against HIV/AIDS, a battle killing men who have sex with men worldwide by the thousands daily and threatening the utter decimation of gay male culture, there was little room for nuance or complexity. Facing an existential threat rife with anxiety and anger, alarm resounded, and only the most devastating and high-stakes historical allusions could meet the moment. The horrors of the concentration camps experienced by some homosexuals in the 1930s and '40s fit that exigency. As such, by the late 1980s, the "pink triangle" eclipsed "the Nazi persecution of homosexuals" completely—a takeover that has only ebbed in degrees in the decades since.

It is exactly for these reasons that this book's investigations are so necessary. For remembering the Nazi persecution of homosexuals remains a pink scar on the American national body we have overlooked for far too long. Prior to HIV/AIDS and particularly in the United States, the diverse and complex ways that different aspects of the Nazi persecution of homosexuals were remembered and used by an assortment of disparate rhetors was staggering. In aim, these memories turned villains into heroes, victims into resisters, and martyrs into monsters—all in ways that required deft and powerful rhetorical work. These transformations in the memory of the Nazi persecution of homosexuals *before* HIV/AIDS merit reconsideration, perhaps even celebration, in a twenty-first-century world in which the pink triangle memory still reigns supreme. At its core, that is what this book has tried to do.

Back to the Beginning

This book began by proposing three related claims about the public memories of homosexuals persecuted by the Nazi regime prior to HIV/AIDS: first, that those memories were well-known and used regularly throughout the period as a central and animating rhetorical resource of the movement; second, that such remembrances were not consistent but rather diverse and even contradictory; and third, that these invocations of the past affected in-group homosexual conversations in key moments, encompassing, but not limited to, homosexuals' experiences in concentration camps. At the project's close, it is important to return to these claims once more and unpack each more fully.

In partial answer to the first claim, the preceding chapters conclusively show that the suffering homosexuals endured under the Third Reich was not some mystery that went unknown for decades, especially within the community of people we think of today as LGBTQ+ Americans. Instead, the book illustrates that these victims were actively remembered from as early as three months following the 1934 Roehm purge. This assertion is certainly supported in the case of Henry Gerber's remembrances of Roehm and his men as "valiant and virile warriors" in the pages of *Chanticleer*—a magazine I argue targeted a significant homosexual readership. But it was also the case that most Americans—homosexual and heterosexual alike—had numerous opportunities to learn how the Nazis attacked, hunted down, and persecuted homosexual men before and during the war. From stray mentions of the "infamous 175's" in regional publications to extensive national coverage of the supposed "second purge" of homosexuals and the crude but wildly popular commentaries of the gossip press, Americans never lacked opportunities to encounter stories of homosexual persecution by the Nazis between 1933 and 1945. And the examples presented here demonstrate that such coverage was not so euphemistic or heavily coded as to be indecipherable to the American reading public. This information was clearly both *knowable* and *known*—and remembered in due course. Arguments otherwise obscure the hard truth that many heterosexual Americans in these decades simply did not much focus on the fate of these homosexuals. This lack of concern among most heterosexuals ranged from ambivalence to rabid agreement that homosexuals were a problem to be solved by the harsh tactics already in use in the United States at the time. Regardless, from almost the moment the Nazis' campaign against homosexuality began, it was impossible for Americans to forget about it.

From that point forward, memories of the Nazi state's persecution of homosexuals would emerge repeatedly in the US homosexual public imagination. As we saw in chapter 2, the campaign of oppression became a fixation for some early members of what would become the Mattachine Foundation and preoccupied both writers and readers of midcentury homosexual publications. Similar memories reappeared in gay Nazi-exploitation pulps in the 1960s, filled with both troublesome fictionalized erotics and important facts not printed elsewhere. These memories surfaced yet again soon after Stonewall in the public writings of the Reverend Mikhail Itkin. Thereafter, supercharged by the "discovery" of the persecution, allusory and extended references to these homosexual victims appeared in various academic and political works of the late 1970s, some with a particularly denunciatory orientation. All of which is to say that at no time between 1934 and 1981 were homosexual activists as a group unaware of the suffering inflicted on their European homosexual kin years earlier. These activists certainly lacked precise details of this past at various times—details that would later be salvaged by academics or lost forever. And any individual homosexual, often emerging into the scene from isolation, could be excused for not knowing this past, at least for a time. But the wider community of homosocials, homosexuals, and lesbians and gays between 1934 and 1981 never forgot key details of the persecution—and who conducted it. For US LGBTQ+ people, the Nazi persecution of homosexuals could sometimes be disregarded, but it would never go away.

The investigations in this book also establish that American memories of the Nazi persecution of homosexuals during these decades were highly disparate and often contradictory. A novice to memory studies might expect that meaningful memories—recollections of events that endure in the face of time—are distinguished by their steadfast consistency. But consistency is not the mark of a powerful and effective public memory rhetoric; rather, one of the most effective dimensions of a durable memory is its malleability or its state of "permanent evolution"—the ability of a memory to be many things to many people in multiple situations.[5] So, too, the malleability in the memories of the Nazi persecution of homosexuals explains the long-standing impact of these past events on the American homosexual imagination over the last century.

In fact, I believe that the realities of the Nazis' anti-homosexual campaign make these events particularly ripe for rhetorical pliability. For instance, because the persecution unfolded over nearly a dozen years, crossed national borders, and swept up thousands of individuals, its narrative offers countless possibilities for interpretation. Similarly, the events are so numerous that these same stories can be told in various ways and at different scales. At the same time, our knowledge of the persecution contained notable gaps, which is where public memory can thrive. Into these gaps, deft persuaders dropped their own details—or invited others to do the same—permitting audiences to interpret these pasts from just the right perspective to make them matter in new and different ways. Meanwhile, the Nazi persecution of homosexuals has now firmly passed from the realm of individual memory to collective or public memory. Going forward, these events will only ever be remembered by those who did not live them. This fact poses significant risks to the past. But critical distance also offers compelling opportunities to remember the Third Reich's repression of homosexuals free from the shackles of overwrought propriety or genuine fears of reprisal. For all these reasons, memories of the Nazis' homosexual persecution have been widely varied, and there is little reason to suspect that will not continue.

This book has revealed a staggering degree of variability in how these events are remembered. Both the complexity and contradictions within these memories are particularly notable, given the relatively smaller community of rememberers this project focuses on. For instance, while 1950s homosexual publications often cast the Nazis' homosexual victims as unjustly persecuted "criminals," 1970s texts attributed their incarceration to an identity-based hate not dissimilar to anti-Semitism. Elsewhere, activists isolated extremely narrow and limited views of these events (e.g., the Roehm purge, the pink triangle experience), while others remembered these events with an expansive scope. Just as jarring are discourses from across the decades showing homosexuals suffering violent and painful ends, while gay Nazi-exploitation pulps of the late 1960s remembered these same men's suffering as erotically charged. These examples cutting across the book do not even account for the major themes for remembering these victims highlighted in each chapter: valiant warriors, outlaws and vagrants, skeptics, defiant martyrs, and lambs to the slaughter. We could easily add further degrees of complexity to this list. But collectively, these examples affirm the book's major argument that memories of the Nazi persecution of homosexuals existed in any number of forms and configurations between 1934 and 1981 exactly because that was necessary for their commemorators to meet their rhetorical purposes.

The preceding chapters also demonstrate that the long-standing practice of American lesbians and gays remembering the Nazi persecution of homosexuals between 1934 and 1981 has gone untold for decades, partly because activists and scholars discounted the significance of these events being remembered within the LGBTQ+ community, even as the wider national public did not. Only by following the rhetorical evidence and disrupting this false assumption can we begin to reclaim this narrative. This trail of discursive clues often leads to well-worn artifacts of the community's internal deliberations on various topics throughout the twentieth century, including texts examined in chapter 2 like ONE, *Mattachine Review*, and *The Ladder*. But stopping here would have suggested that these remembrances were episodic at best. By contrast, this book prioritized engaging different artifacts from within the lesbian and gay community that other such investigations have not. In this vein, texts like the gay Nazi-exploitation pulps and a reconsidered, homosexually attendant *Chanticleer* not only become available for consideration but also serve as rich sites evidencing these memory rhetorics at work. To put a finer point on it, if we only go looking for memories of the Nazis' homosexual victims in the *New York Times* or on American evening news broadcasts, there is no doubt we would find little. This is especially true when scholars hold historical homosexual texts to impossible standards of evidence or impact that render them unworthy of investigation. But when we open our aperture wider and begin to value the rhetoric created by and circulating among homosocial, homosexual, and lesbian and gay counterpublics as worthy of investigation, the stories we can tell about these homosexual forerunners in German history become richer, more complex, and rhetorically compelling in new and exciting ways.

This returns us to the second part of the first claim: that memories of the Nazi persecution of homosexuals should be considered among the most important—and perhaps *the* most important—rhetorical tools in the history of the LGBTQ+ movements, particularly before 1981. Such sweeping claims deserve caution, for other rhetorical idioms, images, and ideas have demonstrated their own potency on the community's behalf. Yet I believe this book shows the validity of this claim for three reasons. To begin, no other rhetorically salient event can be said to have been discursively present at so many turning points in the US LGBTQ+ movement as the Nazi persecution of homosexuals. In this book alone, meaningful references to the Nazi repression appear in the aftermath of the Society for Human Rights, at the founding of Mattachine, during the first homosexual White House picket, amid the earliest post-Stonewall calls for gay power, preceding the removal of homosexuality from the *DSM*, in the consequential months confronting the Religious Right's emergence, and alongside the community's forceful response to HIV/AIDS. As this incomplete list demonstrates, historians of the LGBTQ+ past would be hard-pressed to find another memory so often and vitally reanimated between 1934 and 1981 to advance the cause of US lesbian and gay activism. Relatedly, no other memory of the queer past has been so centrally and repeatedly invoked by the loudest voices in the most consequential venues in the movement. While recognizing that archival limitations often both shape and preserve the past, the surviving documents of the American LGBTQ+ experience place memories of the Nazi persecution of homosexuals at the center of their story.[6] Gerber, Hay, Jennings, ONE, *Mattachine Review*, Kameny, Vincenz, the gay pulp market, Itkin, Milk—these venues and voices were among the most important and consequential of their respective homosexual generations. And each of them made remembering the Nazi persecution of homosexuals central to their reiterative attempts to use speeches, writing, and protests to alter the fate of the US homosexual movement. Last, these memories were put to powerful and important rhetorical ends. The same cannot be said of every community's invocations of Hitler or the Holocaust.[7] But the preceding chapters show that homosexuals reserved invocations of their forebears' suffering under the Third Reich for only the direst circumstances, ranging from inaugurating and sustaining a movement under threat to combating the annihilation of gay people themselves. As such, remembering the Nazi persecution of homosexuals in this era must be understood as not just reiterative or central but also as *epideictic*—a powerful rhetoric of praise or blame reserved by the LGBTQ+ community to inspire people to do hard things.

In all these ways, this book's story of how homophiles, homosexuals, and lesbians and gays remembered the Nazi persecution directly challenges our received wisdom: that these memories were forgotten and unknown for decades. Rather, it makes clear that the homosexual persecution by the Nazi regime has always been an important part of the US LGBTQ+ movement—and has been essential to creating the imperfect but more safe, more just, and more inclusive LGBTQ+ world in which we have lived in the twenty-first century.

Missed Opportunities

Alongside these three central claims, this book also illuminates some reasons why these memories, and their importance to LGBTQ+ rhetorical history, have gone unattended for so long. Numerous factors have helped perpetuate the myth that the Nazi persecution of homosexuals was only knowable in the mid-1970s, including the predilection to look for these memories outside the community rather than inside it. But while there is insufficient space to address each of these explanations fully in the balance of this book, this section highlights some of the most essential reasons. This overdue autopsy of our collective failures to attend to these memories is necessary to ensure these remembrances get their due consideration moving forward.

One factor contributing to this failure is that the LGBTQ+ past in general remains an understudied facet of the human experience. In my previous book, I summarized and added to existing scholarship explaining our ongoing resistance to queer memory, in both the academy and the wider world. Foundational to this resistance is the false but persistent belief that there was no lesbian or gay past to be studied or that, if there was, none of it survived to be investigated.[8] In addition, LGBTQ+ pasts have been subjugated to an ongoing mnemonicide that Charles E. Morris III argues actively works to "assassinate" the queer past through silence and erasure.[9] The queer community today also continues to grapple with the fallout from degeneration at the hands of the HIV/AIDS crisis, which has been particularly pernicious in severing ties binding LGBTQ+ people of different eras.[10] And when LGBTQ+ historical work has been done, various institutions have sidelined or discredited it on procedural grounds, suggesting that the queer past is investigated with insufficient rigor, lacks evidence, is far too ephemeral in form, and does not meet the standards of the archive.[11] These are but a few of the numerous and ongoing ways that LGBTQ+ pasts are rendered unavailable for study or investigation. Remembrances of the Nazi persecution of homosexuals have certainly been stymied by these wider anti-LGBTQ+ processes, both historically and into the present.

Alongside these more general impediments to study the LGBTQ+ past, remembrances of the Nazi persecution of homosexuals in the decades before HIV/AIDS have been deprived of attention for other reasons, at least some of which are unique to these historical events. Among these is the question of how we define the LGBTQ+ "community" or "public" in this type of historical work—and how those definitions do or do not make different kinds of discourses worthy of investigation. Readers will recall that I took issue, in the introduction, with historian Erik Jensen's otherwise outstanding 2002 review of how the pink triangles emerged in collective memory. Key to my angst was Jensen's dismissal—following at least one German scholar—of any memories of the Nazis' persecution of homosexuals that existed prior to the Gay Liberation Movement (i.e., June 1969) because, as he argued, their remembrances were "too small and too hidden from the public to foster a collective memory." Instead, Jensen suggests, a "shared memory of the Nazi persecution of homosexuals emerged in the 1970s."[12] Unstated but heavily implied in Jensen's claim is the belief that there must exist an unknown but consequential number of homosexuals necessary to constitute a public or community before we could take any of their remembrances seriously—a quorum, if you will. I return to this point here because I have disagreed with this unstated idea of a quorum throughout this book. In my disagreement, I have shown there was significant, complex, and meaningful collective and public memory work done by homosexuals before *both* HIV/AIDS *and* gay liberation that warranted scholarly attention. In this regard, I believe the chapters and examples speak for themselves.

But this disagreement returns me to the question of a quorum and its potentially destructive effects on studying the LGBTQ+ past through discourse. I suspect that my disagreements with Jensen on this topic lie in a disciplinary distinction. For some time, terms like *public* linked to a grand vision of social life analyzed by figures like Jürgen Habermas or John Dewey carried a certain cachet in the academy.[13] As a historian, I believe Jensen had something like this notion of public or collective in mind when he discounted nongay liberation homosexual communities as meaningful. But as a rhetorical scholar, I have long been drawn to critiques of these visions of the public, particularly how earlier theorizations ignored both the way publics are inflected with identity and the fact that there are numerous publics and counterpublics at work simultaneously.[14] What's more, as a queer rhetorical scholar, I strongly support the view that drawing hard lines between public and private is unproductive, or perhaps oppressive, anyway. Both points are consequential for scholarly investigations of minoritized LGBTQ+ (counter) publics, who can easily be rendered invisible if standards of a Habermasian public (i.e., quorum) are applied. In my view, all that is needed for a meaningful public worthy of investigation are two people—in fact, it may have no quorum at all. To the extent that publics are created through "mere attention" and the circulation of texts, meaningful publics can emerge in the smallest and most unexpected places, with great consequence.[15] By my definition, homosexual publics have been generated by large circulating texts, like ONE magazine in the 1950s, but also by smaller circulating texts, like *Chanticleer* in 1934. In my view, both texts produce entities in the world worthy of the name *public*—and equally valid for investigation if we are to understand, among other things, how these publics remembered the persecution of homosexuals under the Nazi regime. Indeed, I believe such a view is essential for historical (and contemporary!) homosocial, homosexual, and lesbian and gay communities if they are to be rendered appropriate for academic consideration. It's time to ditch the imaginary quorum in both the study of publics and public memory studies. Otherwise, we are apt to overlook entire memory discourses that hold the potential to radically shift our worldviews.

Another significant reason these remembrances have been discounted for decades is a tendency by activists and some scholars to seek out memories of the Nazi persecution of homosexuals in the wrong places and in the wrong ways. In particular, given the significant differences in how these memories are formulated and deployed before and after 1981, researchers more familiar with the post-HIV/AIDS memoryscape are apt to go searching for more recent instantiations of these memories in the past, where they are unlikely to be found. Jensen's attempts to find a meaningful collective of homosexuals with sufficient numbers and capability is one instance of how this tendency plays out; similarly, pink triangle memories that anticipate a concentration camp–centric framework before the mid-1960s also illustrate this pattern. These are just two examples where the last several decades of remembering the Nazi regime cannot guide our search for earlier such remembrances. The results of this approach are erasure and the false assumption that these atrocities went unremembered or unknown for decades.

Instead, reconstituting pre-HIV/AIDS memories of the Nazi persecution of homosexuals requires making different assumptions and applying different methods to this search, something I have practiced throughout the previous chapters. One strategy includes recognizing the complexities and synergies across and between terminologies in this work. Terminology is always a significant consideration in past-oriented LGBTQ+ research in search of individuals and communities known by a highly variable set of names (*sodomite, invert, third sex*, etc.). But rarely have we applied the same approach to other categories of experience. As a result, when scholars scour online databases and archival finding aids in search of *pink triangles*, they will find little of value before the mid-1970s. By contrast, when we complicate our terminology, to include different terms to describe these persecuted homosexuals pegged to earlier eras, like early US newspapers' use of *175* or Harry Hay's use of *Androgynous Community*, an entirely different set of results emerges. In these ways, deploying different terminologies becomes essential to identifying supposedly unknown stories like these. Similarly, it is also necessary to search for these memories in different texts and artifacts. While acknowledging homosexual publications—*Mattachine Review*, ONE, *Gay Sunshine*—as vital resources for tracing the American homosexual's remembrances of these events, exclusively relying on these outlets places many iterations of these memories out of reach. Instead, a more expansive approach toward texts produces a very different set of possibilities. By examining texts that are, for example, disreputable (gay Nazi-exploitation pulps), unconventional (Itkin's poetry), and not obviously homosexual (*Chanticleer*), we discover different remembrances of the Nazi persecution not seen anywhere else. In short, if activists and scholars are willing to be led by the memories themselves, rather than the presumptions they bring with them, we are much more likely to unlock stories we could not see before.

Similarly stymieing to attempts to study memories of the Nazi persecution of homosexuals before 1981 is an unwillingness to give up the pink triangle as the universal cipher of this past. This book clearly shows how pink triangle memories progressively devoured other, distinctly different experiences of the complex and multifaceted Nazi persecution over the decades, eventually subsuming them completely under its signifier. This state of affairs largely remains, with even the most recent publications in this area content to use the *pink triangle* as their watchword.[16] Nonetheless, to the extent that the pink triangle—as both a symbol and an experience—is what researchers search for, they are unlikely to find homosexuals remembering the Nazi persecution before 1973. For as this book has shown, earlier homosexuals remembered the persecution with different emphases—the Roehm purge, the Gestapo and Kripo, *piepels*, and more—only introducing the concentration camp framework in consistent ways after the mid-1960s. Likewise, the American tendency to remember the Nazi mistreatment of homosexuals through the Jewish experience of the Holocaust—similarly invoked by the pink triangle vantage point—occludes different understandings and memories of the persecution as rooted in discourses of criminality, ethnicity, or medicalized eugenics. Therefore, to the extent that contemporary scholars, researchers, and activists investigate the Nazi persecution of homosexuals in American memory, they are likely to come up empty-handed if they navigate this past with the pink triangle as their North Star.

A final and surely significant reason these memories have gone unacknowledged for years is that they make us uncomfortable. Of course, remembering and its tendency to resurrect the past is often unsettling. But memories of the Nazi persecution of homosexuals are among the most disturbing of those available to the US LGBTQ+ community, leading to a refusal to remember or, more precisely, to remember only in parts. This book reveals these challenges in spades. Most immediately, the facts and details of the abuses inflicted during the Nazi persecution on at least one hundred thousand homosexuals between 1933 and 1945 remain horrific and traumatizing. Facing these facts and internalizing them is chilling, and I fully admit feeling significant trepidation at the prospect of devoting four years of near-daily research to this project. It was debilitating at times, particularly in a global climate where fascism is once again on the rise and the persecution of LGBTQ+ peoples is intensifying in familiar ways. Invoking this past also resurfaces nefarious myths wielded against homosexuals for decades that we would rather leave buried. Chief among them is the myth of the homosexual Nazi that existing research has disproven.[17] Nonetheless, for a century, this idea has persisted as a pernicious thorn in the side of the LGBTQ+ community, and far-right extremists continue today to mobilize this false equivalency for their own purposes in both very new and very old ways. And to a lesser degree, resurrecting earlier remembrances of the Nazis' persecution of homosexuals reminds us of our own community's imprecise, cringeworthy, and sometimes disingenuous ways of using this past—claims that far exceed mere differences of interpretation. Of course, each of these must be judged in the context and evidence in which they were made. But the lionization of Roehm, the reification of the so-called Homocaust, and the brazen and gross overestimation of homosexual deaths in concentration camps—these and other misleading claims about the persecution clash with recent research and our modern sensibilities.

But the most affecting of these limitations is the continued role shame played in remembering these homosexual victims from 1981 onward. As we have seen, American homosexuals remembering the Third Reich did not always feel shame toward their predecessors. Rather, between 1934 and the mid-1970s, US lesbians and gays favored affective responses as varied as anger, shock, sadness, sympathy, empathy, and defiance in their recollections. Some even remembered these victims as heroes and martyrs for the larger cause of homosexual rights. But lesbian and gay Americans' affective orientation to these same victims shifted after Stonewall. With the attendant emergence of gay liberation and its discourse of "pride," the Nazi persecution of homosexuals started to *feel* different. In comparison to Stonewall's notable tone of triumph, the fact that so many homosexuals suffered and died at the hands of the Nazis felt shameful, something to be turned away from rather than toward. As such, when the Nazi persecution was remembered by lesbians and gays after 1978, it was often only to repudiate these earlier homosexuals as disgraceful parts of the community's history that contemporary sexual minorities should define themselves against. I believe this affective orientation explains in part the contours of most post-Stonewall remembrances of the Nazi persecution, which remain tied to the struggle against HIV/AIDS. I suspect the LGBTQ+ community's feeling about the Nazi persecution has changed little in our present moment, though such a claim exceeds the parameters of this book. Today, we certainly have monuments, memorials, and declarations that remember these victims, but there is little evidence that we remember them in any affective register other than shame and sorrow. In this light, devoting time to these earlier memories offers no affective payoff, further deterring our collective attention.

Each of these reasons explains why remembrances of the Nazi persecution of homosexuals between 1934 and 1981 have remained largely unexamined for most of the last century. This book was written to resist this trend, primarily by adopting scholarly dispositions and methods that counter incentives to leave these remembrances in the past. But for reasons that exceed the justice we owe to these past victims, it is increasingly imperative that today's LGBTQ+ community reorient itself to these pasts, lest it risk suffering a similar fate as these homosexuals in the decades ahead.

Queer Pasts, Memory Studies, and Holocaust Memory

In this book, I have related a story of remembrance that has far too long lingered in the background. The key instances, examples, and voices highlighted here have been a prominent focus of this storytelling effort. But in some significant ways, how homosocial, homosexual, and lesbian and gay Americans remembered their European forebears' fate between 1934 and 1981 also highlights several larger implications that exceed the story itself. It seems fitting, both in the book's conclusion and at the moment of its writing, to bring some of these implications to the foreground.

One implication is that this new story of how lesbian and gay Americans remembered the Nazis' homosexual persecution calls for a reexamination of our conventional understandings of the relationship between queer memory and memory studies. With some notable exceptions, the study of queer memory is often framed as a recent amendment to the much longer and deeper work of memory studies proper. In this narrative, memory studies emerged from the works of Maurice Halbwachs, who, in the 1920s, coined the term *collective memory* and shifted academic understandings of memory from an exclusively individual quality to a social phenomenon.[18] This work was later accelerated by the horrors of World War II and particularly the Holocaust, which instilled a moral imperative to remember together in new forms and at new orders of magnitude than previously imaginable. Drawing heavily but not exclusively from Holocaust studies and considerations of the Holocaust writ large, memory studies continued apace, reaching a critical climax in the late 1980s and early 1990s in the works of scholars like Pierre Nora, Eric Hobsbawm, and James E. Young.[19] From that point forward, the cultural "memory boom" and the study of memory both come into their own as dynamic practices and significant scholarly occupations, respectively.

Queer memory is typically framed as an extension and deepening of this century-old memory studies field, one that lesbian and gay thinkers embraced after gay liberation in 1969 and queer activists turned to as a political strategy amid the terrors of HIV/AIDS in the 1980s. Or to put it another way, queer memory is often considered a recent addition to the memory studies portfolio. Yet the stories and examples within *The Pink Scar* demand that this narrative be revisited. For each chapter in this text emphasizes that homosexuals were early adopters of memory work and potent practitioners of its arts. This makes sense, given that Halbwachs's theorization of collective memory in 1920s France happened alongside the early homosexual rights movement in Germany, before the Nazis' rise to power. In fact, the first chapter of the memory studies story might be said to end with Halbwachs's death in Buchenwald, the same concentration camp where approximately five hundred homosexuals were interned between 1938 and 1945.[20] Further, to the extent that the "boom" in memory accelerated after 1945 in direct response to the Holocaust, then this book's examples implicitly make the case that queer memory was intertwined with memory studies early on. For *if*, as Pierre Nora reputedly said, "whoever says memory, says Shoah," and *if* the Nazi persecution of homosexuals is now shown to have always been implicated in Holocaust remembrance, then it seems that queerness has always been embedded with memory.[21] To put it another way, *The Pink Scar* evidences that memory studies has likely almost always been queer. While further study is needed to exhume these fields' coemergence, this provocation leaves us to ask how we would understand memory studies differently if it were understood to have always been at least partially *queer* from the start.

At the same time, as *The Pink Scar* also asks us to consider tectonic shifts undergirding memory studies today, the central question is this: what are we to make of the future of queer memory amid the fluctuating fortunes of Holocaust memory? As I alluded to above, this book was written during a particularly incendiary period in world history, in which the almost unquestioned power of rhetorical appeals to the memory of the Holocaust have begun to diminish. This symbolic decline is complex, but it has been hastened by generational pressures, a reemergent far-right politics, and the aftermath of the October 7, 2023, attacks in Israel. These combined events have significantly degraded the rhetorical force of Holocaust memory, a trend that may accelerate in the decades to come. But in this new world of memory, it is fair to ask what becomes of memory studies when what some call its founding event loses its capacity to signify. And if queer memory is perhaps more deeply ensconced in Holocaust memory than we previously believed, what do these changes in perceptions of Holocaust memory portend for remembrances of the Nazi persecution of homosexuals in particular?

To the extent that the Holocaust has served as both the exigency *for* and moral underpinning *of* memory studies generally, it seems clear that this foundation is now perhaps irrevocably cracked. One might conjecture that a diminished Holocaust memory heralds an existential threat to memory studies, but such alarmism seems unfounded. While the moral imperative to remember the Holocaust has played an unmatched role in memory studies' development, I suspect with other scholars that the turn to memory has long been about more than the Holocaust alone.[22] Yet I do expect memory studies—and memory as a resource for rhetorical action—to change. For one, I believe overtures to memory as a rhetorical strategy may lose some of their luster in the years ahead. In the wake of the depletion of the twentieth century's archetypal memory in much of the public imagination, such appeals may no longer be as reliable or self-evidently appealing as they once were. For another, I anticipate that memory studies will increasingly seek new paradigms for imagining the shape and value of remembering the past in public contexts. For some, losing faith in the meaning of Holocaust memory will foster calls to shift focus to other events and atrocities—calls which may be unproductive if they do nothing beyond swapping the subjects of attention. However, if this search moves beyond "the event" as the organizing principle of the field and instead engenders new assumptions, questions, or infrastructures for making the past meaningful and manifest, such a change could be highly generative. Beyond these two shifts, there will certainly be others outside our present vantage point.

But what does the changing fate of Holocaust memory mean for remembrance of the Nazi persecution of homosexuals in the twenty-first century, and for queer memory as well? Queerness is, of course, capricious, making any attempt to predict the years to come a fickle exercise. Nonetheless, I believe this book's chapters indicate several possible impacts for the future of the queer past. Among the reverberations we might anticipate is a greater emphasis on distinguishing the Nazi persecution of homosexuals from the Jewish Holocaust in queer public memory rhetorics. This would be ironic, given that we have just asserted that the connection between the queer memory and Holocaust memory may be more deeply entrenched than expected. But there are political imperatives that suggest these overlaps are primed to be minimized. Unlike the decades between 1934 and 1981, when homosocial, homosexual, and lesbian and gay activists frequently argued for reading these two events as synonymous, the calculus is simply different today. LGBTQ+ Americans at this moment are notably less likely to look sympathetically on assertions of Jewish victimization in the aftermath of Gaza-Israel conflict, in part driven by a large and measurable turn against Israel among younger members of the LGBTQ+ community.[23] Whether these perceptions will endure and how much present antipathy toward Israel will extend to meaning-making around the Holocaust is unknown. But these data points certainly indicate a potential disidentification in queer memory between the Nazi persecution of homosexuals and the Holocaust.[24]

Alongside efforts to distinguish the Nazi persecution of homosexuals from the Jewish Holocaust in the US memory landscape, we may also see a different emphasis on bringing American remembrances of the Nazi persecution of homosexuals into greater alignment with how homosexual victims have been remembered in certain European contexts. In some parts of Europe, the story of homosexual suffering under the Third Reich has been told to emphasize the parallels between homosexuals and Communists and

Socialists as political prisoners, rather than comparing them to Jews. This alignment reflects different political realities of West Germany's political left after the war and Cold War mentalities that emphasized the suffering of Communists in Eastern European commemorative sites and markers.[25] But there are also some practical reasons for this different mnemonic configuration. Particularly in the first few months after the Nazis claimed power, homosexuals, Communists, and Socialists were some of the earliest communities interned in the emergent concentration camp system. Certainly, the experiences of these victim categories diverged noticeably over the years that followed. But turning toward remembering the Nazi persecution of homosexuals as a political struggle (rather than the victimization of a gay male "ethnic" group) may be one way this memory evolves in a post-Holocaust-centric framework.

But a final lesson remains that we have yet to discuss: the need for a healthy dose of skepticism in powerful claims like "Never Again, Never Forget." For decades, survivors, leaders, and activists have asserted repeatedly that the Holocaust must never be forgotten, and that memory is the essential instrument for resisting the recurrence of the horrors of the twentieth century. But the last two decades indicate that this mnemonic rejoinder has faltered. Forgetting is clearly possible, and the specter of fascism looms larger today than at any point since World War II. With that in mind, it becomes essential that we reconsider the similar imperative to remember the Nazi persecution of homosexuals in the face of a reemergence of anti-LGBTQ+ hate—to the extent that memory remains our only tool for keeping these forces in abeyance. This point is where I turn in the final section of this conclusion.

Remembering to Survive

At the time of this book's writing, evidence of the ongoing persecution of LGBTQ+ people in the United States is everywhere. In the year 2024, 530 anti-LGBTQ+ bills and policies were submitted for legislative consideration across the country, compared to thirty-eight such bills in 2018.[26] These proposed bills target all manner of LGBTQ+ life, including restrictions of transgender people in sports, bathroom bills, book bans, curriculum censorship, requirements that schools "out" their students, slashes to funding for LGBTQ+ programming, the elimination of DEI positions and programs at college and universities, banning or restricting drag performances, creating barriers to LGBTQ+ health care, limiting gender markers on government identification, and redefining sex and gender in government documents to limit LGBTQ+ protections.[27] More than one hundred pieces of such legislation have become law between 2018 and 2023.[28] These measures follow threats by certain conservative members of the US Supreme Court to rescind the federal right to same-sex marriage, and other federal judges have considered permitting government agents to once again use the Comstock Act to police LGBTQ+ content and publications as obscene materials.[29] Meanwhile, white Christian nationalist policies espoused by leading American conservatives promise an agenda focused on rescinding nondiscrimination protections for LGBTQ+ people, expelling transgender and HIV-positive individuals from the US military, slashing access to transgender health care, and prioritizing Christian values in federal policy.[30] And even as election outcomes and political agendas remain uncertain, LGBTQ+ people face increasing levels of violence on a daily basis. FBI data for 2023, tracking the reported number of violent crimes motivated by the victim's perceived sexual orientation or gender identity revealed a staggering 8.6 percent increase from the previous year. This marks the third consecutive annual increase in violence against LGBTQ+ people in the United States and reflects a near doubling of reported violent incidents since 2021.[31] Notably, between 2017 and 2023, 263 transgender or gender-expansive people were murdered in the United States, most of them Black trans women.[32] As a result of these and similar worrisome evidence, the nation's largest LGBTQ+ rights organization declared a "state of emergency" for LGBTQ+ Americans in June 2023.[33] In the face of this demonstrable recidivism toward LGBTQ+ persecution in the United States, much is demanded of those of us who believe in the queerer world we have built and the right of LGBTQ+ people to exist in it. In this work, I believe that remembering the Nazi persecution of homosexuals will be essential. In fact, remembering this past with particular attention to how these memories were understood and marshaled by homosexuals *in the decades between 1934 and 1981* may be among the most important resources available to queer people today as they navigate this next phase of America's recurrent anti-LGBTQ+ onslaughts.

Embedded within the memory rhetorics outlined in this book are several lessons we must learn as we move forward into the next decades of this struggle. Most immediately, contemporary LGBTQ+ activists should recognize that many of the antitrans and antiqueer discourses proffered in this current melee are just repackaged claims from the early to mid-twentieth century. When Florida passed its horrifying "Don't Say Gay" law in March 2022, proponents justified this attack with the same, tired anti-homosexual canards of protecting children that the Nazis once used to take control of German youth groups and organizations.[34] Similarly, when modern far-right activists invade drag story hours or attempt armed riots at pride parades, they borrow a page from the old Nazi playbook that used threats of violence and a culture of fear to garner political power.[35] At the moment, these attacks can feel like a jarring rebuke, a new and outrageous low proffered by a far-right campaign intent on destroying us in the here and now. But when contemporary LGBTQ+ people encounter these discourses armed with memories of the Nazi persecution of homosexuals, they can recognize that such tactics represent only the latest eruption of a century and a half of antiqueer animosity. With that knowledge, LGBTQ+ activists can gain perspective, gird themselves for a larger struggle, and find reassurance in the community's history of overcoming similar attacks and threats. Seeing these abundant allusions and corollaries also affords activists at least one rhetorical tool: the power of the Nazi taint. While charges of Nazi sympathies may no longer generate the universal condemnation they once did, significant value remains in demonstrating to audiences that today's antiqueer and antitrans policies resonate with Nazi-era orientations toward gender and sexual minorities. When LGBTQ+ activists can leverage such claims credibly to their advantage, remembering the Nazi persecution of the past offers the community the raw materials for its own modern defense.

Another significant strategic value modern LGBTQ+ Americans can distill from remembering the Nazi persecution of the past is disrupting the fallacy of the progressive narrative—the belief that things always "get better."[36] For both understandable and problematic reasons, contemporary US LGBTQ+ people assuage their anxieties about the modern world by believing that the horrors of the past cannot be repeated. "That happened back then," we tell ourselves, and it is unimaginable that the same horrors could ever again come to pass. While soothing in difficult times, this belief is dangerous. The cold reality is that it would be all too easy for American LGBTQ+ people to find themselves in a position substantially similar to—or even worse than—the one that befell their homosexual forebears under the Nazi regime. As modern voices continue to parrot fascist talking points of the twentieth century with impunity, we need to confront these risks—not as certainties, but as distinct possibilities. Remembrances of the Nazi persecution of homosexuals can be useful in disrupting this magical thinking. The memories highlighted in this book not only illuminate how these persecutions came about over time and manifested in many forms but also the folly of embracing the complacency inherent in an uncritical progressive mindset. In other words, a long memory of the Nazi persecution of homosexuals reminds us that things do not always get better. Instead, the past shows that the homosocial, homosexual, and lesbian and gay story has always been one of erratic highs and lows. There is no salvation for LGBTQ+ people in the belief that things cannot get worse again; such complacency only invites significant danger.

Relatedly, the memories of the Nazi persecution highlighted in this book remind us that persecution comes in many forms. Few modern American LGBTQ+ people recognize this complexity now. As this book detailed over and over again, when modern Americans invoke memories of the Nazi persecution of homosexuals, they tend to do so only by heralding the experiences of the pink triangles in Nazi concentration camps. This turn makes sense, as such painful histories resonate deeply with audiences and serve as a powerful argument for motivating LGBTQ+ people to act. But a pink triangle memory that conflates the entire Nazi persecution with the horrors of the camps is deeply problematic because it sets the bar too high for what the community should recognize as "persecution." Said otherwise, if we repeatedly use the homosexual experiences in the camps as a rhetorical boogeyman, we are apt to set an unrealistic rhetorical framework for action. This is consequential in two ways. On the one hand, if we invoke the pink triangle at even the slightest offense to LGBTQ+ people, we risk being seen as alarmist and ineffective. On the other hand, when the camps are foregrounded at all times, the many other indignities and harms that befell a far larger number of homosexuals between 1933 and 1945 are missed, permitting a piecemeal path to destruction to unfold unfettered. LGBTQ+ people should be called to arms when politicians declare the return of concentration camps, but they should also pour into the streets when leaders call for identification laws, facial recognition scans, gender identity checks, the firing of LGBTQ+ teachers, and any number of smaller attacks on human rights and dignities. This is one of the particular strengths of the examples in this book: they show how communities in earlier eras wielded a much more complex and nuanced narrative of the Nazi persecution, addressing both existential threats and less severe, yet still deeply problematic, concerns (e.g., police entrapment, snooping, medical experimentation). These previous generations of homosexual activists can teach today's LGBTQ+ defenders how to leverage anti-Nazi memories to effectively confront a much wider set of challenges, ones that are both more pressing and more likely to undermine contemporary queer life.

These earlier versions of remembering the Nazi persecution of homosexuals are also vital for demonstrating to modern LGBTQ+ people that the struggle for freedom requires a deft and dexterous relationship to the past. Above, I noted one reason LGBTQ+ people have avoided remembering the Nazi persecution is that many pre-HIV/AIDS memory rhetorics were made using unhelpful or problematic arguments. I stand by this claim. At the same time, I believe that one of this book's achievements is highlighting just how willing homosexual people of an earlier era were to alter, massage, or manipulate memories of the Nazi persecution to win the day. In this manner, Gerber's remembrances of Roehm were eccentric, Itkin's defiant imagery was often fanciful, and Milk's harsh indictment just felt wrong. But in each of these cases, the rhetors found varying degrees of success by bending these memories to suit their needs. That does not mean modern LGBTQ+ people do not owe their audiences credible evidence and ethical consideration of the Nazi victims' memories. But it does suggest that remembrances of the Nazi persecution of homosexuals may be uniquely capable of withstanding repeated and inconsistent manipulation. This same fact should remind readers that memories dispersed within public debates—particularly those about the survival of marginalized people—are never dictated entirely by truth. Rather, memories' ability to meet a community's most dire needs when needed is what makes them an essential rhetorical resource that must never be forgotten.

Perhaps the most vital reason contemporary LGBTQ+ people need to remember the Nazi persecution of homosexuals as the US homosexual community did between 1934 and 1981 is what it tells us about survival. *Survival* has not often been the key term in more recent debates about American LGBTQ+ life. Since Stonewall, discourses of *pride* and their concomitant messages of *progress* have led LGBTQ+ Americans to understand their current political struggle as one aimed at making the world better, safer, and more welcoming for gender and sexual minorities. Those messages did not always make sense. Particularly with the arrival of HIV/AIDS, the existential threat the virus posed to gay male life and culture demanded that *survival* return to a place of prominence in the community's vocabulary. But with time, political victories, and medical breakthroughs, discourses of survival once again receded in the American LGBTQ+ conversation. In its place, twenty-first-century rhetorics of pride, progress, and power have been rendered, not unproblematically, the prevalent terminologies through which LGBTQ+ Americans see their wider world.

However, given the barrage of anti-LGBTQ+ assaults outlined above, it seems that *survival* must return as the focus of our discourse. Not all LGBTQ+ people in the United States have yet recognized this fact. Many of us have navigated the last decade protected by our privileges, allies, and geographies. Meanwhile, this facade of security and progress has masked the daily struggles of community members, who endure incredible suffering and precarity. For these LGBTQ+ people on the front lines of this battle—transgender and nonbinary folxs, queers of color, queer and trans youth, incarcerated LGBTQ+ individuals, and LGBTQ+ people locked in hostile states by costs, commitments, or consequences—the danger has already come. Many members of the LGBTQ+ community endure routine harassment, torment, violence, and even death at the hands of individual purveyors of hate, but also from governments and authority figures who seek to oppress, legislate, and executive-order them out of existence. These LGBTQ+ Americans already know persecution, and I think it folly if those of us who feel safer at this moment believe we will not also. Today's national and global landscapes are menaced by growing waves of antiqueer and antitrans fascism, with hundreds of thousands of people willfully and glibly goose-stepping us all to a dark future. In the years ahead, genuine dangers haunt the greater queer world that has blossomed over the last century. And should we endure this moment, I fear there is little to prevent a resurgence of these same threats at any time.

In this unfolding world, nearly one hundred years after the Nazi persecution of homosexuals began, remembering these past atrocities as our homosexual kin did between 1934 and 1981 will be vital. For, as this book shows, those memories were not rooted in a narrow recollection of the worst-case scenario long ago defeated. Instead, those memories called to homosocial, homosexual, and lesbian and gay audiences alike to recognize the looming danger that hung over their heads. This threat, they argued, was real, and the Nazi persecution of homosexuals factored into it—not as a distant memory to be recalled and discounted, but as a lesson we should live with every day. Because while the Third Reich eventually fell and the suffering it inflicted on homosexuals changed, the anti-homosexual ideology that underpinned both remains. At their core, the essential message shared by all memories of the Nazi persecution of homosexuals is that, despite these countless horrors, the homosexuals were not snuffed out. They survived. The community's survival is once again at stake, and only time will tell if our memories can match the moment.

Notes

Introduction

1. Between 1934 and 1981, the terminologies used to refer to the diverse people we today call the LGBTQ+ community have changed significantly. To manage these changes throughout this book, I refer to individuals and communities according to either (a) the term(s) they use to refer to themself/themselves or (b) the prevailing term(s) in common usage at the time they were speaking or writing. Typically, I reserve LGBTQ+ to refer to people in our contemporary period. I outline how I address these issues as a methodological concern in the introduction's main text.

2. Harker, "Cuba Against Homosexuals," 2.

3. Hoffman, "Cuban Government Is Alarmed," L2.

4. Randy Wicker organized the first such picket on September 19, 1964, at the US Army Building in Lower Manhattan. See Shockley, "Picket in Front."

5. "Cross-Currents," 22.

6. For example, the White House Historical Association claims that the "consistent deterioration of rights for LGBTQ+ citizens during the 'Lavender Scare' led to the homophile movement and the . . . gay rights picket at the White House on April 17, 1965." See White House Historical Association, "LGBTQ+ Protests in Lafayette Square."

7. Minor discrepancies over the protest's time, duration, and the exact language on the signage are noted between contemporaneous reports and more recent scholarship. See "Cross-Currents," 22, and Cervini, *Deviant's War*, 200–201.

8. For instance, Frank Kameny often drew connections between Nazi Germany's treatment of Jews and the United States' treatment of homosexuals before the protest, but he rarely raised the Nazis' persecution of homosexuals directly. See Cervini, *Deviant's War*, 52, 112.

9. See "Cross-Currents," 22, and "10 Oppose Gov't," 18. On coalitional possibilities, see Cervini, *Deviant's War*, 129. On the *Washington Afro-American*'s history of covering homosexual news in the Black community, see Lvovsky, *Vice Patrol*, 37.

10. "Havana University Ousts 40," L9; Guerra, *Visions of Power*, 227–56; Lumsden, *Machos, Maricones, and Gays*, 68–70.

11. On this trepidation, see Beemyn, *Queer Capital*, 184.

12. Winter, "Generation of Memory," 57; Müller, "Introduction," 14.

13. Nora, "Between Memory and History," 8–9.

14. For a summary of these claims, see Schiappa, "Second Thoughts," 261–64.

15. For instance, significant early research for this project relied on searches in databases, texts, and archives using formal and informal combinations of words, like "homosexual AND Nazi," "Hitler AND invert," and "Homosexuality AND German," to identify leads for further investigation.

16. Memorial to the Persecuted Homosexuals Under National Socialism, "History of the Memorial."

17. Throughout this book, I use the anglicized version of the Nazi captain's name, Roehm, rather than the properly Germanic Röhm.

18. My search of *The Ladder* produced only a few relatively minor results. See *The Ladder: A Lesbian Review*.

19. Admittedly, these searches were not comprehensive, and the context in which I

was researching (i.e., the COVID-19 pandemic) presented several limitations, including a reliance on digital records that often underrepresent intersectional and diverse voices within the LGBTQ+ community.

20. This shift is apparent in the work of Newsome and Tremblay, whose texts both focus on the transnational dimensions of these memories and tend to emphasize the period after 1975. See Newsome, *Pink Triangle Legacies*, and Tremblay, *Badge of Injury*.

21. For instance, see Schoppmann, *Days of Masquerade*, 20–25, and Marhoefer, "Transgender Life and Persecution," 596–98.

22. Marhoefer, "Transgender Life and Persecution," 597.

23. Lusane, *Hitler's Black Victims*, 3–9; Marhoefer, "Transgender Life and Persecution," 597.

24. Ramgopal, "Survey Finds."

25. Beachy, *Gay Berlin*, 52–53.

26. Text and translation from United States Holocaust Memorial Museum, "Paragraph 175."

27. For instance, see Dickinson, "Policing Sex in Germany," 224–25.

28. Plant, *Pink Triangle*, 207.

29. On "passive enforcement," see Beachy, *Gay Berlin*, 13. On spikes in enforcement before 1933, see Dickinson, "Policing Sex in Germany," 224–25.

30. Beachy, *Gay Berlin*, 19–54.

31. Beachy, *Gay Berlin*, 14–15, 86.

32. Steinkopf-Frank, "Publishing Queer Berlin."

33. Sutton, "'We Too Deserve,'" 335.

34. Beachy, *Gay Berlin*, 176–79.

35. Beachy, *Gay Berlin*, 203–8.

36. Hancock, "'Only the Real,'" 632.

37. Hancock, "'Only the Real,'" 616–17, 626–28.

38. Hancock, "'Only the Real,'" 628.

39. Beachy, *Gay Berlin*, 259–60.

40. Parenthetical page citations in this chapter are from Lautmann, "Pink Triangle," 143 (hereafter cited in text as PT).

41. Plant, *Pink Triangle*, 69; Beachy, *Gay Berlin*, 260.

42. The phrase "blood purge" appeared in nearly all US newspaper headlines reporting on the event.

43. Hancock, "Purge of the SA," 682–83.

44. Plant, *Pink Triangle*, 211.

45. Plant, *Pink Triangle*, 211.

46. Beachy, *Gay Berlin*, 260–61.

47. Winchell, "On Broadway," 4; Sherman, *Bent*, 19, 23.

48. Plant, *Pink Triangle*, 7.

49. Whisnant, *Queer Identities and Politics*, 231.

50. Plant, *Pink Triangles*, 143.

51. Goeschel, *Suicide in Nazi Germany*, 87–89, 125–28.

52. Plant, *Pink Triangle*, 108–10.

53. United Press, "Rumors of New German Purge," 13; United Press, "Germany Has New Purge," 2.

54. Marhoefer, "Transgender Life and Persecution," 597.

55. United States Holocaust Memorial Museum, "Paragraph 175."

56. Plant, *Pink Triangle*, 110.

57. United States Holocaust Memorial Museum, "Paragraph 175."

58. United States Holocaust Memorial Museum, "Paragraph 175."

59. Marhoefer, "Transgender Life and Persecution," 597.

60. Hunt, "Frazier Hunt Tours," 9.

61. Röll, "Homosexual Inmates," 21–25.

62. Kogon, *Theory and Practice of Hell*, 35.

63. Schoppmann, *Days of Masquerade*, 20.

64. Marhoefer, "Transgender Life and Persecution," 595–601.

65. Plant, *Pink Triangles*, 143–45.

66. Plant, *Pink Triangles*, 143–45.

67. Argo, "Homosexuality in Germany Today," 9–10; Plant, *Pink Triangle*, 181.

68. Moeller, "Private Acts, Public Anxieties," 529–30.

69. Moeller, "Private Acts, Public Anxieties," 530–31. On annulments and restitution, see Associated Press, "Germany Compensates 249."

70. Evans, "Decriminalization, Seduction," 560; Cottrell, "Old Homosexuality Laws."

71. Hevesi, "Rudolf Brazda."

72. See Alexander Zinn as quoted in Marhoefer, "Transgender Life and Persecution."

73. Bérubé, *Coming Out Under Fire*, 178.

74. Jensen, "Pink Triangle and Political Consciousness," 321–22. Jensen also notes the lack of survivor testimony and the desire of many gay victims to "move on."

75. Stein, "Whose Memories?," 523.

76. Plant, *Pink Triangle*, 6–8.

77. Bérubé, *Coming Out Under Fire*, 178.

78. Bérubé, *Coming Out Under Fire*, 178, 338n14.

79. For examples, see "Nazis Certain of Victory," 3, and "New German Campaign," 2. Search conducted in Newspapers.com database for the year 1934.

80. United Press, "Rumors of New Nazi Purge Fly," 1.

81. Newspapers.com search for (November 1935–January 1936 + Dachau + Hunt).

82. Hunt, "Frazier Hunt Tours," 9.

83. See Associated Press, "Nurmi's Conqueror Jailed," 1, and Associated Press, "Dr. Peltzer Behind Bars," 10. Newspapers.com search for (Otto + Peltzer + arrested) in the year 1935.

84. Associated Press, "Deny Famous German Runner Killed Himself," 1.

85. Pears, "Otto the Strange."

86. Chicago Tribune Press Service, "Seized by Nazi Secret Police," 19; United Press, "Nazis Arrest Von Cramm," 1.

87. International News Service, "German Tennis Star," 1.

88. Associated Press, "Von Cramm, German Tennis Star," D17.

89. Newspapers.com search for ("von Cramm" + "morals charges") in 1938.

90. Winchell, "On Broadway," 4.

91. E. D. H., "Behind the Cables," 348.

92. "Secret Policeman."

93. Giles, "'Most Unkindest Cut,'" 43.

94. On the "lamp" metaphor, see Schwartz, *Abraham Lincoln*, 7.

95. Stryker and Meeker, "Introduction," 11–13; Bronski, *Pulp Friction*, 8.

Chapter 1

1. "In Memoriam on Active Service," 1.

2. Wray, *Pozières*, 203.

3. A search of the *Times* database only reveals notes for 1935 and 1937. However, sightings of these notes to Roehm "year after year" are described in Cassandra, "Times Sheds It Iron Tears," 47.

4. Roehm's only biography is Hancock's *Ernst Röhm: Hitler's SA Chief of Staff* (2008).

5. Hancock, "Purge of the SA," 680.

6. Hancock, "Purge of the SA," 679–80.

7. Hancock, "Purge of the SA," 680.

8. Hancock, *Ernst Röhm*, 167.

9. Unless stated otherwise, quotes in this chapter attributed to Gerber refer to a reproduction of the original "Hitlerism and Homosexuality" in Kepner, "My First 64 Years of Gay Liberation." Kepner's version has some minor discrepancies when compared with the partial reproduction of the original text in Katz, *Gay America History*, 394–96. Kepner's version is used throughout this chapter so that the full essay can be examined consistently. Publication information for the original essay can be found in Gerber, "Hitlerism and Homosexuality," 1–2.

10. On Gerber's anti-Semitism, see Elledge, *Angel in Sodom*, 149, 217 (hereafter cited in text as *AS*).

11. Hancock, "Ernst Röhm Versus General Hans Kundt," 696.

12. Shirer, *Rise and Fall*, 38.

13. Hancock, "Ernst Röhm Versus General Hans Kundt," 696.

14. Hancock, "Ernst Röhm Versus General Hans Kundt," 696.

15. Hancock, "'Only the Real,'" 618–19.

16. Shirer, *Rise and Fall*, 164–65.

17. Baynes, *Speeches of Adolf Hitler*, 309–10.

18. Hancock, "'Only the Real,'" 632.

19. Hancock, "'Only the Real,'" 628–36.

20. Hancock, "Purge of the SA," 669.

21. Hancock, "Purge of the SA," 669.

22. Hancock, "Purge of the SA," 669.

23. Shirer, *Rise and Fall*, 224–25; Baynes, *Speeches of Adolf Hitler*, 323, 309–10.

24. Katz, *Gay American History*, 394.

25. Marhoefer, *Sex and the Weimar Republic*, 154; Whisnant, *Queer Identities and Politics*, 208.

26. E. von H., "On Hitlerism," 4.

27. W. H. H., "Herr Hitler," 10.

28. Straw, "Traffic in Scandal," 950.

29. Chauncey, *Gay New York*, 300. Gaining access to *Brevities* titles can be notoriously challenging. See Chauncey, *Gay New York*, 449n61.

30. "Sexy Sailors Blow," 1, 12.

31. On Communist internment, see Wachsmann, *KL*, 27–35.

32. "Crumbling of the Fascist Front," 3.

33. Hamilton, "Who Is the Mysterious Dutchman," 6.

34. Gannes, "Hitler, God's Deputy," 6.

35. Gold, "Change the World," 7.

36. E. D. H., "Behind the Cables," 348.

37. Gerber, "Hitlerism and Homosexuality," 1–2.

38. Hirschfeld, "Die Homosexualität," 301. This image is reproduced in Katz, *Gay American History*, 390.

39. See note 3 in Katz, "Henry Gerber."

40. G. S., "Dear Friends," 22.

41. Kepner, "My First 64 Years of Gay Liberation," 27 (hereafter cited in text as MFY).

42. Katz, *Gay American History*, 394.

43. Lambright, "Doctor and Patient," 12.

44. Oechsner, "Hitler's Got a Girl," 2.

45. Knickerbocker, "Is Tomorrow Hitler's?," 5.

46. Dunn, *Queerly Remembered*, 13.

47. Greene and Newport, "American Public Opinion."

48. For instance, Plant cites the interpretation of his friend Eric Langer, who resided in Germany in the days after Roehm's murder in 1934: "Have you heard about the Roehm murders? With that it started, the rounding up, the closing of bars, and so on" (*Pink Triangle*, 7).

49. Johnson, *Lavender Scare*, 31.

Chapter 2

1. Katz, *Gay American History*, 411.

2. Hay, "Preliminary Concepts," 1.

3. Hay, *Radically Gay*, 314–15.

4. Alwood, *Straight News*, 27–28.

5. White, *Pre-Gay L.A.*, 39–40.

6. D'Emilio, *Sexual Politics*, 14.

7. Chauncey, *Gay New York*, 301–5.

8. D'Emilio, *Sexual Politics*, 46–49.

9. See Chauncey, "Forgotten History"; Wills, "Gays Bars and Gay Rights"; Marhoefer, "Transgender Life and Persecution," 598; Tully, "Liquor Laws Once Targeted Gay Bars"; Terl, "Essay on the History," 794–801.

10. Silver, "Vag Lewd," 7.

11. For examples, see Silver, "Vag Lewd"; Riccardi and Leeds, "Megan's Law"; and D'Emilio, *Sexual Politics*, 14.

12. Silver, "Vag Lewd," 7.

13. D'Emilio, *Sexual Politics*, 50–51.

14. Kearful, "New Nazism," 7 (hereafter cited in text as NN).

15. Lenn, "Cops Step Up Sex Arrests," 1.

16. On the FBI, see Charles, *Hoover's War on Gays*, 83. For examples of state and local list practices, see Lvovsky, *Vice Patrol*, 152, and Hernandez, "SB 145," 148.

17. Voltz, "Late Spots Face Police Crackdowns," 25.

18. Chauncey, "Forgotten History."

19. *The Ladder*—the first national publication for lesbians—was first published in 1956, but it had little to say about the Nazi persecution of homosexuals.

20. White, *Pre-Gay L.A.*, 52, 55, 59.

21. White, *Pre-Gay L.A.*, 63.

22. For instance, an issue of ONE reminded readers that the magazine "is connected in no way with the Mattachine Society, either legally[,] secretly[,] or ideologically. The January issue will contain the first of a series of criticisms of this organization that does not appear to hold with any of the purposes which motivate this magazine." ONE, back cover, 26.

23. A rare exception is Daniel, "Twelfth Man."

24. The publication excerpted by ONE was a new, postwar magazine named after a defunct Weimar-era homophile magazine. See Samper Vendrell, *Seduction of Youth*, 62, 181n44.

25. World Federation, "Die Insel," 5.

26. Burkhardt, "Letters," 30.

27. See Dickinson, "Policing Sex in Germany," 224–25. Such an interpretation would be wrong, given research showing high homosexual arrest rates prior to the Third Reich.

28. Burkhardt, "Letters," 30.

29. McIntire, "Tangents" (August/ September 1957), 19.

30. Argo, "Homosexual in Germany Today," 9.

31. Barnes, ". . . And the Pursuit of Happiness," 6.

32. Argo, "Homosexual in Germany Today," 9.

33. Church of England Moral Welfare Council, *Problem of Homosexuality*.

34. Jones, "Stained Glass Closet," 133.

35. "Bold Study," 17–18.

36. "Reform of Laws on Homosexuality Urged," 6.

37. American Law Institute, "American Law Institute's Model Penal Code," 12.

38. United States Holocaust Memorial Museum, "Gay Men Under the Nazi Regime."

39. K. L., "Letters from You," 21.

40. Carter, "People v. Martin," 108–9.

41. McIntire, "Tangents" (February 1957), 27; Carter, "Search and Seizures in California," 22–24, 29–33, 23.

42. Carter, "Search and Seizures in California," 30–31.

43. For example, see McIntire, "Tangents" (October/November 1957), 19.

44. McIntire, "Tangents" (April 1958), 18.

45. McIntire, "Tangents" (May 1958), 24.

46. Socrates, "Letters," 31–32.

47. Mr. E., "Letters," 29.

48. One, Incorporated v. Otto K. Olesen, Individually and as Postmaster of the City of Los Angeles, 241 F.2d 772 (9th Cir. 1957).

49. Gellately, Gestapo and German Society, 202.

50. Loftin, Letters to "ONE," 36.

51. Loftin, Letters to "ONE," 112.

52. Disturbed Citizen, "Letters," 29–30.

53. Mr. B., "Letters," 29.

54. Disturbed Citizen, "Letters," 29–30.

55. Stein, "Whose Memories?," 523.

56. K. L., "Letters from You," 21.

57. K. L., "Letters from You," 21.

58. Dunn, Queerly Remembered, 13.

59. White, Pre-Gay L.A., 62.

60. D'Emilio, Sexual Politics, 110.

61. Stein, "Whose Memories?," 523.

Chapter 3

1. Bentley, "Is It Time," D3.

2. Lehmann-Haupt, "Eric Bentley."

3. On pulp scholarship, see Stryker, Queer Pulps, and Bronski, Pulp Friction.

4. Stryker and Meeker, "Introduction," 11–13.

5. On medical experiments, see Röll, "Homosexual Inmates," 21–25.

6. Bourdieu, Logic of Practice, 53.

7. Sender, "Gay Readers, Consumers," 73.

8. Bronski, Pulp Friction, 8.

9. That literature has often been forgotten amid academic debates over how we define literature, and some scholars in the 1990s have searched for a "gay Holocaust literature" they felt certain did "not yet exist." See

Hammermeister, "Inventing History," 18. But several notable works were already in print, including Lannon D. Reed's Behold a Pale Horse (1985), Lesléa Newman's A Letter to Harvey Milk (1988), Robert C. Reinhart's Walk the Night (1994), and Martin Sherman's 1979 play Bent. Still, scholars continue to limit their characterizations to texts published since 1980. See Seifert, "Between Silence and License," 94–96.

10. Bronski, Pulp Friction, 2.

11. Stryker, Queer Pulps, 5.

12. Bronski, Pulp Friction, 4.

13. Bronski, Pulp Friction, 4.

14. Bronski, "Introduction," 11.

15. Magilow, Bridges, and Vander Lugt, Nazisploitation.

16. Pinchevski and Brand, "Holocaust Perversions," 391.

17. Taylor, Return to Lesbos, 49, 110.

18. Abramovich, "Atrocity," 367–68.

19. Previously, US readers may only have encountered the term piepels by passing mention in Wiesel, Night, 60. On tone, see Mikics, "Holocaust Pulp Fiction."

20. American Psychiatric Association, Diagnostic and Statistical Manual, 38–39. On details of considerations, see Dunn, "Dr. H[omosexual] Anonymous," 183–85.

21. For example, see Lehring, Officially Gay, 62–64.

22. Coolen, Concentration of Hans, front cover (hereafter cited in text as CH).

23. Davidson, Go Down, Aaron, 63 (hereafter cited in text as GDA).

24. Röll, "Homosexual Inmates," 21–25.

25. Zilinsky, Middle Ground, 7 (hereafter cited in text as MG).

26. Bronski, Pulp Friction, 7.

27. D'Emilio, Sexual Politics, 232–33.

28. Steakley, "Gay Movement in Germany, Part One," 12.

29. Nealon, Foundlings, 1.

Chapter 4

1. Armstrong and Crage, "Moments and Memory," 724–25.

2. Itkin, "Question Written in Blood," 17 (hereafter cited in text as QWB).

3. The largest collection of Itkin's works is housed at the ONE Archives at the USC Libraries in Los Angeles.

4. Kepner, "Southern California Movement Pioneers," 3.

5. Plaster, *Kids on the Street*, 64–65.

6. Sears, *Behind the Mask*, 318; Young, "Mikhail Itkin."

7. Kepner, "Southern California Movement Pioneers," 3.

8. Young, "Mikhail Itkin"; Plaster, *Kids on the Street*, 62.

9. Young, "Mikhail Itkin."

10. Kepner, "Southern California Movement Pioneers"; Young, "Mikhail Itkin."

11. Young, "Mikhail Itkin."

12. Plaster, *Kids on the Street*, 63.

13. As quoted in Plaster, *Kids on the Street*, 64.

14. Kepner, "Southern California Movement Pioneers," 3.

15. Plaster, *Kids on the Street*, 63.

16. Itkin, *Silent No More*, 5 (hereafter cited in text as *SNM*).

17. Young, "Mikhail Itkin."

18. Young, "Mikhail Itkin."

19. For instance, see Plaster, *Kids on the Street*, 62–65, and Byrne, *Other Catholics*, 156–57, 160, 273.

20. Plaster, *Kids on the Street*, 62.

21. Plaster, *Kids on the Street*, 64–65.

22. Young, "Mikhail Itkin."

23. For example, see Freeman, "Introduction," 159–76, and Freccero, *Queer/Early/Modern*, 69–104.

24. Derrida, *Specters of Marx*, 201–2.

25. Freccero, *Queer/Early/Modern*, 69–70.

26. Freccero, *Queer/Early/Modern*, 70, 5.

27. Freccero, *Queer/Early/Modern*, 13, 70–71.

28. Freccero, *Queer/Early/Modern*, 85–86.

29. Itkin, "Visitors from the Holocaust," 1 (hereafter cited in text as VH).

30. Jensen, Burkholder, and Hammerback, "Martyrs for a Just Cause," 335–37; Dunn, "Remembering Matthew Shepard," 624.

31. Jensen, Burkholder, and Hammerback, "Martyrs for a Just Cause," 337.

32. Jensen, Burkholder, and Hammerback, "Martyrs for a Just Cause," 340–41.

33. Dunn, "Remembering Matthew Shepard," 624.

34. Freccero, *Queer/Early/Modern*, 69.

35. Freccero, *Queer/Early/Modern*, 70.

36. For instance, see Foucault, *Discipline and Punish*, 201–3.

37. Dunn, *Queerly Remembered*, 13.

38. For examples, see Schoppmann, *Days of Masquerade*, 20–27.

Chapter 5

1. Von Neudegg, "Mutiny," 25–26. Von Neudegg was a pseudonym for Leo Classen, a pink triangle imprisoned in Sachsenhausen.

2. The excerpt was taken from a serialized account in the West German homosexual publication *Humanitas* over six issues between February 1954 and February 1955.

3. Von Neudegg, "Mutiny," 25–26.

4. With the possible exception of the execution of a *piepel* described in Wiesel, *Night*, 60.

5. Among them, over thirty-five cities, counties, and states had implemented laws and policies protecting lesbians and gays from discrimination by 1977. See Fejes, *Gay Rights*, 1.

6. Fejes, *Gay Rights*, 1–4.

7. Fejes, *Gay Rights*, 2–4.

8. Fejes, *Gay Rights*, 4.

9. For a reproduction of the full bill, see Tracey, "Proposition 6."

10. Shilts, *Mayor of Castro Street*, 3–5.

11. Shilts, *Mayor of Castro Street*, 50–51.

12. Shilts, *Mayor of Castro Street*, 72, 171.

13. Sharpe, "Angry Gays March," 1, 18.

14. Jensen, "Pink Triangle and Political Consciousness," 322.

15. Shilts, *Mayor of Castro Street*, 213, 223.

16. Dank, "Bryant's Brigade," 5.

17. Shilts, *Mayor of Castro Street*, 241, 240.

18. Shilts, *Mayor of Castro Street*, 220.

19. Black and Morris, "Introduction," 56n125.

20. Shilts, *Mayor of Castro Street*, 10–11.

21. Milk, "That's What America Is," 1.

22. Shilts, *Mayor of Castro Street*, 223, 226.

23. Giteck, "Interview with Harvey Milk," 21.

24. Subtraction is one of the four fundamental operations in the *quadripartita ratio*. It is also known as omission. See [Cicero?], *Rhetorica ad Herennium*, 303–5.

25. In this vein, see Steakley, "Gay Movement in Germany, Part One," and Steakley, "Gay Movement in Germany, Part Two."

26. Hudson, "Brief History."

27. This estimated speech length is taken from the transcript provided by the estate of Harvey Milk to the ONE Institute. See Milk, "That's What America Is," 1–7.

28. The miniseries was watched by more than 120 million Americans in April 1978. See McGuinness, "Holocaust."

29. The term *hysteron proteron* is a rhetorical device in which what should come last is placed first in a chronology or order. See *Oxford English Dictionary*, s.v. "hysteron proteron," accessed September 18, 2024, https://doi.org/10.1093/OED/3160293592.

30. Middleton-Kaplan, "Myth of Jewish Passivity," 3.

31. Isaiah 53:7 (JPS).

32. Middleton-Kaplan, "Myth of Jewish Passivity," 3–4.

33. As quoted in Middleton-Kaplan, "Myth of Jewish Passivity," 6.

34. Feldman and Bowman, "Let Us Not Die."

35. Middleton-Kaplan, "Myth of Jewish Passivity," 7–25.

36. Jews Against Briggs / Proposition 6, "Open Letter," 9.

37. John Paul II, "Address of His Holiness."

38. International Gay Association, "Open Letter to Pope," 5.

Conclusion

1. Kerr, "How Six NYC Activists Changed History.'"

2. Kerr, "How Six NYC Activists Changed History."

3. Centers for Disease Control, "Morbidity and Mortality."

4. For instance, see Newsome, *Pink Triangle Legacies*, 120–27, and Tremblay, *Badge of Injury*, 181–208.

5. See, among other, Nora, "Between Memory and History," 8.

6. On the rhetoric of archives, see Morris, "Archival Turn," 113.

7. For instance, see Goodwin's Law at Goodwin, "Meme, Counter-Meme."

8. Dunn, *Queerly Remembered*, 3–4, 13–14.

9. Morris, "My Old Kentucky Homo," 106.

10. Castiglia and Reed, *If Memory Serves*, 9.

11. Muñoz, "Ephemera as Evidence," 7–10.

12. Jensen, "Pink Triangle and Political Consciousness," 321.

13. In this vein, see Habermas, *Structural Transformation*, and Dewey, *Public and Its Problems*.

14. Most notably Fraser, "Rethinking the Public Sphere," 123, 121.

15. Warner, "Publics and Counterpublics," 50, 60.

16. See the use of pink triangles as "shorthand" in Newsome, *Pink Triangle Legacies*, 5.

17. See this research summarized in Jensen, "Pink Triangle and Political Consciousness," 322–23.

18. Halbwachs, *On Collective Memory*, 43.

19. Nora, "Between Memory and History"; Hobsbawm and Ranger, *Invention of Tradition*; Young, *Texture of Memory*.

20. Röll, "Homosexual Inmates," 13–14.

21. Winter, "Generation of Memory," 57.

22. In fact, some scholarship suggests that there have been numerous "booms" in memory across time in various human societies, many of which preceded the Holocaust and originated from beyond the borders of Europe. See Hass, "Remembering the 'Forgotten War,'" 268.

23. Stack, "Gaza War Is Dividing"; Jones, "Americans' Views."

24. Muñoz, *Disidentifications*, 39.

25. Jensen, "Pink Triangle and Political Consciousness," 342.

26. American Civil Liberties Union, "Mapping Attacks"; Rogers and Radcliffe, "Over 100."

27. American Civil Liberties Union, "Mapping Attacks."

28. Rogers and Radcliffe, "Over 100."

29. Edelman, "Thomas Wants"; Gira Grant, "Conservatives Are Turning."

30. GLADD, "Project 2025 Exposed."

31. Alfonseca, "Hate Crimes."

32. Everytown for Gun Safety, "New Everytown Data."

33. Human Rights Campaign, "For the First Time Ever."

34. Plant, *Pink Triangle*, 102, 109, 125.

35. For two such instances, see Wiggins, "Neo-Nazis Chanting," and Sullivan, "Far-Right Plan."

36. "It Gets Better Project."

Bibliography

Abramovich, Dvir. "Atrocity (Karu Lo Piepel)." In *Reference Guide to Holocaust Literature*, edited by Thomas Riggs, 367–68. New York: St. James Press, 2002.

Alfonseca, Kiara. "Hate Crimes, Particularly Against LGBTQ Community, on the Rise: FBI Data." *ABC News*, September 24, 2024. https://abcnews.go.com/US/hate-crimes-lgbtq-community-rise-fbi-data/story?id=113962673.

Alwood, Edward. *Straight News: Gays, Lesbians, and the News Media*. New York: Columbia University Press, 1996.

American Civil Liberties Union. "Mapping Attacks on LGBTQ Rights in U.S. State Legislatures in 2024." Accessed October 5, 2024. https://www.aclu.org/legislative-attacks-on-lgbtq-rights-2024.

American Law Institute. "American Law Institute's Model Penal Code: Sodomy and Related Offenses." *Mattachine Review* 2, no. 5A (September 1956): 5–25.

American Psychiatric Association. *Diagnostic and Statistical Manual of Mental Disorders*. Washington, DC: American Psychiatric Association, 1952.

Argo, Jack. "The Homosexual in Germany Today." *ONE* 3, no. 6 (June 1955): 9–10.

Armstrong, Elizabeth A., and Suzanna M. Crage. "Moments and Memory: The Making of the Stonewall Myth." *American Sociological Review* 71, no. 5 (2006): 724–51. https://www.jstor.org/stable/25472425.

Associated Press. "Deny Famous German Runner Killed Himself." *Charlotte News*, June 24, 1935. Newspapers.com.

———. "Dr. Peltzer Behind Bars." *Kansas City (MO) Star*, June 25, 1935. Newspapers.com.

———. "Germany Compensates 249 People Persecuted over Nazi-Era Law Criminalizing Homosexuality." *CBS News*, September 14, 2021. https://www.cbsnews.com/news/germany-compensates-249-persecuted-law-homosexuality.

———. "Nurmi's Conqueror Jailed in Germany." *Brooklyn Daily Eagle*, June 25, 1935. Newspapers.com.

———. "Von Cramm, German Tennis Star of the 1930s, Dies in Car Crash at 66." *New York Times*, November 10, 1976. https://www.nytimes.com/1976/11/10/archives/von-cramm-german-tennis-star-of-1930s-dies-in-car-crash-at-66.html.

Barnes, Hollister. ". . . And the Pursuit of Happiness." *ONE* 12, no. 7 (July 1964): 5–8.

Baynes, Norman H., ed. *The Speeches of Adolf Hitler, April 1922–August 1939*. New York: Oxford University Press, 1942.

Beachy, Robert. *Gay Berlin: Birthplace of a Modern Gay Identity*. New York: Vintage Books, 2015. Google Play Books.

Beemyn, Genny. *A Queer Capital: A History of Gay Life in Washington, D.C.* New York: Routledge, 2015.

Bentley, Eric. "Is It Time for the Audience to Shout Back?" *New York Times*, May 14, 1972. https://www.nytimes.com/1972/05/14/archives/is-it-time-for-the-audience-to-shout-back-time-for-the-audience-to.html.

Bérubé, Allan. *Coming Out Under Fire: The History of Gay Men and Women in World War II*. New York: Plume, 1990.

Black, Jason Edward, and Charles E. Morris III. "Introduction: Harvey Milk's Political Archive and Archival Politics." In *An Archive of Hope: Harvey Milk's Speeches and Writings*, by Harvey Milk, edited by Black and Morris, 1–60. Berkeley: University of California Press, 2013.

"A Bold Study by the Church of England." ONE 2, no. 6 (June 1954): 17–18.

Bourdieu, Pierre. *The Logic of Practice.* Translated by Richard Nice. Stanford, CA: Stanford University Press, 1990.

Bronski, Michael. "Introduction." In *Song of the Loon*, by Richard Amory, 9–26. Vancouver: Arsenal Pulp Press, 2005.

———. *Pulp Friction: Uncovering the Golden Age of Gay Male Pulps.* New York: St. Martin's Griffin, 2003.

Burkhardt, Rudolf. "Letters." ONE 7, no. 9 (September 1959): 30.

Byrne, Julie. *The Other Catholics: Remaking America's Largest Religion.* New York: Columbia University Press, 2016.

Carter, Jesse W. "People v. Martin [DISSENT]." 46 Cal. 2d 106; 293 P.2d 52; 1956. https://digitalcommons.law.ggu.edu /carter_opinions/162.

———. "Search and Seizures in California and the Protection of Constitutional Rights." *Mattachine Review* 2, no. 2 (April 1956): 22–24, 29–33.

Cassandra. "The Times Sheds It Iron Tears." *Tucson Daily Citizen*, March 26, 1960. Newspapers.com.

Castiglia, Christopher, and Christopher Reed. *If Memory Serves: Gay Men, AIDS, and the Promise of the Queer Past.* Minneapolis: University of Minnesota Press, 2012.

Centers for Disease Control. "Morbidity and Mortality Weekly Report." August 18, 1989. https://www.cdc.gov/mmwr /preview/mmwrhtml/00001442.htm.

Cervini, Eric. *The Deviant's War: The Homosexual vs. the United States of America.* New York: Picador, 2021.

Charles, Douglas M. *Hoover's War on Gays: Exposing the FBI's "Sex Deviates" Program.* Lawrence: University Press of Kansas, 2015.

Chauncey, George. "The Forgotten History of Gay Entrapment." *The Atlantic*, June 25, 2019. https://www.theatlantic .com/ideas/archive/2019/06/before -stonewall-biggest-threat-was-entrap ment/590536/.

———. *Gay New York: Gender, Urban Culture, and the Making of the Gay Male World, 1890–1940.* New York: Basic Books, 1994.

Chicago Tribune Press Service. "Seized by Nazi Secret Police." *Chicago Daily Tribune*, March 8, 1938. Newspapers .com.

Church of England Moral Welfare Council. *The Problem of Homosexuality: An Interim Report.* London: Church Information Board, 1952.

[Cicero?]. *Rhetorica ad Herennium.* Translated by Harry Caplan. Cambridge, MA: Harvard University Press, 1964.

Coolen, Carl. *The Concentration of Hans.* New York: 101 Enterprises, 1967.

Cottrell, Chris. "Old Homosexuality Laws Still Hang Over Many in Germany." *New York Times*, March 4, 2013. https://www.nytimes.com/2013/03/05 /world/europe/old-homosexuality -laws-still-hang-over-many-in-ger many.html.

"Cross-Currents." *The Ladder: A Lesbian Review* 9, no. 8 (May 1965): 22.

"Crumbling of the Fascist Front." *Daily Worker*, October 29, 1932. Newspapers .com.

Daniel, Marc. "The Twelfth Man." *Mattachine Review* 2, no. 5 (October 1956): 18–24.

Dank, Barry M. "Bryant's Brigade Uses Hitler's Tactics." *Los Angeles Times*, October 23, 1977. Newspapers.com.

Davidson, Chris. *Go Down, Aaron.* San Diego: Ember, 1967.

D'Emilio, John. *Sexual Politics, Sexual Communities: The Making of a Homosexual Minority in the United States, 1940–1970.* Chicago: University of Chicago Press, 1983.

Derrida, Jacques. *Specters of Marx: The State of the Debt, the Work of Mourning and the New International.* Translated by Peggy Kamuf. New York: Routledge, 1994.

Dewey, John. *The Public and Its Problems.* New York: Henry Holt, 1927.

Dickinson, Edward Ross. "Policing Sex in Germany, 1882–1982: A Preliminary Statistical Analysis." *Journal of the History of Sexuality* 16, no. 2 (2007): 204–50. https://www.jstor.org/stable /30114233.

Disturbed Citizen. "Letters." ONE 8, no. 4 (April 1960): 29–30.

Dunn, Thomas R. "Dr. H[omosexual] Anonymous, Gay Liberation Activism, and the American Psychiatric Association, 1963–1973." In *Social Controversy and Public Address in the 1960s and Early 1970s*, edited by Richard J. Jensen, 181–220. East Lansing: Michigan State University Press, 2017.

———. *Queerly Remembered: Rhetorics for Representing the GLBTQ Past.* Columbia: University of South Carolina Press, 2016.

———. "Remembering Matthew Shepard: Violence, Identity, and Queer Counterpublic Memories." *Rhetoric and Public Affairs* 13, no. 4 (2010): 611–51. https://www.jstor.org/stable /41940504.

Edelman, Adam. "Thomas Wants the Supreme Court to Overturn Landmark Rulings That Legalized Contraception, Same-Sex Marriage." *NBC News*, June 24, 2022. https://www.nbcnews .com/politics/supreme-court/thomas -wants-supreme-court-overturn -landmark-rulings-legalized-contrac -rcna35228.

E. D. H. "Behind the Cables." *The Nation*, October 19, 1932. The Nation Digital Archive.

Elledge, Jim. *An Angel in Sodom: Henry Gerber and the Birth of the Gay Rights Movement.* Chicago: Chicago Review Press, 2022. Google Play Books.

Evans, Jennifer V. "Decriminalization, Seduction, and 'Unnatural Desire' in East Germany." *Feminist Studies* 36, no. 3 (2010): 553–77. https://www.jstor .org/stable/27919121.

Everytown for Gun Safety. "New Everytown Data on Transgender Homicides Reveals Concentration in the South." February 13, 2024. https://www .everytown.org/press/new-everytown -data-on-transgender-homicides -reveals-concentration-in-the-south.

E. von H. "On Hitlerism." *Baltimore Sun*, April 29, 1933. Newspapers.com.

Fejes, Fred. *Gay Rights and Moral Panic: The Origins of America's Debate on Homosexuality.* New York: Palgrave Macmillan, 2008.

Feldman, Yael, and Steven Bowman. "Let Us Not Die as Sheep Led to the Slaughter." *Haaretz*, December 6, 2007. https:// www.haaretz.com/2007-12-06/ty -article/let-us-not-die-as-sheep-led-to -the-slaughter/0000017f-e565-da9b -a1ff-ed6f4cd30000.

Foucault, Michel. *Discipline and Punish: The Birth of the Prison.* Translated by Alan Sheridan. New York: Vintage Books, 1991.

Fraser, Nancy. "Rethinking the Public Sphere: A Contribution to the Critique of Actually Existing Democracy." In *Habermas and the Public Sphere*, edited by Craig J. Calhoun, 109–42. Cambridge, MA: MIT Press, 1992.

Freccero, Carla. *Queer/Early/Modern.* Durham, NC: Duke University Press, 2006. Google Play Books.

Freeman, Elizabeth. "Introduction." *GLQ: Journal of Lesbian and Gay Studies* 13, nos. 2–3 (2007): 159–76. https://doi.org /10.1215/10642684-2006-029.

Gannes, Harry. "Hitler, God's Deputy | Against Sodom and Gomorrah | The Real Orgies." *Daily Worker*, July 2, 1934. Newspapers.com.

Gellately, Robert. *The Gestapo and German Society: Enforcing Racial Policy, 1933–1945.* New York: Oxford University Press, 1990.

Gerber, Henry. "Hitlerism and Homosexuality." *Chanticleer* 1, no. 9 (1934): 1–2.

Giles, Geoffrey J. "'The Most Unkindest Cut of All': Castration, Homosexuality, and Nazi Justice." *Journal of Contemporary History* 27, no. 1 (1992): 41–61. https:// www.jstor.org/stable/260778.

Gira Grant, Melissa. "Conservatives Are Turning to a 150-Year-Old Obscenity Law to Outlaw Abortion." *New Republic*, April 12, 2023. https:// newrepublic.com/article/171823

/kacsmaryk-mifepristone-abortion
-comstock-act.

Giteck, Lenny. "An Interview with Harvey
Milk." *San Francisco Examiner*,
November 29, 1978. Newspapers.com.

GLADD. "Project 2025 Exposed." Accessed
October 5, 2024. https://glaad.org
/project-2025.

Goeschel, Christian. *Suicide in Nazi Germany.*
New York: Oxford University Press,
2009.

Gold, Michael. "Change the World." *Daily
Worker*, January 5, 1935. Newspapers
.com.

Goodwin, Mike. "Meme, Counter-Meme."
Wired, October 1, 1994. https://www
.wired.com/1994/10/godwin-if-2.

Greene, Daniel, and Frank Newport.
"American Public Opinion and the
Holocaust." *Polling Matters*, April 23,
2018. https://news.gallup.com/opinion
/polling-matters/232949/american
-public-opinion-holocaust.aspx.

G. S. "Dear Friends . . ." *ONE* 1, no. 7 (July
1953): 22.

Guerra, Lillian. *Visions of Power in Cuba:
Revolution, Redemption, and
Resistance, 1959–1971.* Chapel Hill:
University of North Carolina Press,
2012.

Habermas, Jürgen. *The Structural
Transformation of the Public Sphere:
An Inquiry into a Category of Bourgeois
Society.* Translated by Thomas Burger.
Cambridge, MA: MIT Press, 1991.

Halbwachs, Maurice. *On Collective Memory.*
Edited and translated by Lewis A.
Coser. Chicago: University of Chicago
Press, 1992.

Hamilton, Robert. "Who Is the Mysterious
Dutchman, Van der Lubbe?" *Daily
Worker*, September 28, 1933.
Newspapers.com.

Hammermeister, Kai. "Inventing History:
Toward a Gay Holocaust Literature."
German Quarterly 70, no. 1 (1997):
18–26. https://doi.org/10.2307/407838.

Hancock, Eleanor. *Ernst Röhm: Hitler's SA
Chief of Staff.* New York: Palgrave
Macmillan, 2008.

———. "Ernst Röhm Versus General Hans
Kundt in Bolivia, 1929–30? The
Curious Incident." *Journal of*

Contemporary History 47, no. 4 (2012):
691–708. https://doi.org/10.1177
/0022009412451287.

———. "'Only the Real, the True, the
Masculine Held Its Value': Ernst
Röhm, Masculinity, and Male
Homosexuality." *Journal of the History
of Sexuality* 8, no. 4 (1998): 616–41.
https://www.jstor.org/stable/3840412.

———. "The Purge of the SA Reconsidered:
'An Old Putschist Trick'?" *Central
European History* 44, no. 4 (2011):
669–83. https://www.jstor.org/stable
/41411643.

Harker, Daniel. "Cuba Against Homosexuals,
Beatle Haircuts." *Edwardsville (IL)
Intelligencer*, June 8, 1965. Newspapers
.com.

Hass, Kristin. "Remembering the 'Forgotten
War' and Containing the
'Remembered War.'" In *Transnational
American Memories*, edited by Udo J.
Hebel, 267–84. New York: De Gruyter,
2009.

"Havana University Ousts 40." *New York
Times*, May 27, 1965. https://www
.nytimes.com/1965/05/27/archives
/havana-university-ousts-40.html.

Hay, Harry [Eann MacDonald, pseud.].
"Preliminary Concepts." San Francisco
Public Library, July 7, 1950. https://sfpl
.org/sites/default/files/2019-12
/bachelors-anonymous.pdf.

———. *Radically Gay.* Edited by Will Roscoe.
Boston: Beacon Press, 1996.

Hernandez, Elias. "SB 145: Defending and
Applying Discretion to California's Sex
Offender Registry." *Golden Gate
University Law Review* 52, no. 2 (2002):
145–62. https://digitalcommons.law
.ggu.edu/ggulrev/vol52/iss2/4.

Hevesi, Dennis. "Rudolf Brazda, Who
Survived Pink Triangle, Is Dead at 98."
New York Times, August 5, 2011.
https://www.nytimes.com/2011/08/06
/world/europe/06brazda.html.

Hirschfeld, Magnus. "Die Homosexualität." In
Sittengeschichte des Lasters, edited by
Leo Schidrowitz, 253–318. Leipzig:
Verlag für Kulturforschung, 1927.

Hobsbawm, Eric, and Terence Ranger, eds.
The Invention of Tradition. New York:
Cambridge University Press, 1983.

Hoess, Rudolf. *Commandant of Auschwitz*. London: Weidenfeld and Nicolson, 1959.

Hoffman, Paul. "Cuban Government Is Alarmed by Increase in Homosexuality." *New York Times*, April 16, 1965. https://www.nytimes.com/1965/04/16/archives/cuban-government-is-alarmed-by-increase-in-homosexuality.html.

Hudson, Jonny. "A Brief History of the First Nazi Gas Chamber." Holocaust Centre North, December 7, 2021. https://hcn.org.uk/blog/a-brief-history-of-the-first-nazi-gas-chambers.

Human Rights Campaign. "For the First Time Ever, Human Rights Campaign Officially Declares 'State of Emergency' for LGBTQ+ Americans." June 6, 2023. https://www.hrc.org/press-releases/for-the-first-time-ever-human-rights-campaign-officially-declares-state-of-emergency-for-lgbtq-americans-issues-national-warning-and-guidebook-to-ensure-safety-for-lgbtq-residents-and-travelers.

Hunt, Frazier. "Frazier Hunt Tours German Concentration Camp; Most of Prisoners Are Communists." *Cedar Rapids Gazette*, December 8, 1935. Newspapers.com.

"In Memoriam on Active Service." *Times* (London), June 29, 1935. The Times Digital Archive.

International Gay Association. "An Open Letter to Pope John Paul II." *GALA Review* 2, no. 11 (1979): 4–5. Archives of Sexuality and Gender.

International News Service. "German Tennis Star to Prison for Immorality." *Tulsa (OK) World*, May 15, 1938. Newspapers.com.

"It Gets Better Project." Accessed October 5, 2024. https://itgetsbetter.org/.

Itkin, Rev. Mikhail. "A Question Written in Blood." *Gay Sunshine* 1, no. 1 (1970): 17.

———. *Silent No More: The Pink Triangle*. 1977 pamphlet reprinted in ONE 23, no. 5 (1978): 2–5.

———. "Visitors from the Holocaust." Community of the Love of Christ, 1975: 1. "Holocaust" folder, box 11. International Gay Information Center

Ephemera Files—Subjects. Manuscripts and Archives Division. New York Public Library. Astor, Lenox, and Tilden Foundations.

Jensen, Erik. N. "The Pink Triangle and Political Consciousness: Gays, Lesbians, and the Memory of Nazi Persecution." *Journal of the History of Sexuality* 11, nos. 1–2 (2002): 319–49. https://dx.doi.org/10.1353/sex.2002.0008.

Jensen, Richard R., Thomas R. Burkholder, and John C. Hammerback. "Martyrs for a Just Cause: The Eulogies of Cesar Chavez." *Western Journal of Communication* 67, no. 4 (2003): 335–56. https://doi.org/10.1080/10570310309374778.

Jews Against Briggs / Proposition 6. "An Open Letter to the Los Angeles Lesbian and Gay Community." *Sister* 9, no. 5 (October/November 1978): 9. Archives of Sexuality and Gender.

John Paul II. "Address of His Holiness John Paul II to the Bishops of the United States of America, October 5, 1979." The Vatican. Accessed October 5, 2024. https://www.vatican.va/content/john-paul-ii/en/speeches/1979/october/documents/hf_jp-ii_spe_19791005_chicago-usa-bishops.html.

Johnson, David K. *The Lavender Scare: The Cold War Persecution of Gays and Lesbians in the Federal Government*. Chicago: University of Chicago Press, 2004.

Jones, Jeffrey M. "Americans' Views of Both Israel, Palestinian Authority Down." *Gallup*, March 4, 2024. https://news.gallup.com/poll/611375/americans-views-israel-palestinian-authority-down.aspx.

Jones, Timothy. "The Stained Glass Closet: Celibacy and Homosexuality in the Church of England to 1955." *Journal of the History of Sexuality* 20, no. 1 (2011): 132–52. https://www.jstor.org/stable/40986357.

Katz, Jonathan. *Gay American History: Lesbians and Gay Men in the U.S.A.* New York: Thomas Y. Crowell, 1976.

———. "Henry Gerber: 'I Wanted to Help Solve the Problem,' 1920–1925." OUT

History. Accessed October 5, 2024. https://wiki.outhistory.org/wiki/Henry _Gerber:_%22I_wanted_to_help_solve _the_problem,%22_1920-1925.

Kearful, James F. "The New Nazism." *ONE* 11, no. 5 (May 1963): 5–11.

Kepner, Jim. "My First 64 Years of Gay Liberation: 1933–1942 Circa 1985–1997." Jim Kepner Papers: Writings on Gay and Lesbian History Series. ONE National Gay and Lesbian Archives. Archives of Sexuality and Gender. Accessed September 30, 2024. https://oac.cdlib.org/findaid/ark:/13030/kt8d5nf4c6/dsc/?query=jim%20kepner%20papers#ref107.

———. "'Southern California Movement Pioneers' Circa 1993–1995." Jim Kepner Papers: Writings on Gay and Lesbian History Series. ONE National Gay and Lesbian Archives. Archives of Sexuality and Gender. Accessed September 30, 2024. https://oac.cdlib.org/findaid/ark:/13030/kt8d5nf4c6/dsc/?query=jim%20kepner%20papers#ref107.

Kerr, Theodore. "How Six NYC Activists Changed History with 'Silence = Death.'" *Village Voice*, June 20, 2017. https://www.villagevoice.com/how-six-nyc-activists-changed-history-with-silence-death.

K. L. "Letters from You." *ONE* 1, no. 6 (June 1953): 21.

Knickerbocker, H. R. "Is Tomorrow Hitler's?" *Fort Worth Star-Telegram*, February 2, 1942. Newspapers.com.

Kogon, Eugen. *The Theory and Practice of Hell: German Concentration Camps and the System Behind Them*. New York: Farrar, Straus and Giroux, 1950.

The Ladder: A Lesbian Review, 1956–1972: An Interpretation and Document Archive. Introduction by Marcia M. Gallo. Alexandria, VA: Alexander Street Press, 2010. https://documents.alexanderstreet.com/c/1003264003.

Lambright, E. D. "Doctor and Patient." *Tampa (FL) Tribune*, January 25, 1942. Newspapers.com.

Lautmann, Rüdiger. "The Pink Triangle: The Persecution of Homosexual Males in Concentration Camps in Nazi Germany." *Journal of Homosexuality* 6, nos. 1–2 (1981): 141–60. https://doi.org/10.1300/J082v06n01_13.

Lehmann-Haupt, Christopher. "Eric Bentley, Critic Who Preferred Brecht to Broadway, Dies at 103." *New York Times*, August 5, 2020. https://www.nytimes.com/2020/08/05/theater/eric-bentley-dead.html.

Lehring, Gary. *Officially Gay: The Political Construction of Sexuality by the U.S. Military*. Philadelphia: Temple University Press, 2003.

Lenn, Ernest. "Cops Step Up Sex Arrests." *San Francisco Examiner*, October 17, 1960. Newspapers.com.

Loftin, Craig M., ed. *Letters to "ONE": Gay and Lesbian Voices from the 1950s and 1960s*. Albany: State University of New York Press, 2012.

Lumsden, Ian. *Machos, Maricones, and Gays: Cuba and Homosexuality*. Philadelphia: Temple University Press, 1996.

Lusane, Clarence. *Hitler's Black Victims: The Historical Experiences of Afro-Germans, European Blacks, Africans, and African Americans in the Nazi Era*. New York: Routledge, 2002.

Lvovsky, Anna. *Vice Patrol: Cops, Courts, and the Struggle over Urban Gay Life Before Stonewall*. Chicago: University of Chicago Press, 2021.

Magilow, Daniel H., Elizabeth Bridges, and Kristin T. Vander Lugt, eds. *Nazisploitation! The Nazi Image in Low-Brow Cinema and Culture*. New York: Continuum, 2012.

Marhoefer, Laurie. *Sex and the Weimar Republic: German Homosexual Emancipation and the Rise of the Nazis*. Toronto: University of Toronto Press, 2015.

———. "Transgender Life and Persecution Under the Nazi State: *Gutachten* on the Vollbrecht Case." *Central European History* 56, no. 4 (2023): 595–601. https://doi.org/10.1017/S00089389 23000468.

McGuinness, Damien. "*Holocaust*: How a US TV Series Changed Germany." *BBC*, January 29, 2019. https://www.bbc.com/news/world-europe-47042244.

McIntire, Dal. "Tangents: News and Views." ONE 5, no. 2 (February 1957): 26–29.

———. "Tangents: News and Views." ONE 5, no. 7 (August–September 1957): 17–19.

———. "Tangents: News and Views." ONE 5, no. 8 (October–November 1957): 18–21.

———. "Tangents: News and Views." ONE 6, no. 4 (April 1958): 18–21.

———. "Tangents: News and Views." ONE 6, no. 5 (May 1958): 21–25.

Memorial to the Persecuted Homosexuals under National Socialism. "History of the Memorial to the Persecuted Homosexuals Under National Socialism." Accessed October 5, 2024. https://www.stiftung-denkmal.de/en /memorials/memorial-to-the -persecuted-homosexuals-under -national-socialism.

Middleton-Kaplan, Richard. "The Myth of Jewish Passivity." In Jewish Resistance Against the Nazis, edited by Patrick Henry, 3–26. Washington, DC: Catholic University of America Press, 2014.

Mikics, David. "Holocaust Pulp Fiction." Tablet, April 19, 2012. https://www .tabletmag.com/sections/arts-letters /articles/ka-tzetnik.

Milk, Harvey. "That's What America Is." ONE Institute. Accessed October 5, 2024. https://www.oneinstitute.org/wp -content/uploads/2015/05/1978_harvey _milk_gay_freedom_day_speech.pdf.

Moeller, Robert G. "Private Acts, Public Anxieties, and the Fight to Decriminalize Male Homosexuality in West Germany." Feminist Studies 36, no. 3 (2010): 528–52. https://www.jstor .org/stable/27919120.

Morris, Charles E., III. "The Archival Turn in Rhetorical Studies; Or, The Archive's Rhetorical (Re)turn." Rhetoric and Public Affairs 9, no. 1 (2006): 113–15. https://www.jstor.org/stable/41940037.

———. "My Old Kentucky Homo: Lincoln and the Politics of Queer Public Memory." In Framing Public Memory, edited by Kendall R. Phillips, 89–114. Tuscaloosa: University of Alabama Press, 2004.

Mr. B. "Letters." ONE 10, no. 6 (June 1962): 29.

Mr. E. "Letters." ONE 11, no. 11 (November 1963): 29.

Müller, Jan-Werner. "Introduction: The Power of Memory, the Memory of Power and the Power over Memory." In Memory and Power in Post-War Europe, edited by Jan-Werner Müller, 1–35. New York: Cambridge University Press, 2002.

Muñoz, José Esteban. Disidentifications: Queers of Color and the Performance of Politics. Minneapolis: University of Minnesota Press, 2009.

———. "Ephemera as Evidence: Introductory Notes to Queer Acts." Women and Performance 8, no. 2 (1996): 5–16. https://doi.org/10.1080/0740770960 8571228.

"Nazis Certain of Victory in January Vote." Enid (OK) Morning News, December 28, 1934. Newspapers.com.

Nealon, Christopher S. Foundlings: Lesbian and Gay Historical Emotion Before Stonewall. Durham, NC: Duke University Press, 2001.

"New German Campaign Is Declared Not Purge." Buffalo (NY) News, December 27, 1934. Newspapers.com.

Newman, Lesléa. A Letter to Harvey Milk: Short Stories. Ithaca, NY: Firebrand Books, 1988.

Newsome, W. Jake. Pink Triangles Legacies: Coming Out in the Shadow of the Holocaust. Ithaca, NY: Cornell University Press, 2022.

Nora, Pierre. "Between Memory and History: Les Lieux de Mémoire." Representations 26 (1989): 7–24. https://doi.org/10.2307 /2928520.

Oechsner, Frederick C. "Hitler's Got a Girl, a Bavarian Maid." New York Daily News, June 10, 1942. Newspapers.com.

ONE. Back cover. ONE 1, no. 12 (December 1953): 26.

Pears, Tim. "Otto the Strange: The Champion Who Defied the Nazis." The Guardian, June 28, 2008. https://www.theguard ian.com/sport/2008/jun/29/olympic games.

Pinchevski, Amit, and Roy Brand. "Holocaust Perversions: The Stalags Pulp Fiction and the Eichmann Trial." Critical Studies in Media Communication 24,

no. 5 (2007): 387–407. https://doi.org
/10.1080/07393180701694598.

Plant, Richard. *The Pink Triangle: The Nazi War Against Homosexuals*. New York: Henry Holt, 1986.

Plaster, Joseph. *Kids on the Street: Queer Kinship and Religion in San Francisco's Tenderloin*. Durham, NC: Duke University Press, 2023. Google Play Books.

Plato. *The Banquet of Plato*. Translated by Percy Bysshe Shelley. Boston: Houghton Mifflin, 1908. Google Books.

Ramgopal, Kit. "Survey Finds 'Shocking' Lack of Holocaust Knowledge Among Millennials and Gen Z." *NBC News*, September 16, 2020. https://www .nbcnews.com/news/world/survey -finds-shocking-lack-holocaust -knowledge-among-millennials-gen-z -n1240031.

Reed, Lannon D. *Behold a Pale Horse: A Novel of Homosexuals in the Nazi Holocaust*. San Francisco: Gay Sunshine Press, 1985.

"Reform of Laws on Homosexuality Urged in Oxford." *Oxford Mail*, May 1956. Quoted in "Reform of Laws on Homosexuality Urged in Oxford." *Mattachine Review* 3, no. 4A (July 1956): 6–7.

Reinhart, Robert C. *Walk the Night: A Novel of Gays in the Holocaust*. Boston: Alyson Publications, 1994.

Riccardi, Nicholas, and Jeff Leeds. "Megan's Law Calling Up Old, Minor Offenses." *Los Angeles Times*, February 24, 1997. https://www.latimes.com/archives/la -xpm-1997-02-24-mn-31910-story .html.

Rogers, Kaleigh, and Mary Radcliffe. "Over 100 Anti-LGBTQ+ Laws Passed in the Last Five Years—Half of Them This Year." *FiveThirtyEight*, May 25, 2023. https://fivethirtyeight.com/features /anti-lgbtq-laws-red-states.

Röll, Wolfgang. "Homosexual Inmates in the Buchenwald Concentration Camp." *Journal of Homosexuality* 31, no. 4 (1996): 1–28. https://doi.org/10.1300 /J082v31n04_01.

Samper Vendrell, Javier. *The Seduction of Youth: Print Culture and Homosexual Rights in the Weimar Republic*. Toronto: University of Toronto Press, 2020.

Schiappa, Edward. "Second Thoughts on the Critiques of Big Rhetoric." *Philosophy and Rhetoric* 34, no. 3 (2001): 260–74. https://www.jstor.org/stable/40238095.

Schoppmann, Claudia. *Days of Masquerade: Life Stories of Lesbian Women During the Third Reich*. Translated by Allison Brown. New York: Columbia University Press, 1996.

Schwartz, Barry. *Abraham Lincoln and the Forge on National Memory*. Chicago: University of Chicago Press, 2000.

Sears, James T. *Behind the Mask of the Mattachine: The Hal Call Chronicles and the Early Movement for Homosexual Emancipation*. New York: Routledge, 2012.

"Secret Policeman." *Time*, April 24, 1939. https://time.com/archive/6820428 /foreign-news-secret-policeman.

Seifert, Dorthe. "Between Silence and License: The Representation of the National Socialist Persecution of Homosexuality in Anglo-American Fiction and Film." *History and Memory* 15, no. 2 (2003): 94–129. https://doi.org/10.2979/his.2003.15.2 .94.

Sender, Katherine. "Gay Readers, Consumers, and a Dominant Gay Habitus: 25 Years of the *Advocate* Magazine." *Journal of Communication* 51, no. 1 (2001): 73–99. https://doi.org/10.1111/j.1460-2466 .2001.tb02873.x.

"Sexy Sailors Blow!" *Broadway Brevities*, October 12, 1933. Quoted in Queer Music Heritage, accessed September 30, 2024, https://www .queermusicheritage.com/gayephem eras5.html.

Sharpe, Ivan. "Angry Gays March Through S.F." *San Francisco Examiner*, June 8, 1977. Newspapers.com.

Sherman, Martin. *Bent*. New York: Avon Books, 1979.

Shilts, Randy. *The Mayor of Castro Street: The Life and Times of Harvey Milk*. New York: St. Martin's Press, 1992.

Shirer, William L. *The Rise and Fall of the Third Reich*. New York: Simon and Schuster, 1960.

Shockley, Jay. "Picket in Front of U.S. Army Building, First-Ever U.S. Gay Rights Protest." NYC LGBT Historic Sites Project. Accessed October 12, 2024. https://www.nyclgbtsites.org/site/picket-in-front-of-u-s-army-building-first-ever-u-s-gay-rights-protest.

Silver, Henry. "Vag Lewd: A Criticism of the California Statute." *Mattachine Review* 1, no. 1 (January–February 1955): 3–8.

Socrates. "Letters." ONE 7, no. 9 (September 1959): 31–32.

Stack, Liam. "The Gaza War Is Dividing the L.G.B.T.Q. Community." *New York Times*, June 22, 2024. https://www.nytimes.com/2024/06/22/nyregion/gaza-war-lgbtq-community.html.

Steakley, James. "The Gay Movement in Germany, Part One: 1860–1910." *Body Politic* 9 (1973): 12–16. Archives of Sexuality and Gender.

———. "The Gay Movement in Germany, Part Two: 1910–1933." *The Body Politic* 10 (1973): 14–18. Archives of Sexuality and Gender.

Stein, Arlene. "Whose Memories? Whose Victimhood? Contests for the Holocaust Frame in Recent Social Movement Discourse." *Sociological Perspectives* 41, no. 3 (1998): 519–40. https://doi.org/10.2307/1389562.

Steinkopf-Frank, Hannah. "Publishing Queer Berlin." *JSTOR Daily*, June 7, 2023. https://daily.jstor.org/publishing-queer-berlin.

Straw, Will. "Traffic in Scandal: The Story of *Broadway Brevities*." *University of Toronto Quarterly* 73, no. 4 (2004): 947–71. https://doi.org/10.3138/utq.73.4.947.

Stryker, Susan. *Queer Pulp: Perverted Passions from the Golden Age of the Paperback*. San Francisco: Chronicle Books, 2001.

Stryker, Susan, and Martin Meeker. "Introduction: Mystery as History." In *The Gay Detective*, by Lou Rand, 4–23. San Francisco: Cleis Press, 2003. Google Play Books.

Sullivan, Becky. "A Far-Right Plan to Riot Near an Idaho LGBTQ Event Heightens Safety Concerns at Pride." *NPR*, June 15, 2022. https://www.npr.org/2022/06/15/1104481518/idaho-pride-lgbtq-patriot-front.

Sutton, Katie. "'We Too Deserve a Place in the Sun': The Politics of Transvestite Identity in Weimar Germany." *German Studies Review* 35, no. 2 (2012): 335–54. https://www.jstor.org/stable/23269669.

Taylor, Valerie. *Return to Lesbos*. San Francisco: She Winked Press, 1963. Google Play Books.

"10 Oppose Gov't on Homosexuals." *Washington (DC) Afro-American*, April 20, 1965. Google News.

Terl, Allan H. "An Essay on the History of Lesbian and Gay Rights in Florida." *Nova Law Review* 24, no. 3 (2000): 793–853. https://nsuworks.nova.edu/cgi/viewcontent.cgi?article=1383&context=nlr.

Torrès, Tereska. *Women's Barracks*. New York: Fawcett Publications, 1950.

Tracey, Liz. "Proposition 6 (The Briggs Initiative): Annotated." *JSTOR Daily*, October 28, 2022. https://daily.jstor.org/proposition-6-the-briggs-initiative-annotated.

Tremblay, Sébastien. *A Badge of Injury: The Pink Triangle as Global Symbol of Memory*. Berlin: De Gruyter, 2024.

Tully, Tracey. "Liquor Laws Once Targeted Gay Bars. Now, One State Is Apologizing." *New York Times*, June 29, 2021. https://www.nytimes.com/2021/06/29/nyregion/nj-gay-bars-liquor-laws-.html.

United Press. "Germany Has New Purge." *Columbia Missourian*, December 26, 1934. Newspapers.com.

———. "Nazis Arrest Von Cramm, Tennis Star." *Oakland Tribune*, March 7, 1938. Newspapers.com.

———. "Rumors of New German Purge Are Discounted." *Sacramento Bee*, December 28, 1934. Newspapers.com.

———. "Rumors of New Nazi Purge Fly Despite Denial." *Decatur (IL) Daily Review*, December 28, 1934. Newspapers.com.

United States Holocaust Memorial Museum. "Gay Men Under the Nazi Regime." Accessed October 5, 2024. https://

encyclopedia.ushmm.org/content/en
/article/gay-men-under-the-nazi
-regime.

———. "Paragraph 175 and the Nazi
Campaign Against Homosexuality."
Accessed October 5, 2024. https://
encyclopedia.ushmm.org/content/en
/article/paragraph-175-and-the-nazi
-campaign-against-homosexuality.

Voltz, Luther. "Late Spots Face Police
Crackdowns." *Miami Herald*,
September 2, 1954. Newspapers.com.

Von Neudegg, Classen. "The Mutiny."
Mattachine Review 3, no. 10 (October
1957): 25–26.

Wachsmann, Nikolaus. *KL: A History of the
Nazi Concentration Camps*. New York:
Farrar, Straus and Giroux, 2015.

Warner, Michael. "Publics and
Counterpublic." *Public Culture* 14, no. 1
(2002): 49–90. https://www.muse.jhu
.edu/article/26277.

W. H. H. "Herr Hitler." *Cincinnati (OH)
Enquirer*, May 6, 1933. Newspapers
.com.

Whisnant, Clayton J. *Queer Identities and
Politics in Germany: A History,
1880–1945*. New York: Harrington Park
Press, 2016.

White, C. Todd. *Pre-Gay L.A.: A Social
History of the Movement for
Homosexual Rights*. Urbana: University
of Illinois Press, 2009.

White House Historical Association.
"LGBTQ+ Protests in Lafayette
Square." Accessed October 5, 2024.
https://www.whitehousehistory.org
/lgbtq-protests-in-lafayette-square.

Wiesel, Elie. *Night*. New York: Hill and Wang,
1960.

Wiggins, Christopher. "Neo-Nazis Chanting
'Sieg Heil' Target Drag Queen Story
Event." *The Advocate*, March 13, 2023.
https://www.advocate.com/news/ohio
-nazi-drag-story-hour.

Wills, Matthew. "Gays Bars and Gay Rights."
JSTOR Daily, June 25, 2021. https://
daily.jstor.org/gay-bars-and-gay
-rights/.

Winchell, Walter. "On Broadway." *Johnson
City (TN) Press*, September 27, 1939.
Newspapers.com.

Winter, Jay. "The Generation of Memory:
Reflections on the 'Memory Boom' in
Contemporary Historical Studies."
Canadian Military History 10, no. 3
(2001): 57–66. https://scholars.wlu.ca
/cmh/vol10/iss3/5.

World Federation of the Rights of Man. "Die
Insel." *ONE* 1, no. 1 (January 1953): 4–6.

Wray, Christopher. *Pozières: Echoes of a
Distant Battle*. Cambridge: Cambridge
University Press, 2015.

Young, Ian. "Mikhail Itkin: Tales of a
Bishopric." *Gay and Lesbian Review
Worldwide*, November–December
2010. https://glreview.org/article
/mikhail-itkin-tales-of-a-bishopric/.

Young, James E. *The Texture of Memory:
Holocaust Memorials and Meaning*.
New Haven, CT: Yale University Press,
1993.

Zilinsky, Ursula. *Middle Ground*.
Philadelphia: J. B. Lippincott, 1968.